ABOUT THE AUTHOR

Hal Bock has been a sports writer for the Associated Press since 1963, specializing in ice hockey and baseball. His assignments have taken him to the Stanley Cup Playoffs, the World Series, and the Super Bowl. He is an expert on goaltenders, has co-authored two hockey books and has contributed to many sports magazines.

SAVE!
Hockey's Brave Goalies

by
Hal Bock

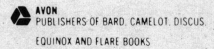 AVON
PUBLISHERS OF BARD, CAMELOT, DISCUS,
EQUINOX AND FLARE BOOKS

To Richard, my favorite goalie

The author wishes to thank John Halligan, publicity director of the New York Rangers, and Maurice "Lefty" Reid, curator of the Hockey Hall of Fame, for their help in the research of this book.

AVON BOOKS
A division of
The Hearst Corporation
959 Eighth Avenue
New York, New York 10019

ISBN 0-380-00135-7

Designed by Vincent Priore.

First Avon Printing, October, 1974.

Printed in the U.S.A.

CONTENTS

INTRODUCTION

His name was Wilf Cude and he was a rather ordinary goaltender for the Montreal Canadiens during the 1930s. He is not listed among hockey's immortals in the Hall of Fame, because he simply wasn't in that class. But for all the legions of men who ever strapped on the tools of a goaltender, Wilf Cude said all there was to be said about their hazardous profession.

Cude was preparing for a game, going through the hockey player's mid-afternoon dinner ritual of eating a king-sized steak. "I poured a hell of a lot of ketchup on it," the goalie said. Just then, Beulah Cude made an offhand remark to her husband about some triviality. Nothing important, you understand, but it hit the goalie the wrong way.

"I picked up the steak," remembered Cude, "and threw it at her."

Beulah Cude's reflexes were every bit as good as her goaltender husband's. The lady ducked and the ketchup-soaked steak splashed into the wall. "The ketchup splattered and the steak hung there on the wall," said Cude. "Slowly it began to peel, and I stared at it. Between the time that steak hit the wall and then the floor, I decided I'd been a touchy goalkeeper long enough. By the time it landed, I'd retired."

Not all goalies end up hurling sirloins at their spouses, but the pressures of the job have resulted in some strange goings-on. There was, for example, Sugar Jim Henry, who tended goal for the New York Rangers and Boston Bruins during some lean years for those two teams. Toward the end of his career, Henry was asked about the goaltending aspirations of his nine-year-old son, Tommy.

"I don't know if he's serious about it," said the proud father, "but if I ever see him with a big stick in his hands, I'll hit him over the head with it."

"You don't have to be nuts to be a goalie," Gump Worsley once observed, "but it helps."

Then, there was the case of Frank McCool, who was

twenty-six when he arrived on the NHL scene in 1944 and led the Toronto Maple Leafs to the Stanley Cup. He was Rookie of the Year that season and turned in four shut-outs in thirteen playoff games as the Leafs won hockey's most cherished trophy. It seemed like the beginning of a long NHL career, but it wasn't. The next season, McCool and his ulcers retired.

"If you lose," he said, "the fans blame the goalie and the reporters take up the cry. After a while, the other players believe what they read and the goalie feels like it's one man against the world. Everybody else who makes a mistake, it escapes the attention of the crowd. But the goalie? If he blows one, they know it. Pretty soon, the goalie feels like an outcast. The only friend he has is the other goalie across the ice. He's the only one who understands."

A popular story when McCool retired was that goaltending had given him ulcers, and driven him out of the game and into the newspaper business in his native Calgary, Alberta.

"I didn't say that," said McCool. "I just know that goaltending didn't quiet the ulcers. I'd much rather write about hockey than play it. In fact, if I had to play it, I'd find some other position."

Chuck Rayner, a Hall of Fame goaltender, understood what McCool meant.

"Goaltending," said the beetle-browed Rayner, "is like walking down a dark alley and never knowing when somebody is going to chop you down."

Some playful opponents occasionally like to use goalies for target practice. Emile Francis, general manager of the New York Rangers, was a pint-sized NHL net-minder during his playing days and had his share of confrontations with too-ambitious forwards. One shooter liked to keep Francis loose by using the little goalie's nose for a bull's-eye.

"One night," recalled Francis, "he skated past me after winging one right by my ear. He stopped for a second and muttered, 'Watch out for me, Emile. I'm shooting a little high tonight.' Next time he came by, I had caught the puck and I threw it way out to my left. While everyone was looking over there, I gave him a fine two-hander with the lumber. Right across the ankles. While they were examining him, laid out on the ice, I skated over."

Francis reached the stricken skater and bent over him. "Hey, I'm sorry," said the goalie. "But I'm hitting a little low tonight."

That little act of retaliation is symptomatic of the long memories goalies have. In this hazardous business, it is a definite prerequisite. Roy Worters, who tended goal for the old New York Americans, demonstrated how important that asset could be. He was engaging in some summer-hockey hot-stove talk with Jess Spring, a defenseman who also played in the NHL. Spring dominated the conversation, relating the attributes of a young prospect he had seen the season before. The kid's name was Ken Doraty.

"He's very good," reported Spring. "Of course, he's too small to make the NHL, and it's a pity. He has an eye like Bill Cook; can skate as fast as Howie Morenz and he's as full of tricks as Aurel Joliat. He's got all those goalies in Regina crazy. They can't stop him. In fact, there's only one way to stop this baby."

"What's that?" asked Worters.

"Well," said Spring, "if a goalie stands absolutely still, this boy will shoot right at him. When he comes in with the puck, he always feints to the right or the left. Invariably, the goalie shifts in the direction of the feint. Doraty sends the puck sizzling in, right at the spot where the goalie was before he shifted."

Worters filed away that piece of intelligence in the back of his head, knowing that it was entirely unlikely that he'd ever need it. After all, Spring had said the kid was too small for the NHL, and Doraty would probably never show up in the big league.

But the years passed and Ken Doraty weaved his way through hockey's minor leagues and, sure enough, he finally made it to the NHL with Toronto. His first game was against the New York Americans, who had Roy Worters guarding their goal.

Doraty sifted through the Amerks' defense several times and every time he headed for the net, Worters was there to meet him, anchored like a stone wall, never moving as Doraty went through his repertoire of fakes and feints. Worters had remembered Spring's scouting report on the young forward, delivered years before. "If the goalie stands absolutely still, this boy will shoot right at him." It worked.

Worters shut Doraty out.

"It's our business to remember things like that," said Worters. "We've got to be thinking, or the cage will be full of pucks."

One of Worters's toughest opponents was Nels Stewart, one of the NHL's first really great scorers. Worters often told of how Stewart once came skating in on his net alone and called to the goalie: "Roy," he said, "you'll find the puck in the left-hand corner of the net." A moment later, that was where Stewart put it with all the preciseness of a Babe Ruth calling his home-run shot.

Stewart was also involved in one of hockey and goal-tending's most dramatic moments—the night Coach Lester Patrick went into the nets for the New York Rangers. It happened during the Stanley Cup playoffs of 1928 with the Rangers facing the Montreal Maroons in the final round.

The Maroons won the first game of the series 2–0, and then in game two, Stewart kayoed the Ranger goalie, Lorne Chabot, launching a shot that hit the net-minder squarely in the left eye. Chabot went down like a man who had been sandbagged. He was carried off the ice on a stretcher, blood spurting from the wound opened by the shot.

In those days, hockey clubs carried only one goaltender. That left Patrick ten minutes to locate a replacement for Chabot. His first thought was Alex Connell, Ottawa's goalie, who was in the stands watching the game. Patrick asked the permission of Eddie Gerard, Montreal's manager. The Maroons' boss snickered. "If I let you take Connell," he said, "it could cost me. Suckers were born yesterday and you're talking to the wrong man. I can't hear you."

Patrick returned to the Ranger dressing room with the news. "Anybody got any ideas?" he asked his players.

"Yeah," piped up center Frank Boucher, "how about you playing goal, Lester?"

Now Patrick had been a pretty good defenseman during his playing days, but those days were long behind him. He was now forty-five years old and, what's more, this was hockey's nitty-gritty—the Stanley Cup playoffs. It was no time for an old defenseman to try imitating a young goalie. "No, I'm too old," said Patrick.

But soon, the other Rangers were caught up in the idea and besides, the team had very little choice. It was Patrick or nothing and eventually the Ranger boss realized it. So he climbed into Chabot's bloodstained uniform, trembling as he considered the task that lay ahead. He stood on jellylike legs as the Rangers threw some warmup shots at him, carefully making sure the boss couldn't help but stop the soft lobs. A few minutes later, Patrick announced he was ready.

The Rangers played like a team possessed, protecting Patrick like a piece of fine china, decking any Montreal player who came within shouting distance of their boss and the net he was guarding. Early in the third period, Bill Cook scored for New York and the white-haired Ranger boss protected the lead until the final minutes. But Stewart broke through the Ranger defense and tied the score, sending the tense game into overtime. The extra period lasted just over seven minutes before Boucher scored the Rangers' winner.

Patrick's dramatic performance captured the imagination of the Montreal crowd, which roared its approval of the New York victory. It also inspired the Rangers who, armed with a real goalie, won two of the next three games to clinch the Stanley Cup.

Twenty-five years later, Lester's son, Lynn, was coaching the Boston Bruins against the Montreal Canadiens in the playoffs. In one game, starting goalie Jim Henry suffered a leg injury and Patrick rushed backup man Red Henry into the nets to replace him. A few minutes later an errant skate, belonging—ironically—to one of the Bruins, cut Red Henry's arm, opening a rather ugly wound. Red was taken to the dressing room, where the doctors started sewing him back together while Patrick paced the floor nervously.

It was then that a Boston sportswriter, who knew a good story when he saw it, suggested that Lynn go into the nets for the Bruins in this goaltending emergency, just as his father had done for the Rangers a quarter century before.

"Are you kidding?" snapped Patrick. "I played only one period of goal in my life, and I missed twenty-five shots."

The journalist drew out a king-sized needle—about the size of the one the doctors were using on Henry. "The present generation must be getting softer," the writer said, recalling Lester's feat.

"It may be softer," answered Lynn, "but it isn't softer in the head."

Lynn's father, Lester, also was in charge of the Rangers when they introduced to the NHL one of the least-talented goalies ever to perform in the league. His name was Steve Buzinski and what he lacked in net-minding talent was made up in enthusiasm for the game. Buzinski loved to play and never believed he was as bad as some of his Ranger teammates said he was.

Patrick imported Buzinski during the war years when NHL talent was scarce. He was a small man whose size was only one of a number of handicaps that he brought to the job. One of the most troubling was the difficulty he had stopping the puck. But you could never convince Buzinski he had any problems.

Once he was on the receiving end of a 7–1 shellacking from Detroit when a Red Wing shot sailed high and wide of the Ranger net. Disregarding the direction of the puck, which was nowhere near goal territory, Buzinski lunged for it and, miraculously, speared it with his gloved hand as teammate Bryan Hextall skated by.

Proud of his accomplishment, Buzinski positively glowed. "Hex," he said, "it's just like picking berries off a tree."

Another time, Buzinski gloved a shot and casually tossed it over his shoulder . . . squarely into the net behind him.

The Buzinski charade lasted just nine games during which time he surrendered fifty-five goals. Patrick, concerned about the sanity of the rest of his hockey players, relieved his rookie of the net-minding burden, but kept him with the hockey club as a sort of jack-of-all-trades, handyman, and good-luck charm.

The Rangers shared Madison Square Garden in those days with their Eastern League affiliate, the New York Rovers. One day the Rovers asked Patrick for some bodies to round out a scrimmage. The Ranger boss, a strict disciplinarian, dispatched a couple of his players, Buzinski included. "Gee, I'd like to help you out, Mr. Patrick," said Buzinski, "but I've got a lot of letters to write."

The next day, Buzinski, armed with a one-way ticket, was on his way home to Swift Current, Saskatchewan.

Most goalies maintain an outward unconcern about the dangers of their jobs even if their stomachs sometimes do somersaults over the notion of spending a night standing up against one-hundred-mile-per-hour shots. Glenn Hall, who once termed a game in the nets as "sixty minutes of hell," regularly suffered from butterflies when he considered what he was about to subject himself to.

Once, Chuck Rayner stopped a shot with his jaw and the save cost him four teeth. He underwent oral surgery to remove the roots of the broken teeth and was back in his cage the next night. He turned the other cheek, blocking another shot and opening another gash in his already well-sutured profile. As he waited for the doctor to do some more hem-stitching, Rayner had a philosophical observation about his job.

"It's a wonder," he said, "that somebody doesn't get badly hurt in this job."

Jacques Plante, the man who introduced the mask to modern goaltending, suggested that the goalie's spot was the best place on the ice. "It's a simple job," said Plante. "You must only watch the puck. If you can see it, you can stop it."

It isn't always that simple, of course. For the first five years of his NHL career, Terry Sawchuk was as close to a perfect goalie as one could imagine. His goals-against average was under two per game for each of those seasons and he won the Vezina Trophy as the league's leading goalie three times.

Then he was traded to Boston and eighteen months later, after a bout with mononucleosis, he announced his retirement from hockey, creating a storm of controversy. Sawchuk's nerves simply got the better of him and he needed a layoff from the game. Most goalies experience the same thing at one time or another in their careers.

Bill Durnan left the Montreal Canadiens in the midst of a playoff series. His successor, Gerry MacNeil, also departed the club suddenly and without warning. Others, like Gump Worsley, blithely go about their risky business without so much as a mask to protect them from the hazards of their job.

Ask them how they got into this crazy business of playing target and you get as many different answers as there are goalies. There is one quality they all share, though. That is the camaraderie of the net-minders. Theirs is an exclusive club. To get in, you must be brave—probably braver than any other athlete. And they wear that badge of courage proudly. They should—they have earned it.

"I thought of myself
as Nureyev on ice,"
said Ken Dryden,
"but on TV I realized
I was a dump truck . . .
an elephant on wheels."
Some elephant!

1
KEN DRYDEN:
STOP IN THE NAME OF THE LAW

The May heat of Chicago's air created a foglike atmosphere that hung heavily over the ice surface. Standing at one end of the rink was a tall lean goalie, number 29 stretching across the back of the *rouge, blanc et bleu* Montreal Canadiens jersey. His face was protected by a grotesque mask that hugged his cheekbones. His long, modishly cut hair stuck out around the straps that held his face protector in place.

A crowd of twenty-thousand fans was squeezed into creaky old Chicago Stadium for the seventh game of the 1971 Stanley Cup championship series between the Canadiens and the Chicago Black Hawks. Fire laws prohibited more than 16,666 in the old building and the Black Hawks dutifully reported that number for every sellout while a good three thousand more watched the games. The fans spent most of this particular evening on the edge of hysteria. The winners of this game would sip champagne from Lord Stanley's mug, an experience the Black Hawks hadn't enjoyed in more than a decade. If the fans had their way, that long dry spell would end this night. The main obstacle to the luxurious drink would be that tall young man guarding the Canadiens' nets. He had played in just six regular-season games before the Canadiens thrust him right into the Stanley Cup pressure pot. It was a bold gamble that had paid off so far with Montreal weaving past Boston, the defending champions and Cup favorites, in the first round and then Minnesota in round two.

It looked like the bubble had finally burst when Chicago

took the first two games of the best-of-seven final. But Montreal battled back to win the next two, tying the series. Game five, usually pivotal, had gone to the Black Hawks, leaving the Canadiens with no margin for mistakes. Montreal won the sixth game and that forced the seventh and final contest. A winner-take-all showdown that could cause a case of rubbery knees in the most grizzled veteran. What would that kind of pressure do to a mere rookie? The answer was absolutely nothing.

Each time play stopped, long, lean Ken Dryden straightened up from his goalie crouch. He set his heavy goaltender's stick in front of him, pointed the blade down on the ice and leaned on the handle, arms folded casually over the knob at the top of the shaft. For all the world, he looked like a farmer, watching over his crops at harvest time. One got the feeling watching the young man that his mind was a million miles away from Chicago Stadium. As the clock ticked off the precious seconds, Dryden stayed cool.

Henri Richard's goal early in the third period had given Montreal a 3–2 lead and now there were less than twenty minutes left to play. The Canadiens battled desperately to protect their narrow edge. But there was no feeling of panic in their actions. If that cool goalie could stand the pressure, so could the rest of them.

Time after time, the Black Hawks charged out of the fog that was quickly settling over the ice. Frantically, they advanced the puck up the ice, battling first the Canadiens, then Dryden, and finally that impossible-to-read clock. And time after time, Dryden met the charge. First Bobby Hull tried, then his brother Dennis. Pit Martin had an open corner and missed. Incredibly, Jim Pappin had the same kind of chance, only to have Dryden whip out his gloved hand like the tongue of a snake to spear the puck. Pat Stapleton boomed a slap shot from the blue line that banged off Dryden's pads. The rebound came to Stan Mikita, deadly around the net, but again Dryden came up with the puck.

By himself, the rookie goalie cut the heart out of Chicago. Hockey players have a tradition of tapping their goalie's pads with their sticks after he has made a good save. Throughout that third period, as each shift of Montreal skaters changed and new legs came on the ice, they skated over to the young goalie and rapped his pads.

Finally, as the game settled into the final minute, Chicago Coach Billy Reay lifted his goalie, Tony Esposito, substituting an extra attacker in a last-ditch try at getting the puck past the octopus in the Montreal nets. Through the fog, Dryden could barely see the vacant Chicago net. But that was all right. He didn't have to worry about *that* net. The one behind him—six feet wide and four feet tall—was the only one concerning him. The Hawks buzzed furiously around him and Dryden turned their shots away. Now the seconds were down to ten . . . nine . . . eight. Martin shot and Dryden cleared the puck to the corner. Seven . . . six . . . five. Bill White sent another low liner toward the Montreal net, but it was blocked by a body in front of Dryden. Four . . . three . . . two . . . one. Pappin launched the last shot, a desperation try from far out that got off just as the siren—that lovely, loud siren—sounded, ending the game and giving the Stanley Cup to the Canadiens.

Now, with the game over, Dryden could come out of the shooting gallery and quit playing bull's-eye. Pappin's shot didn't mean a thing. Dryden had done all the puck-stopping required. He could skate away now. But the goalie didn't do that. Instead, he waited for Pappin's shot to reach the net and then hugged it gratefully. Every other time, after he smothered a puck, he had casually tossed it back to an official for a faceoff. There would be no casual toss this time. Dryden kept this puck—his souvenir of one of the most dramatic jobs of Stanley Cup goaltending in hockey history.

He had been wondering how he could inconspicuously get that last puck without embarrassing himself. Pappin solved his problem. "Fortunately, I didn't have to look like a fool scrambling around for it," Dryden said. The goalie had gotten the puck from his first NHL game a couple of months earlier in the same way. That first game, a 5–1 decision in Pittsburgh, seemed like ancient history by the time Dryden clutched Pappin's shot. He'd been through enough ups and downs in those intervening weeks to last most hockey players a lifetime.

Dryden had started the season in a noble experiment. He had decided to turn pro with the Montreal organization under a complicated schedule that would permit him to combine his hockey playing with his career as a full-time law student at Montreal's McGill University. He rushed from law class at McGill to hockey practice with the Montreal Voyageurs, the Canadiens' farm team in the American Hockey League. On road trips, while other players occupied themselves with paperback novels, Dryden read heavy material like the Civil Codes of Quebec. It was, to say the least, no easy schedule to follow, but then Ken Dryden was no average athlete-scholar. He flourished under the double burden and late in the season when the NHL Canadiens realized that their goaltending might not be sufficient for the Stanley Cup grind, they called up Dryden.

The tall goalie got his first taste of the NHL from the press box, sitting in his street clothes. Coach Al MacNeil didn't even bother putting him in uniform when he was first called up. He was strictly an extra body and he didn't like it one bit. "I watched from the press box," he said, "and I felt like an idiot."

Dryden endured three games of watching and then went to MacNeil and suggested that if the Canadiens didn't plan on playing him, he could certainly do himself more good back in the AHL with the Voyageurs. "Can't you at least dress me for the game, make me feel part of the team?" he asked. MacNeil didn't answer the scholarly goalie, but before Montreal's next game in Pittsburgh Dryden got the word that not only would he dress—he would start.

Off his ice-water playoff show, you'd figure that a nothing regular-season game in, of all places, Pittsburgh, wouldn't jar Dryden, even if it was his NHL debut. Wrong. "My knees were jelly," he said. "My legs were shaking so hard, I thought everybody in the place could see it. For the first time in my life, I stayed nervous through a whole game."

Dryden survived his first-game butterflies to post a 5–1 victory over the Penguins and he even remembered to grab that last puck as a souvenir. He blocked thirty-five shots and was as good as he had to be. Certainly there was in his performance no suggestion of the high drama that lay ahead.

He played five more games, all of them victories, probably the most significant being a 6–2 decision over the Rangers in New York. It was significant because he blocked forty-nine shots. "That was my first big test," he said. "It was the first game where my goaltending was a factor, the first game we might have lost if I hadn't done my job. The big thing as far as my personal development was concerned was that each save bolstered my confidence. I felt none of the nervousness that I had in the earlier games. And I came out of that game with more of a personal feeling that I belonged in the NHL, that I could play in the NHL." It was something like a newly minted lawyer having his first courtroom objection sustained.

In the final week of the season, Montreal played Boston twice and both times Dryden watched from the sidelines. The Bruins, defending Stanley Cup champions, had captured the East crown with a scoring juggernaut that staggered the imagination. Boston was to meet Montreal in the first Cup round and the Bruins did a little psych job on the Canadiens in that final week, running up thirteen goals in a pair of one-sided victories. Led by Phil Esposito's seventy-six goals and seventy-six assists, the Bruins finished the season with an awesome 399 goals, an average of five per game.

Boston was the top-heavy favorite in the opening Cup round against Montreal and it's a cinch that the odds would have been even greater if the bettors had known that the Canadiens would be using Dryden. Here was the highest-scoring team in the history of hockey and the goalie given the assignment of facing this barrage of shooters had a total of six NHL games behind him.

The first game went to the Bruins, as expected, but it was remarkably close. The final score was 3–1 and it could have gone either way. It was that game, said Dryden, that gave the Canadiens the confidence to believe that they could indeed beat the Bruins. "We could just as easily have won," said the goalie. "We lost, but we could have won. I said to myself, 'This is encouraging; this is exciting. We played well. It could have gone either way. We can win this thing.' "

The Canadiens went out and did exactly that. Trailing 5–1 in the second game, Montreal put on a sensational spurt, roaring from behind to beat the Bruins and even the series. "After that first game," said Dryden, "we all seemed to realize that the Boston Bruins were just another hockey club. We talked it over and we agreed that, except for [Bobby] Orr, their team wasn't a bloody bit better than our team."

The series seesawed after that. Montreal took game three,

but the Bruins bounced back to win the fourth and fifth, pushing the Canadiens to the edge of elimination. But once more, Montreal came back, winning game six and extending the series to a seventh and decisive game in Boston Garden. The night before the final game, Dryden was in his motel room, watching television. Suddenly, a filmed show of Bruin highlights flashed on the screen. Now, in Boston, when they show Bruin highlights on TV, you are reasonably certain of seeing those guys in the black-and-gold uniforms filling the enemy nets with shots. And this show was no different. On the receiving end of the show was Dryden. Watching himself beaten time after time on the twenty-one-inch screen was a little nerve-wracking for the six-foot-five-inch goalie.

"This was only the second time in my life I'd ever seen myself on television," he said, "and it shattered a lot of illusions. I looked like a big stiff. What a sobering experience. I always thought of myself as dipping and darting across the goal mouth. I thought of myself as Nureyev on ice. But on TV, I realized that I was a dump truck. I was an elephant on wheels."

Dryden took as much of that show as he could and then wandered out of his room to reflect on the butterflies that had somehow found their way back into his stomach, just as they had before that first NHL start against Pittsburgh. Because he is a deep thinker, Dryden came to terms with his problem and realized that in the overall picture of world events, his Sunday date with the Bruins wasn't life or death. He'd already proven that he could do a good job against the best-scoring team in hockey history. One more game, no matter what the outcome, would not change what he had already achieved.

The butterflies stayed with Dryden right up until the start of the seventh and deciding contest. Then, as soon as the puck was dropped, they disappeared and once again Dryden was the cool-headed customer in the nets, turning back almost everything the Bruins threw his way. Montreal took the deciding game 4–2, eliminating Boston in one of hockey's most memorable upsets. The reason, in no small measure, was Dryden. He made saves that bordered on the miraculous. He left scoring champion Phil Esposito rapping his stick on the backboards, disgusted with himself.

"He has arms like a giraffe," the exasperated Esposito said

later. A nit-picker pointed out to Espo that giraffes are more noted for the length of their necks. "Well," snapped Phil, "we never had a zoo in my hometown."

Johnny McKenzie, another of the frustrated Bruins, remembered Dryden's glove that seemed at times to have a magnet in it. "That bloody hand of his is something else," moaned McKenzie. "We caught him out of position at least a dozen times and shot for three quarters of an open net. Then, zap! That big mitt comes out of thin air. Twice I had my stick in the air and was breaking into my goal-scoring dance when he did that."

After they disposed of the Bruins, the Canadiens suffered a bit of a letdown and Minnesota stretched the semifinal series to six games before falling. Then came the Black Hawks and the seven-game grind that was climaxed by winning the Stanley Cup. The hero, without any question, was the rookie goalie with the eighty-inch reach that sometimes seemed like eighty feet. Ken Dryden, who had played every minute of the twenty playoff games in Montreal's nets, won the Conn Smythe Trophy as the Most Valuable Player of the playoffs.

Barely ten weeks after stepping into a Canadiens' uniform for the first time, Dryden was the toast of Montreal, the newest hero of the NHL. "I just can't believe it's coming all together for me at once," he said. "The pressure wasn't so bad. Nobody expected you to do anything at all, so if you did something, it's groovy." Dryden had done something all right. When the Canadiens' chartered flight landed at Montreal's Dorval Airport at 3:45 A.M., some three thousand Quebecois formed the welcoming committee. And they saved their loudest cheers for the rookie goalie. Included in the crowd was his blonde wife, Lynda. She wheeled her Volkswagen as close as she could to the arrival gate and her elongated husband squeezed in for the trip back to their small apartment. Ken Dryden might be a hockey hero, but he was still just another law student on McGill's campus.

The law and hockey combination is unusual and Ken talks enthusiastically about both. He can get just as excited about a legal brief as he can about a tough save. It was his love of the law and his determination to achieve his degree that almost deprived the Canadiens of his services. And, at the same time, it was his love of hockey that helped Montreal get him. If that sounds confusing, it really isn't.

Dryden had achieved All-America status playing collegiate hockey at Cornell University under Ned Harkness, who, like Ken, later moved on to the NHL, although with less success than his goalie has enjoyed. When he graduated from Cornell in 1969, Ken had to make a decision. The Canadiens had drafted him and were offering him fifty thousand dollars to turn professional. At the same time, the Harvard University law school had accepted his application. Which would it be —Montreal and hockey or Harvard and the law?

First, Dryden turned down the Canadiens' offer because he felt he would be unable to play pro hockey and go to law school at the same time. Then, he turned down the Harvard offer because he would be unable to play hockey while going to law school there.

"The Montreal people wanted me to attend McGill University and at the same time play pro hockey," said Dryden. "But I thought that it would be impossible to combine the two and do them both well. I would be serving two masters and that's tough. The Harvard arrangement would have meant school and no hockey, so it was just as restrictive in its way as the Montreal deal, only the other way around."

The solution was the Canadian National team based, at that time, in Winnipeg, Manitoba. Signing with them meant a substantial salary and free tuition at the University of Manitoba Law School. More importantly, it meant the opportunity to combine both hockey and school. The less strenuous schedule of the National team was a key determining factor in the decision. When he signed, Dryden was convinced he had done the best thing for his own situation.

"I have the best of both worlds," he said. "I have time to study, yet I'll be able to travel with the team to Europe and eventually play in the Olympics. That's something a man doesn't want to miss. I couldn't do that if I signed with the Canadiens. The point is, there are aspects of life I want to explore now before turning pro. For me, big-time hockey can wait. I can always do the NHL thing later, if I'm good enough. And if I never make it to the NHL, I'll still be able to live with myself. I have a natural fascination about playing in the NHL. But right now, I don't know how good I'll be. Who knows? I might be a real big flop. Playing with the Nationals will help me find out where I stand. I think that's important for me."

What Dryden found out was that the National team wasn't the answer for him, after all. For one thing, a squabble between Canada's amateur hockey organization, Hockey Canada, and the International Olympic Committee over ground rules for player eligibilty led the National team to withdraw from Olympic competition. For another, the National team's travel schedule was strenuous enough to throw Dryden's scholastic pursuits out of kilter. Moreover, Dryden's competitive nature just wasn't being satisfied sufficiently by amateur hockey. All of these things added up to a second chance for the Canadiens and, as his contemporaries know, Montreal General Manager Sammy Pollock rarely misses prospects the first time around and never misses when he gets a second shot at them. When Pollock got wind of Dryden's second thoughts, he quickly moved in to repeat his earlier offer that would allow Ken to combine pro hockey and law studies at McGill. This time, Dryden accepted the offer.

"I had an agreement with Hockey Canada and I could have had a comfortable life collecting my money from them and playing at the University of Toronto." The National team had switched base from Manitoba and Dryden had been accepted at Toronto's law school. "But I had had enough of college hockey. I decided that if I was going to continue playing, it would have to be with the pros."

When the Canadiens went to training camp in 1970, the studious goalie was with them. His academic records had been transferred to McGill for his final two years of law school. His pads and mask went to the Voyageurs of the American Hockey League, although some observers in training camp thought he could have stuck with the Canadiens right away. "At training camp, he was our best goalie," said John Ferguson. "But he wanted to go to school, so he went to the Voyageurs."

Pollock planned the prized goalie's schedule carefully so that his studies would suffer a minimum of disruption. Dryden, of course, was grateful. His logistics had been much more difficult with the Nationals. "I think it was tougher than it is here," said Dryden during camp. "We had two seventeen-day trips with the National team and that meant missing two weeks of classes. Here I know that I'll miss the odd cláss, but it's easier to make up one class." Once, during camp, Dryden was "traded" from one team to another in the Canadiens' intrasquad league so that he could attend an afternoon class.

Dryden found that pro hockey forced an adjustment in his approach to the game. "I had to learn to concentrate for the full sixty minutes," he said. "In college, playing on a strong team, there were very few times when I was pressed that heavily. I had to bear down for maybe ten or fifteen minutes in most games, which led to some bad habits." Ken also discovered that his earlier fears about pro hockey producing so much pressure that his studies might be disrupted were unfounded. Instead, his two vocations seemed to benefit each other. "Hockey and my studies stimulate each other," he said, rushing from practice to class. "I couldn't do just one or the other—there's too much other time to fill. I have to combine the two activities. If I waited six years to go to law school, I couldn't adjust to studying again. If I waited to play hockey, my reflexes would be gone. Doing both is best."

The student goaltender played thirty-three games with the Voyageurs that season, three of them shutouts, and had a respectable 2.68 goals-against average on the ice and a just as respectable scholastic average off the ice at McGill. Then came the Canadiens' callup in the final weeks of the regular season. One of the six games he played for the Canadiens before the playoffs was a historic confrontation with Buffalo. It was historic because the Sabres' goalie was Dave Dryden and it marked the first time two brothers had tended goal against each other in the NHL.

After the game, the Drydens skated to center ice. "We didn't have anything to say for posterity," said Dave, "just congratulations." Punch Imlach, Buffalo's imaginative general manager, had arranged the confrontation in the Montreal Forum. He started Dave in the Sabres' goal. But the Canadiens countered with Rogatien Vachon and so, at the first whistle, Imlach lifted Dave. A few minutes later, Vachon was injured and the Canadiens had to send Ken into the nets. Imlach immediately came back with Dave.

Upstairs in the Forum sat Murray Dryden, father of the two goalies. "I know he always wanted it to happen," said Ken, "but I imagine he was going crazy up there when it actually did." Dave, six years older than Ken, had coached his brother through the early days of his goaltending career. "Yes," said Ken, "we had a stacked deck, really. My brother coached and our father managed, so I was always pretty certain of making the team."

Ken was always big for his age and when his older brother played hockey, he would tag along. The fact that the rink was located in the Dryden backyard in Etobicoke, Ontario, didn't hurt either. Dave would guard one net at one end of the yard and Ken would take the other. "We played from September until May," said Dave. "Eight guys to a side and away we'd go. Neither Ken nor I ever wanted to play anything but goal. I think what helped us both was that we played ball hockey when we were kids. Not too many boys can lift a hockey puck when they are starting out, but they really could zip a tennis ball at us. Ken has fast hands and stopping that tennis ball coming at him from a kid six years older made them even faster."

The Drydens were good goaltenders, but hockey was strictly for fun. "We never ever thought about playing against each other in the NHL," said Dave. "We never considered pro hockey when we were kids. I was going to be a schoolteacher and Ken was doing so well in school he didn't think about becoming a pro athlete either." Their schooling always came first for the Dryden brothers. Many of today's top professional players left home to play their junior hockey. When Ken had that opportunity, he turned it down, strictly because of educational considerations.

"When I was playing Junior B in Etobicoke, I was drafted by Peterborough," he said. The Petes played in the prestigious Ontario Hockey Association and it would have been a good opportunity for Ken. "They had Chuck Goddard as their number-one goaltender and they felt they had a good chance to win the Memorial Cup. They needed a backup goalie, but I was in grade thirteen and I felt I should stay in Toronto and finish my schooling."

A year later, Dryden was ready for college. He had his share of his scholarship offers from colleges and universities throughout the United States and Canada. He received visits and calls from alumni and coaches, including Cornell's Ned Harkness. They all rolled off Dryden's broad shoulders. The most effective recruiter was a distinguished professor of government, the late Clinton Rossiter, whose presence on the faculty helped lead Dryden to the Ithaca, New York, institution. There was no scholarship, because Ivy League schools don't give them for athletes. Financial help is based on need and the Drydens were able to handle Ken's expenses themselves.

"Had Ken been thinking about a pro-hockey career," said brother Dave, "he would have gone elsewhere. Eastern hockey was not that big then and Cornell wasn't even at the top of the East."

With Dryden performing brilliantly in goal, Cornell won two national championships in his three varsity seasons. He was named to the collegiate All-America squad in each of those seasons. Harkness called him "the greatest goalie I ever coached." Cooney Weiland, long-time coach at Harvard and before that a standout player and coach in the NHL, said, "I simply cannot remember a better hockey goalie." In his three varsity seasons, Cornell lost only four games. His goals-against average was 1.60. "It was pretty easy behind the bench when he was in goal," said Harkness.

The Canadiens, who owned his professional rights, kept tabs on Dryden from a distance during those collegiate days. "I never even knew they were alive," the goalie said. Then, toward the end of his senior year, Sammy Pollock and his operatives began buzzing around the tall, thinking man's goalie. One night, Toe Blake watched him against Boston University. Another time, Pollock showed up at Ithaca to study the elongated net-minder. The consensus of opinion was that Dryden had the stuff for stardom in the NHL. The only problem would be getting him there. It took two years to achieve that goal. Then, all at once, he was a hero, leading Montreal to the Stanley Cup with his scintillating performance against Boston, Minnesota, and Chicago. It all happened so fast that it took a while for Dryden to assimilate the impact he had made on the world of hockey. He made the adjustment in, of all places, Washington, D.C.

Three months before becoming a Stanley Cup sensation, Dryden had applied for summer work with consumer crusader Ralph Nader. He would be one of Nader's Raiders, an unpaid volunteer soaking up experience—invaluable experience for a budding attorney. There would be no hockey camps cashing in on Dryden's sudden fame. There would be no golf and very little relaxation—the usual summer occupations of hockey stars. Instead, there would be a summer of intensive and rewarding work on ecology problems.

Dryden's was one of two thousand applications for thirty-five positions with Nader that summer. Salaries averaged $450 for ten weeks so the applicants obviously weren't there for money. Dryden, who declined the fee, was assigned to a project concerned with water pollution. "My area was to try to organize sport and commercial fishermen into a national group," he said. "The idea is to gain them a strong voice against industries and government agencies that pollute the waters, destroying their livelihood and their way of life. Every day, you look up at the air and see that it isn't what it should be. The water has smells, or looks terrible. You find crud coming out of the drinking water and fish are dying. You can't avoid it."

The goalie first became fascinated with Nader's work when he read the consumer advocate's book, *Unsafe At Any Speed*. And in his summer with the Raiders, Dryden found satisfaction in doing something he considered important and helpful. "Suddenly finding yourself in the position of doing something about all the things you've seen going on and have been frustrating you is most satisfying," he said.

"If I learned one thing," Dryden continued, "it is that one man—you or I—can make a big difference in a bureaucracy, with a surprisingly limited personal sacrifice. Organizations like the National Rifle Association have shown that pressure groups can bring about results that—to me—are undesirable. Nader is trying to organize people to bring about desirable results. He's the kind of concerned lawyer I hope to be."

Dryden measured his opinions carefully before delivering them, fearing that his athletic success might cause people to listen to him rather than to what he was saying. "One very dangerous thing is for a person in the spotlight to speak out on these issues when he has a forum just because of his athletic ability. That's irresponsible," he said. "To go on a TV show and speak out like this . . . why should people be listening to him? If he really knows what he's talking about, fine. Otherwise, it's irresponsible."

Dryden returned from his summer in Washington, anxious to resume his career with the Canadiens. "After a couple of weeks in Washington," he said, "I started to miss Montreal. I'd call Montreal information on the phone, just to hear the operator answer in French and English." There was another thing bothering the young goalie. There was a chance, albeit a slim one, that he was a flash in the pan. "It enters my mind," he said. "I've proven myself over six regular games and twenty playoff games, but I haven't proven myself over thirty or forty games, or a whole season of seventy-eight games, or more than a whole season. You have to take all the knocks and bruises and bad spells and the whole scene, over and over again, and I haven't done that yet in the NHL. That's why the pressure will be on me this season—to see if I can do it."

Dryden proved he could do it all right. At a time when most teams employed the two-goalie system to preserve their net-minders in the bull's-eye world of the NHL, Dryden was an ironman. He played in sixty-four games, more than any other goalie in the league, and produced a 2.24 goals-against average with eight shutouts. The fourteen games he missed were because of a persistent back problem that had him in traction for a while and, without him in the nets, the Canadiens floundered. When he returned, the team straightened out again. His performance earned him the Calder Trophy as NHL Rookie of the Year, this on top of his playoff MVP of the year before. NHL rules stipulate rookie eligibility and Dryden's playoff experience did not disqualify him from the first-year award in 1971–72.

Dryden was a gold mine for writers. He rarely answered a question with a simple "yes" or "no" so widely used by less articulate athletes. Once, a newsman asked him about Bobby Hull's slapshot and Dryden, who has turned goal-tending into a personal science, admitted that if it were aimed well, Hull's slapper could be unstoppable.

"Hull's slapshot has been clocked at just under one hundred twenty miles per hour," said Dryden. "If he blasts at my upper left-hand corner from our blueline and my glove is two feet below the point of entry, it is quite impossible to stop it. Why? It takes less than half a second for the puck to travel from stick to nets, which is less time than is required for my brain computer to decide what to do, to tell my glove hand to lift and to have the glove lift."

While he was backstopping the Canadiens and operating his brain computer on the ice, he was also running it at McGill in his third and final year of law school. He laughed at suggestions that he couldn't combine the two careers competently—a suggestion that had sent him off to the National team just a couple of years earlier. "They have this great myth that anyone who has anything else to do obviously does not approach hockey with the proper frame of mind, but to me it's just the opposite," said Dryden. "Hockey as a twenty-four-hour job, 365 days a year, is absurd."

Dave Dryden knows just what his brother means. "If he were just a hockey player," said Dave, the schoolteacher-goalie, "his intelligence would work against him. There's too much free time to worry if you're as thoughtful as he is. If he's frustrated by hockey, he has school as an outlet."

"Hockey is enjoyable, and a challenge," said Ken. "That's why I play it. Believe me, I couldn't live with law alone."

Ken and Lynda Dryden were summering in Vienna after his first full NHL season, when he got the phone call from Rochester, New York. The caller was Harry Sinden, who would be coaching a team of NHL All-Stars in an eight-game, pre-1973 season series against the Russian National team. Sinden wanted Ken as one of Team Canada's goalies and it didn't take long for the moonlighting lawyer to accept. The series began with four games in Canada in early September and then concluded with four in Moscow later in the month.

"It was a great experience," said Dryden, whose original interest in international hockey had helped lure him to Canada's National team after Cornell. Canada won the eight-game series, 4–3–1. "I knew they were good, but I was surprised that they held up so well against this level of opposition." Dryden found himself changing his concepts of goaltending as a result of the Russian experience. "My attitudes changed daily," he said. "I would discard ideas almost as fast as I was getting them when I found they didn't work. I'm really glad one thing came up, because it affected my basic approach to playing goal. I found that you just don't play outside the crease against a team like Russia.

"I've been tempted to roam in the NHL. It seems sensible, but you often gamble unnecessarily. Against Russia, I was going out from the cage, assuming that the man coming in with the puck was going to shoot. But the Russians think equally of passing or shooting in that situation. A team like Russia that can make crisp position passes in close can ruin a roaming goalie."

So Dryden altered his style a bit, not roaming as much as he might have before the Russian confrontation. Did it work? Well, the scholarly goalie returned to the NHL and played fifty-four games with the Canadiens, turning a 2.26 goals-against average and a 33–7–13 won-lost-tied log. Again, his back gave him mid-season problems, but young Wayne Thomas and Michel Plasse filled in admirably, and when the season was over Montreal had surrendered fewer goals than any other team in the NHL. That meant the Vezina Trophy for Dryden and his helpers. Then the Canadiens capped the season with still another Stanley Cup, the second with Dryden in the nets.

The Vezina joined his Rookie of the Year Calder Trophy and playoff MVP Smythe Trophy on the Dryden mantelpiece. Not a bad haul for the young attorney. "You don't win awards without help," said Dryden. "I played most of our games in goal, but Plasse and Thomas played a lot too, and had great records. We had great defensemen in front of us and great forwards who monopolized the puck. Maybe it's a cliché, but you don't win much without the help of others. Few forwards could score much without getting the good passes. And few goaltenders could stop scoring without getting support from their defensemen and backchecking forwards."

Dryden remains the picture of coolness under the pressure of tending goal. He prepares for each night in the nets with a calm composed schedule. "I like to take walks on the day of a game, then attempt to have a little snooze in the afternoon," he said. If he has a problem getting that nap, Dryden keeps a law book handy. Usually one on trusts. "There's nothing like trusts," the counselor said, "to put you to sleep."

Before the 1973–74 season, Dryden decided he would not be taking any afternoon snoozes. He announced he was retiring from hockey to devote his full time to practicing law. Some saw this as an attempt at obtaining a better contract from the Canadiens and were sure he'd be back on the ice. Others, impressed with the goals of the summertime Nader Raider, felt Dryden had made a thoughtful decision and would stick to it.

And that's exactly what he did, spending the year fulfilling his law internship duties. But he wasn't completely removed from hockey. The Toronto Toros of the World Hockey Association hired him as a broadcaster and he found himself a local league where he could satisfy his need to stop pucks. When play lapsed, he would lean on his big goalie stick in the same casual style he had when he was playing for the Stanley Cup. He was the same Ken Dryden as always.

But, after sitting out the 1973–74 season while he completed his law internship, Dryden announced his comeback with the signing of a multi-year contract with the Canadiens in May, 1974.

Montreal Canadiens

**Boyish Ken Dryden,
a summertime Nader Raider,
has mastered the art
of stopping pucks that
are "Unsafe at any Speed."**

Georges Vezina has his
skates on, but he preferred
guarding the nets
without skates.

2
GEORGES VEZINA:
THE CHICOUTIMI CUCUMBER

Every year the National Hockey League salutes its leading goaltenders with the presentation of the Vezina Trophy in recognition of the best defensive record. The trophy honors the memory of Georges Vezina, one of the league's first outstanding goaltenders, who enjoyed a brilliant fifteen-year career with the Montreal Canadiens from 1910 to 1925.

Georges Vezina played his hockey in a different era. Goalies in his day were not allowed to drop to the ice for a save. If a net-minder went down, he was subject to a penalty and a fine as well. So Georges Vezina never went down. He stood straight and tall in front of the Canadiens' net and from the first day he climbed into a Montreal uniform until the last day he never missed a scheduled game. Game after game, Vezina played goal, a tall, gangly, poker-faced man who rarely betrayed the emotions of his job.

The Canadiens found Vezina in his native Chicoutimi, Quebec, a tiny lumber town on the Saguenay River. Georges was born there in 1887 and grew up playing hockey. He developed into a first-rate goaltender, but he had an odd hang-up. Wearing skates bothered him, so he tended the nets without them. It wasn't until he turned twenty that Vezina began wearing blades regularly. And when he finally conceded to that hockey convention, it had no effect on his goaltending. He was still the best net-minder in Northern Quebec.

In February 1910, the big-city Montreal Canadiens scheduled an exhibition game visit in little Chicoutimi. Their opponents would be the local amateur team, a squad of hockey Lilliputians led by a lanky goaltender named Vezina.

The Canadiens came north with some of the best scorers in the National Hockey Association, forerunner of the NHL. Included in the cast were Newsy Lalonde, Didier Pitre, and Jack Laviolette—all future Hall of Famers. In goal, the Canadiens used Joe Cattarinich, who also doubled as the team's coach. If Vezina was impressed by the pros, he certainly didn't show it. The goalie leaned lazily against his net during lapses in the action and when play resumed he stopped every thrust the Canadiens tried.

Once, Lalonde had him at his mercy, or so it seemed. As the Canadiens' top scorer zoomed in on him, Vezina never gave an inch. He refused to be lured by Lalonde's fakes and finally the Montreal forward had used up all his options and had run out of maneuvering room. He threw a desperate shot that Vezina deflected deftly into the corner, out of danger.

Again and again, the Canadiens swarmed past the amateur team's flimsy defense to test Vezina; again and again the tall goalie kept the puck out of his net. At the other end of the ice, Cattarinich was experiencing conflicting emotions. There was frustration over the Canadiens' failure to score against this amateur team and admiration for the goaltending performance that tall kid was putting on in the Chicoutimi nets.

Finally, the amateurs broke through Cattarinich for one goal and then another. Now the Canadiens threw everything they had at Vezina, but Georges stood tall, kicking out every Montreal shot. Each time the Canadiens fired, Vezina would either smother the shot or block it with his stick and turn it toward the corner. Rarely did Montreal get a rebound opportunity. Soon time ran out and the little Chicoutimi amateurs had scored a major upset over the Canadiens. Cattarinich was embarrassed by the loss, but he knew that he had come across something special on that trip to Chicoutimi. When the Canadiens returned to Montreal, the coach wasted no time contacting George Kennedy, owner of the club.

"There's a goalie up in Chicoutimi we have to get," Cattarinich told his boss, knowing that he was putting his own net-minding job in jeopardy. The following winter, Georges Vezina was in goal for the Montreal Canadiens.

Vezina's debut came on New Year's Eve, December 31,

1910, in Montreal and the Ottawa Senators beat him, 5–3. But the goalie from Chicoutimi rebounded and went on to lead all net-minders in the NHL that season with a 3.9 goals-against average. His goaltending was marked by the same composure Cattarinich had noticed in the amateur game the previous February. Vezina had an uncanny ability to stay cool even though the area around his net sometimes resembled the eye of a hurricane. His calm posture earned him the nickname of "The Chicoutimi Cucumber." It described Georges perfectly.

Vezina was a man of few words who moved purposefully through his goaltending chores and left the job behind him when the game was over. He was a devoted family man who fathered two sets of triplets in his first two years of marriage and eventually had twenty-two children. One of his sons was born on March 30, 1916, the night the Canadiens defeated Portland 2–1 to clinch the Stanley Cup. Vezina dutifully christened his son, Stanley, to commemorate the victory.

The Canadiens' goalie was at his best in the clutch show-down games. Once, in a match between Montreal and Ottawa with the league championship hanging in the balance, Vezina blocked seventy-eight of seventy-nine shots. Performances like that made Vezina one of the Canadiens' most beloved performers.

He was a private man who never smoked or drank. His career with the Canadiens was never bound by a signed contract. He preferred to seal his relationship each season with a handshake. He was something of a philosopher who liked to express his thoughts in essays that belied his limited formal education.

Although Vezina guarded his privacy with a passion, he also was a good team man. When the Canadiens won the Stanley Cup again in 1924, Leo Dandurand, one of the owners, invited the team to a party at his home. In those days, the Stanley Cup was more than the symbolic trophy it is today. When a team won the Cup then, it really won it. The players could cart the prize home with them.

When Dandurand issued his party invitation, a group of Canadiens, including Vezina, hopped in a Model T Ford and headed for the owner's home. They carried the Stanley Cup with them. When the Tin Lizzie began to balk on a steep Montreal hill, the players hopped out to push. Since it is difficult to push a car while lugging the Stanley Cup, the hardware was put down on the sidewalk. It was still there, on the sidewalk, when Vezina and the others got back into the car to continue the trip to Dandurand's home. And, fortunately, it was still there, on the same sidewalk, when the players discovered their oversight a few hours later and rushed back for it.

Five times, Vezina led the league's goaltenders. In 1925, he finished with a sparkling 1.9 goals-against average for his fifth defensive title. But there was something not entirely right with the goaltending giant. Beads of perspiration formed on his forehead for no apparent reason. Now and then he suffered heavy coughing spells. There was pain in his chest.

When Vezina showed up for the 1925–26 NHL season, he looked like a man fighting a battle with disease. He was pale and had lost weight. His uniform hung loosely on his six-foot frame. He did not resemble the goaltending stone wall his teammates had remembered so well from past years.

On November 28, 1925, the Canadiens were set to open the season against a new NHL team, the Pittsburgh Pirates, at the Mount Royal Arena. It was a rainy night and when Vezina arrived for the game, he looked absolutely terrible.

Leo Dandurand approached his goalie. "Georges," he said, "are you all right?" Vezina shook off the Canadiens' general manager. "I'm okay," the goalie replied softly, as chills and fever whipped through his body.

Vezina skated out to the Canadiens' nets as he had done 367 consecutive times since George Kennedy first brought him to Montreal fifteen years before. His body operated on reflex through a pressure-packed first period as he held off the Pittsburgh club. Once, at a break in the action, he staggered over to the Canadiens' bench for a breather, but then returned quickly to the nets.

When the period was over, Vezina barely made it to the dressing room. Inside, he collapsed, suffering an arterial hemorrhage. Dandurand moved to replace his goalie, but Vezina would not allow it. And as the second period began, Vezina returned to the Montreal nets.

By now, his uniform was soaked. His brain was pounding,

seemingly ready to explode from the fever that soared through his body. Fighting back gamely, Vezina tried to continue, but his legs just would not respond to his commands. The end, he knew, was near.

Suddenly, the crowd of six thousand fans gasped. There, sprawled in the Montreal nets, lay the great Vezina. His body had simply given its last ounce of energy and he finally had collapsed, exhausted. A ghostly silence hung over the arena as the great goalie was carried off the ice.

A few days later, a physician gave Vezina the dread news: he was suffering from an advanced state of tuberculosis and had only a few months to live. The unobtrusive Vezina quietly packed his bags and returned to Chicoutimi. He wanted to live out his last days in the little lumber town that was his home.

On March 26, 1926, almost four months to the day after he had collapsed on the ice in Montreal, Vezina died. Death came quietly to the great goalie. But the Canadiens were determined that his memory be perpetuated. The next year, Leo Dandurand, Louis Letourneau, and Joe Cattarinich, the owners of the Montreal club, presented a trophy to the NHL to be presented to the leading goalie each season. Ever since then, the Vezina Trophy has been the measure of goaltending greatness, named for the goaltender who may have been the greatest of them all.

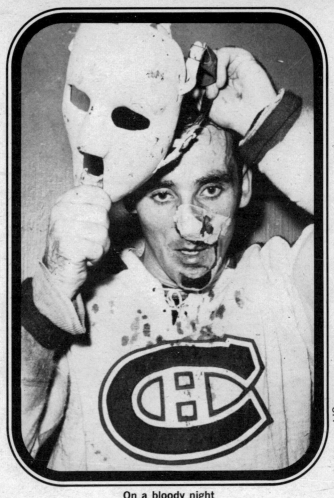

On a bloody night
in November 1959,
Jacques Plante donned a mask
for the first time.

UPI

3
JACQUES
PLANTE:
THE INNOVATOR

The puck was in New York's end of the ice and, for a moment at least, Jacques Plante could relax. The Canadiens buzzed around Ranger goalie Gump Worsley, applying the kind of pressure they had made famous. The puck zipped from stick to stick, and Worsley darted from side to side. up and down, trying to block the shot before it could hit the net behind him. At the other end of the ice, Plante watched and hoped his teammates could keep the puck in New York's zone for a while so that he could relax.

No such luck. A misplaced Montreal pass had been intercepted and now it was the Rangers' turn to attack. They rused out of their zone with the puck, not in any way as precisely as Montreal's machinelike attack, but moving up-ice nevertheless. Over the blue line they swarmed and Plante, stationed in front of the Canadiens' net, crouched, ready to meet their attack. At the other end of the ice, it was Worsley's turn to take it easy and watch Jacques work. Gump stood casually, one elbow resting on the crossbar, as his teammates worked on Plante.

First, a long shot from inside the blue line thumped off Plante's pad and toward the corner. A Ranger forward grabbed the rebound and tried to stuff it between Plante and the goalpost, but Jacques anticipated the move and shifted quickly to cut it off. Again, the puck banged off his big stick. A Montreal defender tried to clear the rubber out of danger, but couldn't and it fell back into New York hands. A quick flip shot and Plante flicked out his gloved hand and snatched the puck like a first baseman, holding it to his chest and forcing a faceoff. The Rangers' first thrusts had been thwarted as the referee's whistle blew, halting play.

Now the two teams lined up in front of Plante, ready for the linesman to drop the puck in the circle on the right side of the ice. Plante crouched low, one knee almost touching the ice, the other a bit higher, waiting for the action to start again. As the rubber dropped, the sticks of the two center icemen banged together, as they tried to gain control. Finally, it bounced loose toward the middle of the ice. Plante straightened up, following the flight of the puck. In front of him, a dozen hockey players jockeyed for position, tugging and shoving at one another, all intent on getting at that bouncing black puck.

Finally, New York's Andy Bathgate reached it, controlling on the blade of his stick. Now some form began to develop out of the chaos in front of Plante. The Ranger skaters tried to break free, set themselves up for a pass or screen Plante, blocking his view of Bathgate and hoping perhaps to tip a wide shot past the goalie. Meanwhile, the Montreal players tried to clear the Rangers away from the net and at the same time attempted to anticipate Bathgate and get the puck away from the talented Ranger right wing. For Plante, it made little difference what the players in front of him tried. All he knew was that they blocked his vision. All he could see was a tangle of bodies and legs and, beyond it, Bathgate, controlling the puck on the blade of his stick. Jacques could see Bathgate, but not the puck. And any goalie will tell you that he has to always see the puck to do his job properly.

Jacques bobbed and weaved, trying desperately to shove the bodies away from the front of his net so he could see what Bathgate was up to. But it was no use. The crowd in front wasn't cooperating and neither was Bathgate. Plante could see the Ranger star drop his shoulders and lean into the puck. Immediately, Jacques knew Bathgate was not passing. He was shooting. But there was one very important problem for Plante. He couldn't see the puck. He would need a little bit of luck on this shot.

Bathgate's powerful arms brought his stick down on the puck with tremendous force. He hit the rubber squarely, sending a sizzling backhander toward the Montreal net. Somehow, the small rubber disc weaved its way through the mass of bodies in front of Plante and headed straight for the Montreal net. Plante was still playing peek-a-boo, searching for it, when the puck emerged from the crowd in front of him. It was a rising shot and it was on him before he could move. The disc crashed into his face with a dull thud and the goalie crumbled to the ice, blood gushing from the wound.

Quickly, the Canadiens gathered around Plante. The trainer was on the ice immediately to examine the damage. The puck had caught Plante above his lip, at the corner of his nose, and the blood was flowing freely. His teammates got him on his feet and helped him to the dressing room, where seven stitches were taken in the wound. As the doctor stitched Plante, Montreal's coach, Toe Blake, paced nervously. Hockey's two-goalie system had not yet been introduced. Jacques was the Canadiens' only goalie. If he could not continue, the Montreal club would have to use the home team's house goalie, on call for just such emergencies. In New York, the house goalie was Joe Schaefer, who would never be mistaken for an NHL player. When Schaefer, a fine fellow, had to play you knew the other goalie was in pretty bad shape. If Plante could stand up, reasoned Blake, his Canadiens would have a better shot with a wounded Jacques than with a healthy Schaefer.

While Blake was considering his options, his fallen goalie motioned to the coach. Plante was seated on the first-aid table and the doctor was just finishing his needlework when Blake approached.

"I won't go back without the mask," the goalie said grimly.

Plante had been using an eery, milk-white fiberglass contraption during practice sessions to protect his face. In six big-league seasons, the Montreal goalie had absorbed more than two hundred stitches in his face. He had suffered a broken nose four times and twice his cheekbone had been shattered. Both cheekbone fractures had occurred in practice sessions when a teammate's shot had crashed into Jacques's profile. After the second one, Plante had an awkward plastic mask designed and used it during practices. During the 1958–59 season, a letter was sent to Plante that changed his career.

"It was from the head of a fiberglass company," said

Jacques. "He told me he could make a fiberglass mask that would fit snugly on my face. That was just what I wanted." A tight face-mask could be used in a game and Plante wanted to do just that. When he presented the idea to Blake, though, the coach turned him down. "Plante tells me the mask will keep him in the league after his reflexes and eyesight aren't as sharp as they used to be," said Blake. "But it seems to me that neither his sight nor his reflexes have been impaired. So why the mask?"

The debate had gone on through the first month of the 1959 season. Now, as he sat on the first-aid table, the thirty-year-old goalie ended the argument once and for all. If Blake wanted Jacques back in the nets, it would have to be with the mask. The coach realized that his goalie had made his mind up once and for all not to expose his face to shots like Bathgate's any more. Without a word, Blake nodded and turned away. Plante reached into an equipment bag and came up with the mask. He adjusted the straps and pulled it over his face, trying not to disturb the blood-spattered gauze covering his cut. Now he waddled out the dressing-room door, down the rubber mat, and through the entranceway to the Madison Square Garden ice. A huge ovation greeted his return and then, when the fans saw the mask, there was a stunned silence. The date was November 1, 1959, an historic date for all goalies. A balcony fan, aware of the calendar, leaned over the railing and shouted at the masked goalie. "Hey, Plante," he yelled. "Take that thing off. Halloween's over."

Jacques, of course, did not take it off. He stopped everything the Rangers threw at him and the only goal New York got came on a rebound by Camille Henry after Plante had done a split to stop Bathgate. Montreal won by a score of 3–1, stretching its unbeaten streak to eight games. The streak continued for ten more games, a total of eighteen in all, eleven of them with Plante sporting the mask. In those eleven games, Plante surrendered just thirteen goals. He was every bit as good with the mask, perhaps even better, as he had been before putting it on. He knew that he was on the spot with the face covering. He had to show that it did not hinder his efficiency and, in fact, that it even helped him.

"It's been in people's minds that masks are no good for

goalies," said Plante. "If I wore a mask when Boston beat us 8–4, they would all say, 'See, it was the mask.' I had to show good results to keep the mask." The results were so good that even the doubtful Blake was impressed. "He wore it in training camp," said the coach, "and I didn't think he was sharp with it. But I think it's coming. I think they'll get a better mask and eventually all the goalies will wear it."

Plante's original mask was an all-but-indestructible affair. He delighted in displaying it to dressing-room visitors. "Here, feel it," he would say. "That's hard fiberglass. We tested it, hit the thing with a hammer, and couldn't break it." Those tests convinced Jacques that the mask would provide him with the protection he needed to face the one-hundred-mile-an-hour shots that NHL goalies must live with game in and game out. He also knew that he'd have to win with it in order to have it accepted. He knew that Blake was a conventional coach—a traditionalist. And traditionally, goalies played bare-faced. "If we had started to lose, he would have ordered me to take off the mask," said Plante. "As long as we were winning, I was okay."

Plante proved to be a prophet. When the Canadiens hit a slump late in the 1959–60 season, Blake blamed the mask. "I've said before that Plante won the Vezina Trophy four years in a row without the mask," said Blake. "I'm wondering if he really needs it now. If the mask is affecting his play, perhaps he should try to do without it." Plante agreed to try playing without the mask. The experiment lasted one game. The Canadiens lost 3–0 to Detroit and Jacques never played another game without it. "I play just the same with it or without it," he said, "and I have just as much guts whether I wear it or not. The first duty of a goalie, of course, is to stop shots. But there's also a natural instinct to guard against injury. Look at the way the hockey fan, protected by unbreakable glass, ducks and put his hands to his face when the puck strikes the glass in front of him."

When Plante first put on the mask, some other players suggested that the Canadien's goalie had lost his courage. Plante sneered at that kind of talk. "If you jump out of a plane without a parachute," asked Plante, "does that make you brave? No, I think that makes you stupid. I will never play without the mask again."

Plante had spent too many nights in hospitals after stopping pucks with his bare face. "Until you have a broken cheekbone," he said, "you don't realize what it's like. Cuts don't mean anything. But the feeling you get when a bone is broken . . . you take it home with you. You're in the hospital and you say to yourself, 'I'm never going to play again.' You can see the puck hit you in your sleep and you wake up and figure you've just been hit again. Then, two weeks later, you want to go back and you're out there again. Before I wore the mask, I'd go home after a game and say if a shot had been two or three inches closer, I'd have been in the hospital again."

Once Glenn Hall, one of the last goalies to adopt a face mask, asked Plante what it felt like when the puck hit the mask. Plante smiled. "It's like not having one on," he said. "It doesn't cut, but it burns. Once I got hit twice, back to back, in a game with Toronto. Red Kelly shot and hit me in the face and the rebound went to Frank Mahovlich. I dove for the puck and his shot hit me right where the mask protects my nose."

"You weren't scratched or anything?" wondered Hall.

"I had a nosebleed, that's all. But my nose was sore for about two weeks," said Plante.

Plante had led National Hockey League goalies four times before putting on the mask. After he started wearing the protection, he added three more Vezina Trophies to his collection, sharing the last one with Hall in St. Louis, playing for an expansion team in 1968–69. He was still playing in the NHL at the age of forty-four and credited the mask with prolonging his career far beyond expectations.

"The mask did it," he said. "Without it, I could never have played so long." Plante never was short on confidence, but the mask gave him even more of that valuable commodity. "I am the best goalie in the league," he said, shortly after putting it on, "and with the mask, I am even better. I can laugh at getting hit in the face. I can use my face to stop pucks. Look, I don't care how brave you are. You are going to put your arm up to protect your face when you dive into a pileup. That means you can't have your eye on the puck. With the mask, you don't worry and you can keep watching the puck. Before the mask, you would go home and lie awake in bed, thinking about the shot that just missed your face. You know if one hits your eye, your career is over. Once I put on the mask, I didn't worry—not on the day of the game and not afterwards either."

The mask became as much a part of Plante as Plante was a part of Montreal's vastly successful Canadiens. Jacques played nine seasons for Montreal, and set a record with five consecutive Vezina Trophies. During his term in the Canadiens' nets, the team won the Stanley Cup five consecutive years, the same five years that Plante won his Vezinas. And then, one June day in 1963, he was gone, traded to the New York Rangers in a mammoth seven-player deal that rocked the hockey world. Plante and forwards Phil Goyette and Donnie Marshall moved to the lowly Rangers in exchange for goalie Gump Worsley and three young forwards—Dave Balon, Len Ronson, and Leon Rochefort. Ranger General Manager Muzz Patrick appeared to have come out on top in the deal and even Frank Selke, Montreal's GM, agreed that "Worsley never saw the day he could play like Plante when Jacques was at his best." The problem was that Plante wasn't always at his best. "We got rid of Plante," continued Selke, "because we couldn't depend on him any more."

The problem was Plante's ailments, real or imagined. He suffered from asthma throughout his childhood and it was real enough to force him to sleep sitting up, coughing long into the night. As a teenager, the asthma disappeared, but in his later years with the Canadiens it reappeared. He suffered most in Toronto and claimed that a disinfectant used in the hotel where the Canadiens stayed was the cause of his problem. Reluctantly, management agreed to let him stay at another hotel. But he had to join the rest of the players for the pregame meal and meeting, and as soon as he set foot into the regular hotel, he'd start wheezing all over again.

"Plante had become a disturbing, upsetting influence on the rest of the team," said Ken Reardon, a vice president of the Canadiens. "His asthma was bothering him and in the dressing room before the game, he'd be breathing hard. Sometimes gasping and using a nasal spray. That's not the way for a goalie to make the other players confident." Selke, too, was troubled by his goalie's health problems. There was always some doubt in the minds of the club's management as to how real Plante's problems were. "How can a man be all right Friday night and show up sick Saturday morning?" wondered Selke.

Another time, Plante complained about his knee and was sent to have it X-rayed. The doctor's examination and pictures of his leg showed no damage, but Plante continued to complain, insisting he was hurting. Finally, the doctors agreed to operate. "They opened up my knee, not my head," said Plante, "and they took out three pieces of cartilage. Only then did they believe I was really hurt." The constant parrying between management and goalie reached its peak in the 1962 playoffs when Toronto eliminated Montreal in five games. The Maple Leafs won the deciding game 5–0, and Toe Blake was livid afterward.

"That's it," stormed Blake. "I'm through with him. If Plante is back here next year, I won't be. How can you run a team when you're never sure if your goalie is going to play?" Blake left the decision squarely up to the Canadiens. They would have to choose between their hypochondriac goaltender and the coach. The club chose the coach and within a few weeks Plante and his mask were traded away. The deal was a blockbuster and left a bad taste in Jacques's mouth. He heard he'd been traded while driving along in his car, listening to the radio. It left him speechless—but not for long. He composed himself quickly and was ready for the barrage of reporters' questions.

"I was really hoping to be traded to the Rangers," he said. "This is a big challenge for me. A lot of people said I had a good record only because I was with a great team. This is my big chance to prove it isn't so. A lot of people said I won the Vezina trophies because Doug Harvey was always in front of me. But I won the trophy and the Most Valuable Player award after he went to the Rangers. I played my best that year, too, because it was a big challenge."

As happy as the Canadiens were at getting rid of Plante and his problems, the Rangers were just as thrilled to acquire Jacques. "He is absolutely the greatest goalie who ever played this game," said GM Muzz Patrick, who engineered the deal. "You can't give the guy enough credit," said Andy Bathgate, the man who drove Plante to the mask and who now was his teammate. "He came in here new and he's showing our guys why he's the best." The ultimate tribute to Plante during his first training camp with the Rangers came from Ulf

Sterner, a Swedish player who had been invited to work out with the Rangers. After Jacques had stopped the Swede repeatedly, newsmen asked Sterner what he thought of the goalie. "Plante," he said, "he's impossible."

Jacques's Madison Square Garden debut in a Ranger uniform came on October 16, 1963, and Plante rose to the occasion with a 3–0 shutout of the Detroit Red Wings. A crowd of 15,240, largest to watch a Ranger home opener in sixteen years, showed up and gave Plante an enormous standing ovation when the game was over. Jacques, enjoying every moment, thrust his hands over his head in triumph, another of the little habits that had left Montreal management disenchanted with him. "I was keyed up for my first appearance in New York," the goalie said. "All I wanted was to play well for the New York fans and for the Rangers. The win couldn't have been better. And the crowd at the end . . . it left me with a chill between the shoulders."

Plante compared that Madison Square Garden bow with the first game he ever played in the National Hockey League. "I was every bit as nervous," the goalie said. The circumstances, however, were quite different. Instead of October, it was April 1953, when hockey's cherished Stanley Cup was on the line. Plante had spent the season playing for Buffalo of the American Hockey League. When the AHL season ended, the Canadiens called him up as a standby goalie for the playoffs to back up regular Gerry McNeil. After five games of the semifinal series, the Canadiens found themselves trailing Chicago three games to two, only one loss away from Stanley Cup elimination. Coach Dick Irvin was desperate and he made a drastic decision. He would insert his rookie goalie, Plante, into the lineup.

"On the morning of that sixth game," said Plante, "the coach came over to me when I came down from my hotel room. He said, 'You're playing tonight, and you're going to get a shutout.'" Plante spent the rest of the day getting nervous. He would be breaking into the NHL under less than ideal circumstances, with no margin for mistakes.

By the time he got to the dressing room, Plante was in a terrible state. "I was so nervous I couldn't tie my skates," he said. "My hands were shaking so much, I didn't know if I could play." Across the room, Maurice Richard, captain of the Canadiens, noticed the young goalie and his problem.

"The Rocket must have realized how I felt," said Plante. He walked over and held out his hands. 'Look at them,' he said. 'They always shake before a big game. You'll feel better when you get out on the ice.'"

Plante strapped on the heavy pads and climbed into the Montreal sweater with the "CH" on the front. Now he struggled up the narrow staircase from the dressing room to the Chicago Stadium ice. "There was a full house," he said. "Some of the fans didn't even know who was in goal for us. A few of them yelled, 'You're a bum, McNeil.' I was still pretty shaky." Then a good thing happened to Jacques. Shortly after the game started, Jimmy McFadden of the Black Hawks broke into Montreal's ice all alone with the puck on his stick. It was shooter against goalie—the ultimate test of a netminder. McFadden faked once, then dropped his shoulder and fired. Plante did a split and the puck plunked harmlessly off his pad.

"That calmed me down," said Plante. "I felt as though I was in the game." He certainly was in the game. Montreal won 3–0, and Irvin had called the shutout. That tied the semifinal series at three games apiece and Irvin stayed with Plante for the seventh and deciding game. Again, Jacques won and the Canadiens moved into the finals against Boston. Plante played the first two games of that series, winning the opener but losing the second, before Irvin went back to McNeil. The veteran, refreshed from his rest, went on to backstop Montreal to the Cup.

The next year, Plante was back in Buffalo and was leading all AHL goalies when McNeil suffered an injury in the final month of the season. Montreal summoned Jacques and his seventeen games produced five shutouts. The next season the Canadiens' goaltending job was Plante's from the start. "McNeil was having weight problems during training camp," said Plante. "In the practice games, he gave up seventy-two goals and I allowed only thirty-five. One day, Gerry didn't show up for practice. The same thing happened the next day. I heard that he had quit, but I wasn't sure. One night after an exhibition game in the Forum, Mr. Selke called me into his office and told me the job was mine. Later, McNeil came over and said, 'Jacques, I can't beat you. Good luck.' In a way, I felt sorry for him."

That was the start of a fabulous decade in the Canadien

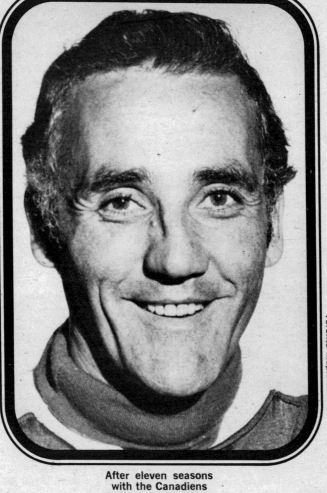

After eleven seasons
with the Canadiens
and stints with the Rangers
and St. Louis Blues,
Jacques Plante became
a Toronto Maple Leaf in 1970.

nets for Plante. Six Vezina Trophies as top goalie and one Hart Trophy as Most Valuable Player in the league would follow before his trade to the Rangers ended an era for him and for the Canadiens. Winning the Vezina in those days was no simple task. The six-team league was loaded with outstanding goaltending talent. Glenn Hall, Terry Sawchuk, Gump Worsley, Johnny Bower, and Harry Lumley were all first-class net-minders. Plante's first Vezina came in 1955–56, when he hooked up in a duel with Hall that was not settled until the final weekend of the season.

"I was two goals behind him," said Jacques. "But I had only one game to play and Hall had two. We played our final game in the Forum on Saturday night against Chicago while the Red Wings [and their goalie, Hall] were in Toronto. We started our Saturday night games at eight-fifteen and the Leafs at eight o'clock. When I came out on the ice, I looked at the scoreboard and saw that Toronto was leading, 1–0. That put me only one goal behind Hall. Halfway through the second period, Toronto scored again. That made us even. We were in the third period when the final score from Toronto was posted. The Red Wings had won 6–3, and now I was one goal in front. I was shutting out the Hawks, but there still was plenty of time for them to score."

Plante knew that if he could hang on and blank the Hawks, the Vezina would be his. The tension built as the clock ran down. "I couldn't watch the scoreboard clock because it was behind the goal in the Forum," said Plante. But a fan sitting on my left kept shouting, 'Come on Jacques. There's only nine minutes left . . . eight . . . seven.' It seemed like a long time, but the game finally ended. We won 3–0, and I had my first Vezina."

His years at Montreal were full of dramatic high spots like that first Vezina. He had come a long way from his days as a fifty-cent-a-game goaltender for the factory team in his hometown of Shawinigan Falls, Quebec. Plante's first experience at playing target for ambitious shooters came when he was twelve years old. His father came home from an office Christmas party carrying a goalie stick and young Jacques was a net-minder from then on. He was a student at Ecole St. Maurice School in Shawinigan when he first tried organized hockey shortly after getting that stick.

"Our hockey team consisted of boys seventeen and eighteen years old and I used to watch them play all the time on the outdoor rink. On this day, I remember it was very cold and I was looking at the game while standing indoors with my back against a stove. The goalie was having trouble and the coach accused him of not doing his best. The goalie got mad and took his skates off. I rushed toward the coach and volunteered to take his place. There was no other goalie around, so I went in the net and played with them for the rest of the season."

By the time he was fifteen, Plante had advanced to the factory team. "We didn't get paid, so one day my father suggested that I ask the coach for some money. The coach agreed to give me fifty cents a game if I didn't tell any of the other players about it. Even fifty cents meant a lot to me in those days," he said. "I was the oldest of eleven children. We couldn't afford a radio or luxuries of any kind. The only time we had soft drinks was at Christmas."

Because he was the oldest, Jacques often helped his mother with chores at home. She taught him to knit and he made sweaters, stockings, and caps for his younger brothers and sisters. In fact, when he first turned professional, he would knit to pass the time on long minor-league bus rides. He often wore the toques he knitted and when he reached the National Hockey League, it took considerable coaxing by management to get him to give them up. He switched to knitting turtleneck sweaters which he always wore under his jerseys, claiming they were more comfortable than the standard long underwear most hockey players favor. "That was Jacques for you," a former teammate once said. "He had to be different. He always had a new idea to change things. He was a freethinker."

The trade from Montreal to New York did nothing to change that aspect of Plante. Early in his Ranger career, he insisted that Madison Square Garden's nets were not regulation size. Their dimensions, he said, were an inch or so off the required six feet by four feet prescribed in the rule book. A hasty check was made and Plante was discovered to be right. The nets were changed with a minimum of fanfare and Jacques moved on to another project. He suggested that the Rangers were defending the wrong end of the ice for two periods of every game at home. Because of the configuration of the Madison Square Garden ice surface and location of the player benches, the home club's bench was a few strides further away from the net New York defended in the first and third periods than the visitor's bench was.

Plante argued, and logically, that New York should defend the net closest to its bench for two periods so that the goalie could get off more quickly on a delayed penalty. It was farfetched to believe that it could ever make a difference, but logic *did* support Plante's idea. The Rangers never did change ends, mainly because season-ticket subscribers, who picked their locations specifically to watch the club attack at their end for two periods, wanted two periods of attack, not one. That was okay with Plante, but if the Rangers weren't going to take his suggestion, well, he couldn't be expected to come tearing off the ice on every delayed penalty.

It was little conflicts like this one that made Plante's two seasons in the Ranger organization probably the stormiest of his career. On one occasion, he popped off to a New York newspaperman, saying the Rangers were riddled with dissension and blaming management for a variety of shortcomings. The story rocked the organization and eventually led to the dismissal of Muzz Patrick as general manager. In only two years in New York, Plante had bagged a GM. That was more front-office turmoil than he managed in ten years in Montreal.

After the 1964–65 season, Plante, age thirty-six, announced his retirement from hockey. "I've been away from my wife and family an awfully long time," Plante said. "I believe it's time to spend more time with them." When he was asked if his health—he had just undergone knee surgery—had entered the decision, Jacques said it had not. "I feel fine and maybe I could play another four or five years. I'm sorry to quit and I know I may never make as much money as I'm making now."

Plante's old friend, Gump Worsley, predicted Jacques's retirement would be only temporary. "Wait until the greenbacks start flashing," said Worsley. The Gump had a firsthand familiarity with Plante's affection for money. It happened shortly after the huge 1963 trade that saw the two goalies switch teams. A television producer called Plante and said he wanted Jacques and Worsley on a show to discuss the controversial trade.

"How much?" asked Plante. "Normally," replied the producer, "we don't pay anything, but we'll pay you and Worsley fifty dollars apiece."

Jacques agreed and then hurried to the nearest phone to call Worsley. "Are you going to appear on the television show tomorrow?" he asked.

"Yeah," replied the Gump.

"Are they paying you one hundred dollars too?" continued Plante.

"Yeah," answered Worsley.

Quickly, Plante called the producer back. "I won't appear on your show," he snapped. "You offered me only fifty dollars. Worsley's getting one hundred." The producer calmed Plante down and, after several minutes, convinced Jacques that Worsley was getting the same fifty dollars they had agreed on earlier. The next morning, Plante showed up at the studio, but not Worsley.

A few days later, their paths crossed and Jacques asked Gump why he hadn't shown up. "Why should I?" snapped Gump. "They were paying you a hundred dollars and I was only getting fifty."

After Plante's retirement, he moved from the ice to the press box, authoring a weekly column for a French-language newspaper in Montreal. Two years after he quit, the NHL added six new teams and the two-goalie system came into style. Suddenly twenty-four net-minders instead of only six were earning NHL salaries. Plante, meanwhile, had stayed in shape playing in weekend leagues and oldtimers' games. He would sit in the Montreal press booth and watch a variety of less than awesome athletes station themselves in front of NHL nets. It soon became apparent to him that the best goalie in the building wasn't on the ice, but up in the press box, writing stories.

So Plante dropped the hint, not so casually, that he would consider strapping on the pads for an NHL team again. He was chatting with Montreal scout Ron Caron during the league's 1968 summer meetings when Scotty Bowman, then general manager-coach of the newly minted St. Louis Blues, came along. "Hey, Scotty," said Caron, "you're looking for a goalie, why not draft Jacques?"

Bowman looked at the slender goalie. "Would you play?" he asked him.

"Draft me," replied Plante.

The next day, Bowman packaged thirty thousand dollars of the Blues' money for delivery to New York in exchange for Plante. Jacques got the news at his office and called home. "When I phoned my wife to tell her, she already knew it. Some newspaper fellow phoned and she told him I couldn't come back because my 'legs were too rubbery.' She didn't realize that you're not necessarily signed when you're drafted. I'll report to training camp next fall if I can come to terms with the Blues. From what I've heard, St. Louis is a tremendous organization. If I'm going to come back, I couldn't have come back with a better team."

The Blues not only had a fine organization, they also had Glenn Hall, like Plante one of the giants of modern goal-tending. "I expect I'll have a great year," said Jacques. "It's the first time I ever had such a good backup man." A generous salary and Hall's presence to share the work brought Plante to the banks of the Mississippi.

Bowman, always a master at maneuvering his men, alternated his aging goalies. Hall played one game while Plante sat in the stands and a rookie dressed as the Blues' backup man. Then Plante played with Hall in the stands and the rookie at the end of the bench. Once Hall was injured and forced to leave the game. The referee forced Bowman to use his backup while Plante made a beeline for the dressing room. Soon the rookie was hurt, or so he claimed, and Jacques played. Plante loved the idea of not having to sit on the bench on the nights he wasn't playing.

"It was much easier that way," he said. "There is not the pressure. I relaxed when Glenn played and he did the same when I played. What a life. When I broke into the league, I had to play every game and every practice."

Bowman pampered his two senior citizens. They enjoyed every luxury he could provide for them. "Why not?" he said. "It's like having Bob Gibson and Sandy Koufax on the same pitching staff."

When the season was over, each of the old goalies had appeared in thirty-seven games. Hall had a 2.17 goals-against average and Plante's was 1.96. Together, they had backstopped the Blues to the West Division championship and together they shared the Vezina Trophy—the same trophy they had battled each other for so bitterly right down to the final weekend of the season thirteen years before.

Plante was in goal for the final game, and when it was over he pulled off his mask in triumph. As the players left the ice, Plante trailed his teammates. Then, as he neared the runway that led to the dressing room, he thrust his arms high in his famous victory salute, his face enveloped in a huge grin. The theatrical Jacques was celebrating his seventh Vezina, an all-time record, and his joy was shared by the partisan St. Louis crowd, which rocked the building in a thunderous roar.

The partnership was equally successful the next year, although the tandem did not capture the Vezina again. But Bowman's skillful juggling of the two goalies helped the Blues to another West Division crown. Plante played in thirty-two games and had a goals-against average of 2.19. He also had five shutouts, the same number he had produced the year before. That meant that in two seasons, totaling sixty-nine games, the old master had ten blankings, about one every seven games.

The Blues reached the Stanley Cup finals for the third straight year and faced Boston for the Cup. In the opening game in St. Louis, Plante was in goal. It was a 1–1 game early in the second period with Boston putting on the pressure during a power play. Fred Stanfield lined up the puck at the blue line and leaned into it, much the way Andy Bathgate had leaned into a puck against Plante eleven years earlier. Stanfield's shot was a low liner and Phil Esposito, stationed in front of Plante, got his stick down, catching the puck with his hooked blade. The rubber shot up at a forty-five-degree angle and Plante, already on the way down to handle Stanfield's shot, never had a chance. The puck crashed into his mask with a crack heard all over the building. Plante went down as if shot, losing consciousness immediately.

Later, he remembered seeing Stanfield and getting set for the shot. After that—nothing. "The next thing that happens, all I know is the pain. It is like somebody coming up behind you and hitting you with a sledgehammer. The pain . . . and then I open my eyes and see all those legs around me. Something is squeezing my tongue. It's burning. I didn't know what was happening. The cool air is in my mouth and that was the oxygen they had brought on the ice." Then Plante stopped and thought for a moment. "You know," he said, "the mask saved my life."

That was the last game Plante played for St. Louis. The next season the goalie, by then forty-one, was sold to Toronto, of all places. Toronto, where he suffered those terrible asthma attacks early in his career. "Oh, that's old stuff," said Plante. "I was younger then and nervous and little things used to upset me. Now I'm much older and wiser. I gave up smoking cigars—five a day—a couple of months ago and I will live in the northern part of the city. I think I can beat the problem."

He did, of course. Wearing a new mask which he built himself, Jacques led the league with a 1.88 goals-against average including four shutouts in forty games. He also launched his own mask company, selling copies of his fiberglass creation to goalies throughout North America. "It's a beauty," said Jacques, displaying his masterpiece. "I spent all summer with my arms in plaster of paris up to the elbows. Most days, I worked from 8:00 A.M. until midnight. But when my mask was finished, I had a great sense of accomplishment. It was worth all the hard work. This was the first time I had a hand in the making of a mask. I just designed and tested the others. This one is foolproof. We tested it with pucks shot from an air cannon."

Plante's show lasted for almost three seasons in Toronto and then, in March 1973, the Leafs traded him to Boston. The Bruins were desperate for goaltending help. Jacques supplied his oldtime magic, playing eight games and coming up a winner seven times. Two of his victories were shutouts, the last one against his old friends, the Rangers, which all but clinched second place for Boston and doomed New York to a third-place finish. It wasn't bad for a guy who had forty-four candles on his most recent birthday cake.

Plante arrived in Boston with a two-year contract and, despite his age, the Bruins were counting on him for heavy work in the 1973–74 season. But Jacques, always the innovator, always ready for a new challenge, had other ideas. The Quebec Nordiques of the World Hockey Association offered him the job of general manager-coach and the proposal appealed to Jacques so much that he decided to jump to the younger league.

Did this mean that his active playing career was over. Not at all. "I can't play this season because Boston owns my playing rights," announced Plante when he took the Quebec job. "But next year. . . ."

And sure enough, Jacques carried out his threat to strap on the pads again. After piloting Quebec to a struggling fifth place finish, Plante announced his resignation from the Nordiques. A few days later came the announcement that he would return to the ice for the 1974 season with the WHA's Edmonton Oilers.

You get the feeling that a man must really enjoy playing target if he's willing to do it at Plante's age. Plante won't argue that. "You must be born a goaltender," he said, "a man alone. The eyes are upon you. You are the target of the game. If you make a mistake, they turn on a red light behind you, a siren goes off and thousands of people scream. There are nights I go home and I tell my wife I don't know how they could score. I filled the net tonight. I blocked it all and every time they shot, I scooped up the puck and laughed, 'Aha, look what I found.' It is nights like that that keep me going. Nights like that that I know I love what I do."

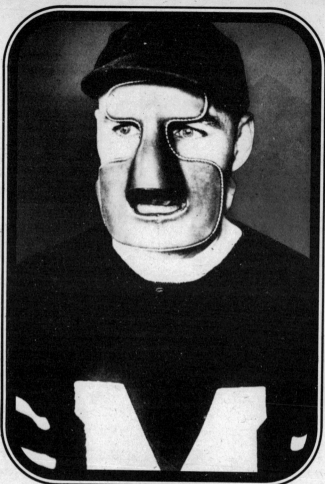

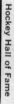
Hockey Hall of Fame

**The Montreal Maroons'
Clint Benedict was hockey's
first masked goalie—
in the 1929–30 season.**

4
CLINT
BENEDICT:
FIRST MASK

When Jacques Plante dramatically skated onto the ice at Madison Square Garden in November 1959, wearing his revolutionary goaltender's mask, he was saluted as a pioneer, a trailblazer whose initiative would forever change the face of goaltending. In Ottawa, Ontario, an old goalie named Clint Benedict just sighed and recalled hockey's first mask— the one he had worn thirty years before Plante did.

Traditionally, Plante is credited with introducing the mask to hockey and he has received the gratitude of scores of goaltenders, and their families, for the innovation. But when Plante first put on the mask, he was only introducing the modern version of an idea that Benedict had introduced three decades earlier.

Benedict, like Plante, was a great goalie, and, like Jacques, he was concerned about having his face serve as a bull's-eye for the National Hockey League's hardest shooters. And, like Plante, Clint did something about it. The only difference was that Benedict's mask did not work as well and Clint, at the end of an outstanding NHL career, decided to retire totally from the game rather than try to perfect the face protector.

"You know," said Benedict after Plante had reintroduced the goalie's face covering, "if we had been able to perfect the mask, I would have been a twenty-year man. I broke in when I was seventeen and I played seventeen seasons." At that time, Benedict's longevity was a record for goalies. It was in his seventeenth season that Clint tried the mask, an awkward-looking leather contraption. It happened after a game between Benedict's Montreal Maroons and their crosstown rivals, the Montreal Canadiens. No love was lost between those two teams and bodies were often scattered around the ice when they met. It was not unusual for the goalies to be included among the casualties.

Benedict was stationed in the Maroons' net when the Canadiens' legendary Howie Morenz broke through the defense and zoomed in on the goalie. Benedict, never noted as a standup goalie, fell to his knees as he shifted to meet Morenz's thrust. Howie, seeing the goalie go down, changed his plan at the last minute. He switched the puck to his backhand and scooped it off his stick, much as a cleaning lady might sweep at dust with a broom. The puck snapped off Morenz's stick point-blank in front of Benedict. The goalie had no time to react and the rubber crashed squarely into his nose. Save—the hard way!

Benedict tumbled to the ice, blood spurting from the wound Morenz's shot had opened up. He was helped to the dressing room and the crowd was surprised not to see him return a few minutes later. Benedict and other goalies of that era were hard rocks who usually shrugged off injuries. "I lost count of the number of stitches they put in my head," he once said. "I remember at least four times being carried into the dressing room to get all stitched up and then going back in to play. There were other times, too, but I don't remember them."

But Clint could not continue this time. Morenz's shot had made sure of that. "He did a great job," the goalie muttered. "I was in bed for a month."

While the doctors put Clint's nose back together, a Boston leather-goods firm was commissioned to create a mask for the goalie. It produced a primitive covering patterned after the football models popular at that time. Because it was designed specifically to protect Benedict's tender nose, the mask concentrated on the middle of the goalie's face. The area around the eyes was completely exposed with the mask covering the forehead, narrowing at the eyes and then protecting the nose, cheeks, and chin.

Benedict was game and put it on for a game against the Chicago Black Hawks. "After we lost 2–1, I threw the darn thing away," said the old goalie. "I blamed it for the loss and that was that. It just didn't work out. The nosepiece protruded too far and obscured my vision on low shots. I also experimented with wire ones, like a baseball catcher's, but the wires distracted me. That's when I gave up."

Another thing that distracted Benedict was Morenz's amazing accuracy when it came to shooting the puck at Benedict's head. After he had recovered from the nose job, Clint took another shot from the Canadiens' star, this one in the larynx. However the damage he absorbed from Morenz did not affect the off-ice relationship between the two men.

"He and I were the best of friends before and after. It was all part of the game. He didn't shoot at my face. Actually, I jumped into the shot. Jim Ward cut in front of me, trying to break up the play, and Morenz got his shot away using Ward as a screen. I saw it at the last split-second and lunged. Wham! I'm out like a light and wake up in the hospital."

That was the end of a career which had begun in Benedict's hometown of Ottawa in 1913. Clint was only seventeen years old when he joined the Senators of the National Hockey Association. The team's regular goalie at the time was Percy Lesueur, who was twelve years older and not nearly as proficient a goaltender as young Benedict. For two years, Lesueur and Benedict shared Ottawa's goaltending with the veteran often starting games and the youngster coming in to relieve him in the second or third period.

By 1915, Benedict had developed into a first-class goalie and Ottawa sold Lesueur to the Toronto Shamrocks. Clint began to carve an impressive record despite the bumps and bruises which were a routine part of a goalie's life even in those days. Primitive equipment was part of the net-minder's problems.

"The sticks in those days weighed a ton," he said. "Goalies used cricket pads. I liked them and never did use heavier padding. And we had five-fingered gloves, not those padded mitts and trappers they use today. My fingers were as badly hurt as my face or legs."

There is evidence that hockey players of Benedict's era were sturdier than their present-day successors.

"Getting hurt was nothing," said the goalie. "I've been hit so hard with a puck that it bounced off my head and into the seats. They just stitched me up and put me back in. They didn't have a goal crease in those days and the forwards would come roaring right in and bang you as hard as they could. If they knocked you down, you were supposed to get back on your feet before you could stop the puck—those were the rules."

Actually, the rules were even stricter than that. Not only weren't goalies allowed to sprawl on the ice to make a save, but referees could impose a fine of two dollars on those net-minders who tried to bend that rule. And one of the best benders was Benedict. He would flop on the ice regularly. "If you made it look like an accident," he said, "you could get away without a penalty. If you did it a little bit sneaky, you could fall on the puck. We [goalies] all watched each other's tricks and that's one of mine which was copied and eventually became part of the game."

Soon Benedict wasn't the only swooning goalie in the league. The fans heckled him when he sprawled, shouting, "Bring your bed, Benny!" But other net-minders adopted his method. The sprawlers had referees perplexed. If the officials enforced the rule against going down, the game would become a farce. The rule would make the game a laughingstock, they said. And so, in 1918, the rule was changed. Goalies no longer were forced to stand up to stop shots. They were now allowed to assume any position they wanted. Clint Benedict and the sprawlers had won a point.

Strangely, the change in rules which he precipitated did not seem to help Benedict's performance at all. In fact, there is evidence that he was hurt by the change. He had led all goalies in the old National Hockey Association in 1915, 1916, and 1917. Then, in 1918, playing in the new National Hockey League with the new sprawling rule, he had a luckluster 5.2 goals-against average and finished third.

But Benedict recovered his form and led the league's goalies for the next five consecutive seasons, giving him a string of eight years out of nine in which he had paced his league in net-minding. In 1920 there were five shoutouts posted in the NHL and all belonged to Benedict. The same thing happened in 1922 when there were but two shutouts and Benedict achieved both of them.

He capped his career with another goaltending crown in 1927, his ninth. That was the first season goalies competed for the Vezina Trophy, named for one of Benedict's goaltending contemporaries who had died the previous year. And although Benedict's 1.51 goals-against average was the best in the league, he lost the Vezina to George Hainsworth of the

Canadiens. The difference was in the obscure wording defining presentation of the trophy. It goes to the goalie of the team allowing the fewest goals. Hainsworth played all of the forty-four Canadiens' games that season and surrendered all sixty-seven goals allowed by the team for a 1.52 goals-against average. Benedict allowed sixty-five goals in forty-three games for a 1.51 average. But his replacement for the one game he missed was Jim Walsh, who gave up three goals, pushing the Maroon's yield for the season to sixty-eight —one more than the Canadiens had given up—and costing Benedict the trophy.

Benedict obviously was an outstanding regular-season goalie as shown by his career 2.49 goals-against average and sixty-one shutouts in 433 games, an average of a shutout every seven games. But he was also a standout in Stanley Cup playoff competition. In fifty-six career Cup games, he had sixteen shutouts and a 2.16 goals-against average. Most of those were achieved before 1927 when the Cup was a challenge trophy competed for between the NHL and teams from Western Canada. Official records for Cup competition begin in 1927, when the trophy came under sole jurisdiction of the NHL. The shutout leader since then has been Jacques Plante with fourteen. Benedict's sixteen blankings are not mentioned in the NHL record book.

Clint did manager one line in the list of Cup records. His four shutouts in the 1927–28 playoffs set a single season Stanley Cup record. He allowed eight goals in nine playoff games that year for a skimpy 0.89 average. Two years before that, he had allowed eight goals in eight games and also achieved four shutouts. That performance, too, is left out of the NHL record book because it was pre-1927.

Benedict's four shutouts and 0.89 playoff average in 1928 would seem to have been enough to carry the Maroons to the Stanley Cup singlehandedly. But they did not. Montreal bowed to the inspired New York Rangers in the finals that year after Lester Patrick, forty-four-year-old general manager-coach of the New York club, had gone into the nets to replace injured Lorne Chabot. The incident is one of the most memorable in hockey history. What is forgotten is that the goalie at the other end was Benedict. He surrendered a goal to Bill Cook and then was beaten in overtime by Frank Boucher for the Rangers' winner.

That proved to be the last hurrah for Benedict. The next year Howie Morenz bounced those two rockets off him that caused, first, his introduction of the goalie's mask and, ultimately, his retirement from hockey.

Because so many of his achievements occurred in hockey's dark ages when recordkeeping was imprecise at best. Benedict was rarely recognized as one of the game's outstanding goalies. But numbers don't lie and leading the league in the goals-against average nine times in seventeen seasons is no small accomplishment. Remember Clint Benedict for that. And the next time Jacques Plante is honored as the man who introduced the mask to goaltending, you might suggest the insertion of the word "modern." After all, Benedict did it thirty years earlier.

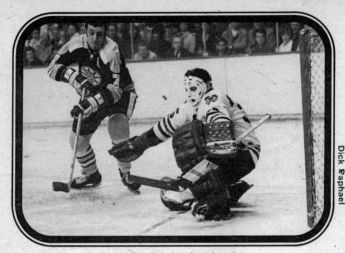

**It was brother against brother
as Boston's Phil Esposito
tries to get one past
Chicago's Tony Esposito.**

Dick Raphael

5
TONY
ESPOSITO:
THE RELUCTANT
BACKSTOP

The telephone jangled, disturbing the mid-afternoon peace hockey players like to enjoy on the day of a game. Phil Esposito of the Boston Bruins lifted the receiver and immediately recognized the voice at the other end. It was his kid brother, Tony, the family goaltender. A week earlier, the younger Esposito had made his National Hockey League debut for the Montreal Canadiens, coming off the bench and surrendering three goals to the Oakland Seals. Brother Phil commiserated with Tony and told him not to worry and that he'd have other chances.

The goalie chuckled and agreed. There would be other chances, starting that very night when the Canadiens were playing the Bruins. At center ice for Boston would be Phil Esposito. In the nets for Montreal would be his brother Tony, making his first NHL start. "Well, good luck," Phil said, "and don't be too tough on the star of the family."

The date was December 5, 1968, and papa Pat Esposito couldn't have been happier with the results of the confrontation between his hockey-playing sons. Tony starred in the Canadiens' nets, backstopping Montreal to a 2–2 tie with the Bruins, always roughest on their home ice at Boston Garden. Both Boston goals belonged to Tony's brother, Phil. Phil was pleased and so was Tony, although the goalie claims to this day that his brother's goals were both lucky shots.

When they met for the first time on an NHL rink, Phil Esposito was an established big-league star with more than one hundred career goals and on his way to the first of many scoring titles. Tony, on the other hand, although only fourteen months younger, had only one minor-league season behind him. That's because the younger Esposito had spent four years playing collegiate hockey at Michigan Tech where he earned All-America honors.

The Espositos grew up in Sault Ste. Marie, Ontario, and from the start, Phil was the scoring hero and Tony the goaltender. "He was younger," Phil once explained, "so he got to be goalie for me." They played hockey endlessly, pausing only for dinner and never even unlacing their skates while gulping down their meal. Now and then, an errant puck would smack into a window and their father paid the bill. And there were the endless nights of lying in their room, listening to hockey games on the radio and dreaming of some day playing in the NHL.

The chance of that dream becoming reality seemed remote, especially for Tony, whose nearsightedness required that he wear thick eyeglasses. After he'd allowed a seemingly easy shot to hit the net, more than one neighborhood teammate, Phil included, raged at him, "You're blind!" It was not the very best way for a goaltender to build his confidence.

As a boy, Tony rooted for the Montreal Canadiens and brother Phil liked the Detroit Red Wings. That too caused a few shouting matches between the brothers Esposito. But when they played hockey together, the differences were forgotten. Then Tony's glasses would fog up on the ice, an easy one would get by and Phil would be on his brother's back again. They played together until Phil was fifteen and Tony fourteen, coming up through Sault Ste. Marie's youth-hockey program. Later, they were teammates for one more season in juvenile hockey before going their separate ways. Along the way, Tony discarded his horn-rimmed glasses for contact lenses.

Phil had left home to play junior hockey in St. Catharines, Ontario, because there was no junior team in Sault Ste. Marie. With his brother gone, Tony's interest in the game dwindled and he concentrated on football. Hockey was all but forgotten when Tony's father and some other local people decided that Sault Ste. Marie should have its own junior-hockey team. So they founded the Soo Greyhounds and went looking for players. Too bad about Tony Esposito, though. He would have been a good goalie for the Greyhounds.

Tony had heard the whispers around town and didn't like

their sound. People were saying he was a quitter and Tony set out to prove them wrong. He went to his father and although Pat Esposito wanted Tony for the Greyhounds, he wouldn't pressure his son into playing. "If you want to play hockey again," he said, "it has to be your decision and yours alone." Tony mulled it over and decided to go ahead. "I said I would give it a whirl," he said, "and everything worked out."

It was a hectic year because Tony was still playing high-school football and between going to classes and practicing both sports, he had little spare time. Often he'd grab a sandwich while climbing into his hockey pads. That would be dinner. There was no time for a formal meal. There was barely time for his schoolwork.

Once, the Greyhounds played a game in Sudbury when Tony halted the action. One of his contact lenses had slipped and pretty soon the whole Sault Ste. Marie team, Tony's father included, was pawing its way around the ice, searching for the errant lens. Tony retreated to the dressing room while the search continued. He casually fingered his eye and there, in the corner, he found the missing lens. He hadn't lost it, after all. It had just shifted a bit. Tony rushed out to tell his father he didn't have to creep around on all fours any more—news that was greeted enthusiastically by the senior Esposito. There were two reasons for his joy. First the Greyhounds needed the game badly and Tony was vital. And second, the contact lenses cost one hundred twenty dollars.

The next year, at nineteen, Tony made a decision. He had two college-scholarship offers, one to play football at a small school near Boston and the other to play hockey at Michigan Tech. The determining factor turned out to be size. At five feet, eleven inches, and one hundred eighty-five pounds, Esposito didn't think he had the build to take the pounding a football player must absorb. "I felt I could develop into a better hockey player," he said. So Tony accepted the scholarship at Tech and played hockey for four years at the school in Houghton, Michigan. In his sophomore year, Tony backstopped the team to the National Collegiate championship and gained All-America honors for the first of three straight varsity seasons.

After his big sophomore year, Tony learned that he had been placed on the negotiation list of the Montreal Canadiens. That was tantamount to drafting the young goalie. If he wanted to talk about pro hockey, it would have to be with the Canadiens. Ironically, brother Phil had by now migrated to the Chicago Black Hawks and when they heard about his goaltending brother, they decided to have a look-see at Tony. "By the time we got around to it," said General Manager Tommy Ivan, "he was already playing at Tech and he was already the property of Montreal."

Tony wasn't thrilled with that situation, but there wasn't very much he could do about it, except apply what he had learned in four years of studying business administration at Tech to his first pro-contract negotiations with the Canadiens. He needed all the help he could get.

There was no World Hockey Association in those days for youngsters to use as a lever to extract more attractive contracts from NHL teams. Today a promising rookie can demand and get one hundred fifty thousand dollars for turning pro. The Canadiens weren't even offering Tony Esposito one tenth of that figure. But Montreal had one important factor going in its contract negotiations with the young goalie: Tony wanted very much to play pro hockey. In the end, it was this desire that helped the Canadiens break him down.

At first, Tony rejected their first and second contract offers as too small. "But I wanted to prove that I could play hockey in the big leagues," said Tony. So he agreed to come to training camp and continue negotiations there. He was assigned to Montreal's American League farm team, the Cleveland Barons, and enjoyed a fine training camp. Only then, after much bickering, did he agree to terms with Sammy Pollock, the Canadiens' general manager. For a while, early in their talks, Tony refused to sign and Pollock refused to raise his final offer. But both gave a bit and finally agreed to terms.

Tony began his professional career with Cleveland, where he shared the goaltending with Gerry Desjardins. The Barons opened the 1967–68 season with Desjardins in goal and Gerry played so well that Coach Fred Glover kept him there. Meanwhile, Esposito sat on the end of the bench, waiting for his turn. It came soon, but with Vancouver, not Cleveland. The Canadiens, concerned about getting Esposito some work, arranged to lend him to the Vancouver club of the Western League. Tony reported to his new team in Rochester, New York, and played his first game on November 4, 1967.

"I was really worried," he said. "I didn't know whether I

could play in the pros or not. Aside from exhibition games, I never had had real pros firing at me. I wondered what it would be like." Also wondering about Tony was Jim Gregory, coach of the Vancouver club. His team had lost eight straight and maybe a new face in goal would help turn things around. "Just go out there and do the best you can," Gregory advised Esposito. "Don't worry about a thing." Tony, however, worried plenty. He was shaky in the knees as he skated out to start his professional career. His All-America credentials wouldn't mean much now.

The first goal he allowed was scored by Milan Marcetta, who Tony remembered from his junior-hockey days in Sault Ste. Marie. Esposito surrendered two more goals and escaped with a 3–3 tie that ended Vancouver's long losing streak. Gregory, who later moved up to the NHL as general manager of the Toronto Maple Leafs, patted his new goalie on the back. A couple of weeks later there were more pats when Tony recorded the first of consecutive shutouts against San Diego and Seattle.

Esposito improved Vancouver's defensive picture, but he couldn't pull the team into contention by himself. The problem seemed to be a combination of too much age and too much youth. The inexperienced youngsters were learning the pro ropes and the older members of the team were just playing out their string. It all added up to a last-place finish and plenty of work for the goaltender. "I learned all about losing that season," said Tony, "and how I didn't really enjoy it. I also learned a great deal from Jim Gregory. He's a good hockey man and gave me great encouragement and considerable knowledge. I owe him quite a lot, in fact." Tony played sixty-three games, finishing with four shutouts and a 3.20 goals-against average. Meanwhile, his brother, Phil, had totaled eighty-seven points for Boston, finishing second in the NHL scoring race. Clearly, Tony was still "the other Esposito."

When the brothers met during the summer, Tony was solemn. Phil knew something was wrong and they sat down to talk it over. "I want to make the NHL," Tony said, "but I don't want to kick around in the minors for years, waiting for that chance. I'm going to give myself one more year down there. Then, if I don't make it, I'll quit." Tony had always been the more intense of the brothers. Their father noted that quality even when they were growing up. "He was always a worrywart, a very nervous boy. Phil took a loss better. He forgot about it. Not Tony."

Maybe that's because Tony is a goaltender. "Sure I'm nervous every time I'm out there," said Tony. "Even when I was a kid, I felt the pressure. All the guys—Phil was the worst—were blaming me when we lost and after a while, I was blaming myself. It's still torture. It's a job, that's what it is, a job. There is pressure every time you are in there. That's the name of the game—pressure. It was torture for me when I was a kid in the bantams, Phil and the other kids bitching and moaning when a puck went by me, and it's still torture when one goes in."

It's one thing to suffer that kind of pressure in the major leagues, but to do it at the minor-league level was more than Tony could endure. So he made his decision. One more year to make it to the NHL—or else he would pack his pads in mothballs for good. He got there sooner than he expected, although again he was not thrilled with the circumstances following his promotion.

Tony began the 1968–69 season playing for Montreal's Central League farm club at Houston. He was to share the Apollos' net-minding job with another promising young goalie, Phil Myre, while Rogatien Vachon and Gump Worsley divided the goaltending for the Canadiens. Both Myre and Esposito were playing well for Houston, but in Montreal there were problems. Coach Claude Ruel was giving most of the work to Vachon and spent a considerable amount of time grumbling over Worsley's less than enthusiastic performances during practices. Before too very long the conflict between the pudgy goaltender and his pudgier coach reached a head. And the repercussions were felt all the way to Houston.

Toe Blake, one of Sammy Pollock's trusted aides, was dispatched to Houston to assess Esposito and Myre. He watched a couple of games and then returned to Montreal with his report. A few days later, the Worsley-Ruel conflict played its final note. Gump, shaken by a particularly bumpy plane ride between Montreal and Chicago and dejected over his lack of playing time, announced that he was going home. The Canadiens now had only one goalie—Vachon. Pollock put in a rush call to Houston and talked to player-coach Al MacNeil. Already armed with Blake's scouting report, the Canadiens'

GM now asked MacNeil his advice. The coach recommended Esposito, who had lost only one of eight games and was sporting a fancy 1.80 goals-against average. The recommendation coincided with Blake's assessment of the two Houston goalies. Pollack was satisfied. "Fine," he said, "We're calling Tony up. Tell him to get packed and report to Ruel in Los Angeles."

The news hit Tony like a thunderbolt. His wife Marilyn and infant son had arrived in Houston only a week or so earlier, and now he was on his way to the airport, headed for Los Angeles and the Canadiens. His head swam as he climbed into an NHL uniform for the first time. He spent his first game in the big leagues on the end of the bench, watching Vachon beat the Kings, 4–2. The next morning the team headed for Oakland, but Tony overslept and missed the team bus to the airport. What a way to break into the NHL, he thought as he dressed quickly and grabbed a cab to the Los Angeles airport. When he arrived, Tony rushed from one airline to another, trying to locate the Canadiens. When he finally did, Esposito strolled up to the knot of players as if nothing unusual had happened. Ruel didn't say a word.

Montreal's next game was in Oakland. Again Vachon was in the nets and Esposito on the bench. Late in the second period, with Oakland leading 3–2, a shot cracked into Vachon's forehead and the Canadien's goalie was forced to leave the game. Ruel approached Esposito. "Tony, get in there," he said, "and don't be nervous." Tony wasn't nervous at all. He was petrified. "I was shaking in my pads," he said. It showed. He faced only six shots in his NHL debut and two of them wound up in the net.

The critical Montreal press jumped right on Esposito, blaming him for the Oakland loss and suggesting that he needed more minor-league experience before stepping up to the big time. It was, thought Tony, just like old times. When he was a kid growing up, it was standard procedure to blame the goalie when the puck went into the net. Apparently, things were no different in the NHL. "That's why I never really wanted to play goal," said Tony, reminiscing on his days back at Sault Ste. Marie.

Ruel figured the best way to deal with a case of rookie shakes would be to get Tony back into action as soon as possible. So he gave Esposito his first NHL start six days later against the Bruins. Starting Tony was as much a matter of necessity as an effort at restoring his confidence. Vachon had broken a bone in his hand during practice and with Worsley still out of the picture, Montreal called up veteran Ernie Wakely from Cleveland to join Tony. Wakely faced the New York Rangers in the next game and his shakiness contributed to a 4–2 defeat for the Canadiens. The Bruins were next and Ruel went to Tony. "I'm giving you another chance," he told his goalie. "I know the Bruins are tough," he continued, "but give it your best—and try to relax."

The speech must have sounded to Tony something like the advice the Romans gave the Christians before tossing them to the lions. Waiting to chew up the rookie were the boisterous Bruins, who, led by brother Phil, were developing into one of the NHL's best-scoring teams.

Tony was alone with his thoughts as he strapped on his bulky pads. Most of those thoughts concerned Boston's number seven, brother Phil. But there were other problems, too. There was Bobby Orr to deal with. And Derek Sanderson. And Ken Hodge. And Johnny Bucyk. One had to forgive the Montreal goalie making his first NHL start if he shuddered just a little bit. Early in the game, Esposito calmed down a bit, thanks to a bit of carelessness on the part of one of the Bruins.

Boston had rushed out of its own end and the Canadiens were slow coming back. At the blue line, Fred Stanfield found himself with the puck and took a couple of strides before booming a shot at the Canadiens' net. Tony threw out his gloved hand and caught the puck in the webbing. Then he dropped it to the side of his net—a routine move the NHL goalies make countless times in every game. This time, though, the first stick to reach the puck belonged to a Bruin. But instead of snapping it into the net, the Boston player hesitated. In that split second, Tony dove to his side and covered the puck. Save!

There was little Tony could do about brother Phil that night. First Phil bounced one off both posts and into the net for the opening Boston goal. Then he unloaded a fifty-footer that caught the corner of the net for Boston's other goal in the 2–2 tie. After the game, the brothers met momentarily. "You were lucky on the first goal and lucky on the second goal," said Tony. Phil shrugged. "What the heck, Tony, I'm just a lucky guy," he said.

His performance against the Bruins in Boston earned Tony another start, this time against the Chicago Black Hawks and Bobby Hull. The Canadiens won this one 6–3 for Tony's first big-league victory. And he was officially introduced to the Hull slap shot. Bobby boomed one that hit Tony in the mask and sent him down, not quite for the count. Fortunately, the mask absorbed most of the shock and Esposito escaped with only a scare. It is a scare that he shares with many goaltenders. "Hell, I'd be scared to play without a mask. I'm scared with one," he said. "It's only natural to be afraid of getting hurt. You can get hurt even wearing the mask."

The victory was a milestone for Esposito and for the Canadiens. Without Vachon available, Ruel depended on Tony to handle the bulk of the net-minding and he started Montreal's next nine games. There was a shutout in Philadelphia and another one at home against, of all people, brother Phil and his Boston buddies. That one was a 0–0 tie —a classic goaltending duel in which Tony blocked forty-one shots including five by Phil. The game was the first of a weekend home-and-home series against Boston and the next night was a complete turnabout. The goals came hot and heavy and when it was over, Boston had seven and Montreal five. The Bruins had bombed Tony with fifty shots and wiped out a 3–0 Canadiens' lead, leaving Montreal and its young goalie shaken. Two of the goals belonged to Phil Esposito.

December turned into January and soon Rogatien Vachon, his hand mended, rejoined the Canadiens. Once Vachon was ready, Esposito returned to the bench. In the eleven games he had started since Vachon's injury, Montreal had lost only twice. But after Vachon returned, Tony got only one more start for the Canadiens. Then Worsley returned as well and suddenly, from Montreal's starting goalie, Esposito was relegated to number three status. He was not thrilled with the situation, especially when the Canadiens kept him sitting around, doing little more than practice, while his family was two thousand miles away in Texas.

Finally, the Canadiens returned him to the Central League and he finished the season as he had started it, alternating in goal with Phil Myre. He lost only one of his final eight games and finished with a 2.42 goals-against average for nineteen games with the Apollos and 2.73 for thirteen games with Montreal. When Worsley banged up a hand during the play-offs, he was summoned back to the Canadiens to sit and watch while Vachon led the club to the Stanley Cup. Tony was a sad sight in the lobby of the Canadiens' St. Louis hotel the day Montreal clinched the Cup. He sat alone, a member of the team but not feeling like one.

But things began looking better for him. June was only one month away—June and the annual league drift where the Canadiens would have to make a decision. They could protect only two goalies from the draft. If they chose to hang on to Worsley and Vachon, then Tony would be available for the thirty-thousand-dollar draft price. Tony figured he had to have impressed some team enough for them to risk that amount. And he was right.

Two years before, Chicago had traded Tony's brother, Phil, to Boston in a deal that backfired on the Black Hawks when Esposito emerged as an NHL superstar. General Manager Tommy Ivan absorbed considerable criticism over the swap. The Black Hawks had sunk into the East Division cellar, assuring themselves of the number two choice in the draft. Asked about his selection on the night before the draft, Ivan smiled. "Well," he said, "I've always liked the name Esposito. If there's someone by that name available tomorrow, I might just give it some thought."

As usual, there was predraft conversation among the general managers. Ivan wanted a goalie and the Canadiens would make Esposito available. The only problem was that the Black Hawks owned the number-two choice in the draft. Minnesota had the worst record in the league the previous year and would pick first. Sammy Pollock had the answer to that problem, though. Minnesota owed him a favor and he collected. The North Stars opened the draft by choosing a rather obscure forward, Dick Sentes. That left the Black Hawks with the opportunity to draft Esposito. They exercised it.

"I don't know if Tony can play in the big leagues or not," said Ivan after the draft. "But we liked what we saw of him with the Canadiens and he sure was good enough in the minors. I went down and watched Tony play a few games with Houston and he played well down there. Mostly, I liked the fact that he was big and moved well."

Ivan was happy to be able to draft Tony and Tony was glad to be moving to the Chicago organization. "With the Black Hawks I knew I would get greater opportunities to play and prove to them and to myself that I was a major-league goalie." Tony battled head-to-head with Chicago's holdover goalie, Denis DeJordy, during training camp, splitting the games. Before the Hawks' opening game, Coach Billy Reay made his goaltending decision. Esposito would be his man—for openers, at least. The first game was a disaster. St. Louis blasted seven goals past Tony and DeJordy got the call in the next game, a 2–1 setback against Oakland.

It was Tony's turn back in the box for game three and again Chicago lost—this time by a score of 4–1. Tony had become totally disgusted and disenchanted with himself. That's when he heard from his big brother again. Phil phoned and tried to cheer up his brother. "Don't worry so much," he told Tony. "Just hang in there."

DeJordy started the next three games, managing just one tie and so the Black Hawks went into Montreal having played six games and having won none of them. Esposito got the goaltending call against his old friends, the Canadiens. Montreal had not lost a game at home in the last twenty-four starts. Chicago had not won a game all season. It seemed like a mismatch and Tony Esposito knew it. "I was a bundle of nerves when we showed up at the Montreal Forum," recalled Tony. "I had given up eleven goals in my first two starts. How long could I hold them? Would they embarrass the life out of me?"

Tony's questions were answered fast. He stopped everything the Canadiens threw his way. Meanwhile, the Black Hawks scored five goals and when the final horn went off Chicago had its first victory and Esposito had his first shutout of the season. "I felt like the whole world had been lifted off my shoulders," said Tony. "The pressure on me before the game had been tremendous. I hadn't played well in my first two starts and then I was thrown in against a team I had been with the previous season. But I came out of it smiling again because I had shown myself and my coach that I could handle the pressure."

The Montreal shutout turned everything around for Esposito. The Hawks spun off six straight victories with Tony in the nets. Two of them were shutouts—one of these a repeat performance against the Canadiens. In the six-game stretch, Tony permitted just five goals. "I can't remember any time in my six years here," said Coach Billy Reay, "when we've gotten such consistently fine goalkeeping over as long a stretch as Tony has given us in these six games." And that fine goalkeeping kept up too. One shutout followed another and before he knew it, Tony Esposito was leading the league in whitewashings and had the best goals-against average in the NHL.

"What makes him so good," said Reay, "is his alertness. He's very much in the game at all times, watching the puck, and for that reason, he's a split-second ahead of everything that happens. Instead of reacting a split-second afterward, he's on top of every situation." But there was criticism of Tony's style. He is undoubtedly unorthodox. He stands with pads apart, giving the shooter a triangular target to shoot for. He sprawls on the ice more often than hockey purists say he should. But he also keeps the puck out of the net and that, after all, is what goaltending is about. "You know," said Reay, "I get tired of people knocking his style. He may be awkward, but he's rarely out of position. He keeps the puck out . . . and that's what counts."

Esposito doesn't try to explain his style. "Don't ask me," he said when a newsman did just that. "I stay up if I think I need to and if I figure the shot calls for me to flop, I do that. I just think it's my job to stop the puck and I'll do anything I think seems best to do it."

As one shutout led to another, Chicago fans tagged their goalie with the nickname "Tony-O" and compared him with Mr. Goalie, Glenn Hall. "He's a lot like Hall," said Reay. "When he's behind that face mask and yelling, you'd swear it was Glenn. And he has a lot of Hall's moves." That is no accident. Tony patterned his style after Hall and Johnny Bower. "Hall was a reflex goalie and they call me unorthodox maybe because I depend a lot on reflexes. From Bower I picked up the way he used his stick. I try to poke check with it and I guess I use it more than most guys. I like to use the stick a lot and I'm not too proud to accept a little help from the goal posts."

By mid-season, Esposito had earned a berth in the All-Star Game. He had ten shutouts and had taken dead aim on the NHL modern record of thirteen set by Harry Lumley of To-

ronto in 1954. He tied the record on March 22 and then
added two more shutouts before the season ended to erase
Lumley's mark. "Tony's record is unbelievable," said Reay.
"In these days of faster hockey and harder shooting, I never
thought it could happen."

Tony said that shutouts never entered his mind on the ice.
"Shutouts? That's something you don't think about," the
goalie said. "You like to have confidence going into a game
that you'll be hot, but you can hardly say 'I'm going to get a
shutout tonight.' Here again, I've been lucky. In a couple of
those shutouts, a shot or two has bounced off the post. Besides, a shutout means a complete team defensive effort. The
team has been doing a fine checking job. The defense has
improved steadily and the forwards are backchecking really
well. A goalie's secrets are a little luck and a lot of help.
I've had both."

When the season was over, Esposito had been voted the
NHL's Rookie of the Year and his miniscule 217 goals-
against average had earned him the Vezina Trophy as well.
What's more, his goaltending had led the Black Hawks to the
division championship—a major reversal for a team that had
finished in last place the year before. "If I had to single out
one factor for our success," said Reay, "I guess it would be
Esposito. Time and again, he has made what you would call
the big save for us, the one that gives us a lift. So many
times you get that kind of save and bang, you go right down
into the other team's end and score one of your own."

Esposito had proven that he was indeed a big-league net-
minder. He backstopped Chicago to the East title in his first
season there and then the Hawks won three straight West
Division championships, after switching to that division. There
was another Vezina Trophy in 1971–72 when he again led
the league with nine shutouts and a sparkling 1.76 goals-
against average. In 1973–74, he tied for the Vezina with
Philadelphia's Bernie Parent. But the pressure of playing
goal in the NHL has taken its toll. "I'm nervous," said Tony.
"Nervous all the time. I'd worry if I wasn't. I think you're
sharper when you're nervous. The older you get, the more
afraid you get. To be playing well as a goalkeeper, you have
to be afraid. Not afraid that you'll get hurt, but afraid they're
going to score on you. Every time they come down the ice
with the puck, I'm afraid the puck is going to go in. It's a

job. I have to do it. But it's tough. I don't like it."

If Tony doesn't like his job, opposing players don't exactly enjoy working against him either. He has lightninglike reflexes—quickness you wouldn't expect from a goalie as bulky as he is. He challenges the shooter and more often than not, he wins the showdown with a flick of his stick or a thrust of his big leg pads. "He flops all over the place," said Bobby Orr. "He will even open his pads for a shot through the middle. But he's so quick with his arms and legs, he'll close up the opening. You've got to hit the puck and hope." Tony's inverted Y stance has an uncanny way of closing up as soon as an enemy shooter tries to put the puck between his legs. It can be frustrating.

One forward on the New York Rangers zoomed in on Tony-O during the playoffs two years ago and Esposito bided his time, leaving the inviting target open. As soon as the shot came, Tony's legs clamped together. "I couldn't believe it," said the Ranger. "I'd swear that shot had him beaten and it just bounced off his damn pads. I couldn't believe it."

A few times, Esposito's inverted Y hasn't closed fast enough and the result has been enemy goals. When that happens, Esposito tries to erase the debacle from his mind by thinking of the next game. "I think it's better to play two nights in a row, especially if you lose the first night," he said. "It doesn't affect you as much. You haven't got time to think about it—if you know what I mean. You win the next night and everything that happened before is out of your mind."

Early in his career, Tony had trouble taking those bad games in stride. He brooded over them instead. "A shot would bounce in on me and I'd either brood about it or lose my temper. A goalie can't afford to do either. The worst thing that can happen to a goalie is to get mad. But now when I let a bad goal in I try to put it out of my mind. You can't always succeed, but you try."

Esposito's success made Tommy Ivan look like a genius. But Ivan admits that Tony's instant stardom was something of a surprise to him. "Don't get me wrong," the Hawks' general manager said. "We didn't expect him to do as well as he did in his first year, getting fifteen shutouts and all. Now, he's not simply a very good goalie. He's a great one. The thing you have to like about him is that he's a fighter. He wants to be number one. If he isn't number one, you don't get as much out of him as you'd like. But when he puts on that uniform, he fights you for everything. He dares you to beat him."

Every forward carrying the puck into the Chicago zone is toting a challenge that Esposito meets head-on. That is the job of the goalkeeper. Sometimes the job isn't pleasant. But that's the job. "The pressure is unreal," said Tony. "Most of the goalkeepers feel the pressure. I haven't met one who did a good job and didn't worry. The only ones that don't worry are the ones too dumb to understand what's happening to them."

Tony says his nerves are in better shape now than they were when he started his NHL career. "I'm not as nervous off the ice as I was a few years ago," he said. "When you play regularly, you are more relaxed, knowing you have a job. But I still get very emotional before a game. It's important. You've got to be psyched up because a goalkeeper's game isn't physical—you're not skating out there. It's emotional."

You could never mistake Esposito for a carefree, nonchalant character. "I don't joke around a lot," he said, frowning. "I don't want to be distracted. There's nothing funny about goaltending."

Especially when you're the forward and the goaltender is Tony Esposito.

Chicago Black Hawks

Tony owns the NHL record for the most shutouts in a season, fifteen.

Hockey Hall of Fame

Frankie Brimsek, a Yank
in a sport dominated
by Canadians, played nine
of his ten NHL years
with Boston.

6
FRANK
BRIMSEK:
MR. ZERO

Eveleth, Minnesota, is a town so small it would be easy to miss it if you didn't know it was there, nestled in the northeast corner of the state. The population numbers less than six thousand—when everybody's home. And on one frigid night back in December of 1939, very few of the local citizens were at home. Most of them had journeyed over to Chicago to watch a showdown between two of their own boys—Mike Karakas and Frank Brimsek—a couple of goaltenders who had made it all the way to the National Hockey League.

Karakas tended goal for the Chicago Black Hawks and had held that job since 1935. Brimsek, who had followed Karakas into the nets at Eveleth High School, was breaking in with the Boston Bruins. The game stuck in both goalie's minds, not only because of the ironic duel of two youngsters who grew up in the same small town, but because it marked the start of one of the great goaltending feats in history.

The story really started a few years earlier when Karakas was about to graduate from high school and Eveleth needed a goaltending replacement. John Brimsek was being groomed to take over the post, but he wasn't exactly thrilled with the idea of standing in front of a net and letting the other kids take pot shots at him. No, thank you. John envisioned himself instead as a burly, bruising defensemen who could belt the other kids and lug the puck out of his own end. "Now if you want a goalie," reasoned John, "why not use my brother, Frankie?" That was okay with Frankie, already a star on

Eveleth's basketball, softball, and football teams. And it was fine with Cliff Thompson, the school's hockey coach, especially after he had watched Frank operate in the goal. The boy seemed absolutely fearless, almost daring the shooters to try and put the puck past him.

"He just stood in the net and waited for the puck to come to him," said Thompson. "Most kids want to come out and meet the puck too soon and too often, but it was a long time before I could get Frankie to come skating out of the net and cut down the angles of the shot." Thompson kept working on the youngster and in the back of his head thought that the boy had professional potential.

Brimsek moved on to St. Cloud Teacher's College and in 1935 decided to try his hand at pro hockey. His friends had been badgering him to give hockey a whirl and he finally consented, trying out with the Baltimore club in the Eastern League. He gambled everything he had on the try. He hung on grimly through training camp, but shortly before the season started he got the bad news: he hadn't made the team. All he had for his troubles was a handshake and a pat on the back.

The goalie's spirit was about as low as it could be at that point. "I got kicked out," he said. "Not good enough even for the amateurs. I thought I was through with hockey." And he probably would have been too—if an empty stomach and pockets in the same condition hadn't intervened.

When Baltimore gave Brimsek its regrets, the goalie started making his way home to Eveleth, which was a thousand or so miles and several hitchhikes away. He got as far as Pittsburgh when his hunger was such that he detoured to Duquesne Garden, home of the EHL's Pittsburgh Yellow Jackets. His hope was that he'd find a friendly hockey man who might be willing to underwrite a meal or two for a goaltender down on his luck. He found something better than that.

Dinny Manners, who ran the Yellow Jackets, was desperate for a goalie. Brimsek and his pads arrived at just the right moment; before he could get his thumb up looking for another ride, Frankie had a net-minding job. Brimsek wound up staying two seasons.

He impressed people all around the EHL with his goaltending prowess and it was only a matter of time before Brimsek's skills caught the attention of NHL executives. The catalyst was Herb Mitchell, boss of another EHL club, the Hershey Bears. Mitchell had logged two seasons in the NHL with the Boston Bruins a decade before and his career scoring total of six goals in fifty-three games testifies to his appreciation of fine goaltending. And Brimsek was clearly a fine goaltender. Mitchell owed a favor to his old coach, Art Ross, coach of the Bruins, and one day he called Boston.

"Art," said Mitchell, "there's a goalie in our league I think you ought to look at. His name is Brimsek and he's playing for Pittsburgh." Ross had never been overly impressed with Mitchell's talents as a player, but he had demonstrated astute judgment concerning hockey talent in the past and so the Bruin boss decided to follow up the tip.

The year was 1937 and the best goalie in the Western world was Cecil "Tiny" Thompson, who happened to be working for the Boston Bruins. Thompson had won the Vezina Trophy three times. He was cool and agile in the nets. If there was one position that the Bruins didn't have to worry about, it was goal. Tiny Thompson was like the Great Wall of China and he showed no signs of cracking.

Still, Ross thought, Tiny was thirty-two years old, a dangerous age for an athlete. You never knew when you might need somebody to fill in for him because of an injury. So Ross took the advice of his old friend, Herb Mitchell, and signed Brimsek for Boston's American League farm club at Providence. The remarkable thing was that Ross was so busy with the Bruins that he never even saw Brimsek play before giving the go-ahead to sign the young goalie.

Brimsek fulfilled Mitchell's buildup with a sensational season in the AHL. He surrendered only eighty-six goals in forty-eight games for a glittering 1.79 goals-against average, and he posted five shutouts—all fine and dandy except for one thing. Over in Boston, Tiny Thompson captured the Vezina Trophy for the fourth time with an equally skimpy 1.85 goals-against average and seven shutouts.

Thompson clearly still had all the skills that had earned him the nickname of "The Goalie Without A Weakness." And he also had a special place in the hearts of Bruin fans. He had spent ten seasons in Boston and was one of only four players still on the club from the Bruins' first and only Stanley Cup championship team of 1929. He was as popular in Boston then as Bobby Orr is today.

When the Bruins went to training camp in 1938, Brimsek was invited to work out with the big club. In camp, Thompson was as good as ever but Ross's attention was riveted to the rookie from Eveleth. Brimsek was doing some unbelievable things in the net at the other end of the ice and even a grizzled hockey veteran like Ross was favorably impressed. So the Bruins' boss decided on a little experiment. He beckoned his two goalies to one end of the ice and grabbed a hockey stick.

Standing no more than ten feet away from the net, Ross rifled twenty-five shots at Thompson—high, low, all over the place. Tiny blocked nineteen of the boss's drives. Next it was Brimsek's turn. Again, Ross fired. Brimsek went up, down, and all around, darting from one side of the net to the other. And when he was through, the kid from Eveleth had blocked every one of Ross's shots.

The little demonstration was hardly a definitive test, but it made Ross think. Brimsek had been impressive—no, sensational. "The kid had the fastest hands I ever saw," said Ross. "Like lightning." It was clear that the youngster had major-league goaltending credentials and his fine work continued through training camp.

When Thompson developed an infected eye, Ross gave Brimsek the word: the youngster would open the season in the Boston nets. Was the normally cool goalie shaken by the prospect? He was just petrified. "I was so jittery when we got to Toronto for that opening game," said Brimsek, "that I couldn't eat. My hand shook so much that my roommate, Jack Crawford, started to feed me."

Brimsek pulled himself together well enough to defeat Toronto 3–2, and three nights later he backstopped the Bruins to another victory over Detroit. By then, Thompson's eye had healed and he reclaimed his job. Brimsek was dispatched to Providence, but the image of the acrobatic young goalie stuck in Ross's mind. The AHL was no place for this talented kid, thought Ross. And, after all, Thompson was now thirty-three. Was it time to consider a permanent change in goal for the Bruins?

Ross debated the consequences of dealing away Thompson. He'd have all of Boston on his back; Tiny was one of the club's most popular players and still at the top of his game. And what if Brimsek failed? That would really be trouble.

Imagine the clamor if the Bruins got rid of one of the best goalies in the business and his replacement was a dud. But Ross remembered Brimsek's training-camp show and decided that his first judgment was correct. There was no way this kid couldn't do the job.

Ross went over to Providence to watch Brimsek. Frankie was still every bit as impressive as he had been in camp and in those first two games of the season. Then and there, Ross made up his mind. Brimsek would be Boston's goalie. The Bruin boss called his old friend Jack Adams in Detroit. Would the Red Wings be interested in a goalie, asked Ross. Sure, replied Adams, unprepared for what came next. The man Ross offered was not some minor-leaguer, but Tiny Thompson, the defending Vezina winner and the previous year's all-star goalie. Adams managed not to drop the phone in shock and offered Ross fifteen thousand dollars—a sizable amount of cash in those days. "It's a deal," said the Bruin boss.

Next, he wired Providence, ordering Brimsek to join the Bruins in Montreal for their next game, December 1, 1938. Then he released the news of Thompson's sale and Brimsek's recall to the press, stunning all of Boston. The city and the team were deeply shocked. The Bruins had surrendered a proven star and replaced him with an untested rookie. Brimsek had his work cut out for him.

Brimsek started against the Canadiens and everything that could have gone wrong for him that night went wrong. He surrendered only two goals, but the Bruins, perhaps still in shock over the Thompson deal, neglected to score any and Frankie came up a loser. Meanwhile, the same night in Detroit, Thompson made his debut in the Red Wing nets and beat Chicago 4–1. The result was dutifully noted by the disgruntled Boston fans.

Ross shrugged off comparisons. "Don't worry," he said. "This kid has the stuff to be great. You'll see." And Ross was right. The NHL saw plenty, for in the next seven games Frankie Brimsek became a hockey legend.

The Bruins moved from Montreal to Chicago, where they met the Black Hawks and Brimsek's old goaltending buddy from Eveleth, Mike Karakas. The clash of the two neighbors captured the imagination of the small Minnesota town and both goalies had their own cheering sections led by their mothers. There was another touch of irony to the game because one of Chicago's top goal snipers was Paul Thompson, who happened to be the brother of the man Brimsek replaced in the Boston nets. And the Black Hawks, defending Stanley Cup champions, were in no mood to make life easy for a rookie goalie just breaking into the NHL.

Chicago came at Brimsek in swarms and he turned back attack after attack. Once, swift-skating Earl Seibert unloaded a rocket from the blue line. Brimsek had the puck lined up when Paul Thompson skated in front of the net and got his stick down to deflect the shot. The rubber flew off at an angle, but Brimsek sprung with it and knocked it aside with a sparkling move. Save!

Art Ross poked trainer Win Green on the Bruins' bench as Brimsek kept stopping everything the Black Hawks threw at him. When the game was over, Boston had outscored Chicago 5–0, and some of the pressure had been lifted from Brimsek's shoulders. But it was right back in place two nights later when the Bruins returned home to play Chicago again. It would be Brimsek's first appearance before the hometown fans, who were still seething over the deal that had deprived them of their favorite, Tiny Thompson.

As Frankie led the Bruins onto the ice, he heard only a smattering of polite applause from the crowd. "I don't think they were glad to see me," the goalie said. It was almost as if the Bruin fans were telling Brimsek to show them what he could do. They were reserving judgment, but he'd better be good. After all, he had replaced Tiny Thompson. "It was so quiet that I could hear the fans breathing and feel their cold eyes on the back of my neck," said Brimsek.

Frankie warmed up the fans with another scintillating job in the Bruins' nets. For the second straight game, he held the Hawks scoreless and this time Boston beat Karakas and company 2–0. When it was over the fans gave the goalie a warm ovation. In the dressing room, Ross approached his rookie net-minder.

"You'll make them forget Thompson," said the coach. "From now on, you're their goaltender."

Next, it was the New York Rangers' turn and they really put the pressure on Brimsek, testing him with thirty-three shots. But Frankie blocked them all and the Bruins won 3–0, for his third straight shutout. By now, hockey fans began to sit up and take notice of the twenty-three-year-old goalie.

His three straight shutouts had given him 192 minutes and forty seconds of scoreless hockey. The modern record for the longest shutout skein was 224 minutes and forty-seven seconds and Brimsek was closing in on it. Ironically, the mark belonged to Tiny Thompson.

Brimsek would go for the record at home against the Montreal Canadiens and this time he received a decidedly warmer welcome from the Bruin fans than he had the first time he skated onto the home ice. During the warmups, Brimsek was just as cool as ever. His placid approach earned him nicknames such as Frigid Frankie and the Human Icicle. He stood deadpan in the nets, daring, it seemed, opponents to try and put one past him. He was poised and unruffled. "Maybe I look like that," he said, "but inside, butterflies are fluttering all over the place." They had good reason to flutter on this night because, in only his fifth game since being called up, Frankie was going for a line in the record book.

The string of shutouts had convinced the Bruins that Ross's assessment of Brimsek had been valid. The team had seen the rookie goalie kick out everything sent his way and that earned their confidence. So much so that they often neglected their checking chores, launching five-man attacks up-ice and leaving him to his own devices in Boston's end. Frequently, the goal-hungry Canadiens took advantage of the offense-minded Bruins to sneak in for attacks on Brimsek. And each time, Frankie stopped them.

Bobby Bauer and Gordie Pettinger scored for Boston in the first period and Brimsek kept the Canadiens off the scoreboard, stretching his streak to 212 minutes, forty seconds. The rookie was barely twelve minutes away from Tiny Thompson's record.

The tension built through the early stages of the middle period as the clock in ancient Boston Garden ticked off the seconds and minutes, tacking them onto Brimsek's streak. Five minutes went by with no goals against the Boston netminder. Then five more. Just past the twelve-minute mark, the pressure exploded in a deep-throated roar from the crowd. Brimsek had done it! He had eclipsed Tiny Thompson's shutout record. For another seven minutes, Brimsek kept the Canadiens off the scoreboard.

Then, with less than one minute left in the period, Montreal's Herb Cain and George Brown broke up a four-man

Boston attack and turned the flow of play toward the Bruins'
end. Brown carried the puck in on defensemen Jack Portland
the only Bruin between the two Montreal skaters and Brimsek. He faked once and then again, before shoveling the puck
to Cain who zoomed in alone on the Bruin net. Cain fired
and Brimsek never had a chance. The goal ended the rookie's
remarkable shutout skein at a record 231 minutes, fifty-four
seconds.

Montreal added another goal in the third period, but Boston won the game, 3–2. Afterward, Brimsek, who was now
being called Kid Zero, was asked about the string. "It's nice,
of course, to have a string of goose eggs like that to your
credit," the rookie said. "But after all, a goaltender can't
whitewash a team all on his own. Look what a defense we
had." And it was true that Eddie Shore, Jack Portland, Dit
Clapper, Johnny Crawford, and Flash Hollett had been making life miserable for ambitious forwards in the Bruins' zone.
But the fact remained that young Mr. Brimsek had been
pretty impressive.

Now that the shutout string was ended, observers expected Brimsek to settle down to the business of simply playing winning hockey. After all, it's not necessary for a goalie to
shut out the other team to win. But what happened next may
be even more remarkable than his record shutout string. He
came right back and started another string.

Boston's next game was in Montreal and Brimsek stood
tall in a 1–0 blanking of the Canadiens. Then it was on to
Detroit for a face-to-face showdown with Tiny Thompson.
Both goalies played shutout hockey for two tense periods. But
the Bruins broke their ex-teammate down in the final twenty
minutes, scoring twice. Final score: Boston 2, Detroit 0.

The New York Americans were next and Coach Red Dut-
ton tried unorthodox strategy. He threw five forwards at
Brimsek, hoping to generate scoring punch. But the strategy
didn't upset Frankie at all. The Bruin goalie blocked twenty-
three shots and Boston won again, 3–0.

That gave Brimsek another string of three shutouts and
six in seven games, an unbelievable performance for any
goalie and even more remarkable because Frank was a rookie. His latest shutout string was 195 minutes, fifteen seconds
and now he would go after his own scoreless record, established only a week or so before. The New York Rangers

were next up and a capacity crowd jammed Boston Garden on Christmas night to see if Brimsek could do it again. Through the first period, Brimsek stood the Rangers off. Now the streak was at 215 minutes, fifteen seconds. Then, five minutes into the second period, Dutch Hiller sped down-ice with Bryan Hextall and Phil Watson. Hiller was bottled up in a corner and centered to Hextall who spied Watson at the corner of Brimsek's net. The pass was perfect and Watson scooped the puck past Brimsek, ending his latest shutout siege at 220 minutes, twenty-four seconds.

His second streak ended, Brimsek went about the task of keeping Boston on top in the NHL pennant race. He tacked on four more shutouts, finishing the season with ten in forty-three games and a league-leading 1.60 goals-against average that won for him both the Vezina Trophy as the top goalie and the Calder Trophy as Rookie of the Year. And by the end of that dazzling season, Bruin fans rarely mentioned Tiny Thompson.

Kid Zero had matured into Mr. Zero and the rookie kept his poise throughout a heart-thumping semifinal playoff series against New York. The series went the full seven games and three of the games stretched into overtime. Each of those sudden-death games was won by Boston and each of them on a goal by lightly regarded Mel "Sudden Death" Hill. But Hill's heroics never would have had a chance if it hadn't been for Brimsek's nearly airtight goaltending. After their life-and-death struggle with the Rangers, the Bruins found the finals against Toronto much easier. They eliminated the Maple Leafs in five games, nailing down Boston's first Stanley Cup in a decade. In twelve playoff games, Brimsek surrendered only eighteen goals for a miserly 1.50 average. Many years later, Frankie remembered that sensational rookie season. "I guess that first year was my biggest thrill in hockey," he said, "especially when we won the Stanley Cup."

Brimsek backstopped the Bruins to regular-season titles in each of the next two seasons and another Stanley Cup in 1940–41. The year after that, he captured his second Vezina Trophy and, ironically, he did it with a 2.38 goals-against average—higher than his figure for either of the previous two seasons when he had been beaten out for the award by Davey Kerr of the New York Rangers and Turk

Broda of Toronto.

On the ice, Brimsek maintained a deadpan expression that belied the nervousness he felt inside. Some opponents like New York Ranger boss Lester Patrick realized that Mr. Zero's cool look was only a put-on. "Where do they get that Frigid Frankie stuff?" snapped Patrick. "He's nervous and high-strung. His words spill out of him. He's a bundle of nerves."

Fidgety Frankie might have been a better description of the Bruin goalie. In the dressing room, he often complained of not feeling well. His teammates, however, knew that when Brimsek was griping, it usually meant a first-rate goaltending performance by their man. He was the first player dressed and was very finicky about his equipment. He preferred a pair of comfortable old pads that were held together by twine, safety pins, adhesive tape, and anything else trainer Win Green could come up with for the job.

But Brimsek's nervousness never showed on the ice. If anything, it was his presence in front of the Boston net that made other teams nervous. Lynn Patrick, one of Lester's sons, admitted that Brimsek shook him up.

"He was unbeatable as far as I was concerned," said Patrick, a long-time hockey executive who termed Brimsek the best goalie he ever played against. "I remember one time when I came in all alone on him and was too terrified to shoot. I figured he'd stop my shot just as he always did when we played the Bruins. So I passed the puck back to Bryan Hextall." Just to prove Brimsek wasn't infallible all the time, Hextall whipped the shot past him.

"Brimsek was a dedicated goaltender," Patrick continued. "He was very quick and had a terrific pair of hands. He had no weakness that I could detect. They say he always complained about his health and that the worse he felt, the better he played. I guess he must have been dying most of the time when he played against the Rangers."

But Mr. Zero didn't pick only on Patrick's Rangers. He made life miserable for other teams too. Once, he stopped Montreal's great Maurice Richard on a fistful of close-in chances. After one particularly frustrating save against him, the Rocket skated through Brimsek's crease. "Hey," he said, "did you catch that puck or did I shoot it into your hand?"

In 1943, Brimsek, like so many other players, exchanged

his hockey uniform for a military one. He joined the United States Coast Guard, serving for two years in the South Pacific. Some old NHL friends like Art Coulter of the Rangers, Alex Motter of the Red Wings, and Chicago's Johnny Mariucci, another Eveleth, Minnesota, product, served with him. When the war ended, he rejoined the Bruins immediately. That turned out to be a mistake.

"It took me nearly two years to get back to my old form," he said. "When you spend two years aboard a ship, you soon lose your ice legs. When I came back to Boston I had to play myself into condition. That's not so good. I should have stayed at home for a while to get into shape, but I rejoined the club as soon as I got out. It was my legs that bothered me most. It's not so much your eye you lose, but it's more your nerve. I was a little shaky when I first got back into the game."

Brimsek returned to a changed game. The center red line had been introduced to the NHL while he was in the service and the device helped open up attacking patterns and put more pressure on the goalies. Mr. Zero noticed. "It's a lot different all right," he said. "A goalie has a much harder time trying to stop them today. When you have about ten players milling around in front of you, it's hard to tell where the puck is going to come from."

The readjustment was agonizing for Brimsek. A nervous man to start with, he had his problems. The puck found its way past him more frequently than it ever had before and it was a situation that troubled him. He thought about it all the time. It was during this period that Brimsek's obsession with his goaltending problems overflowed one day.

He was walking along a downtown Boston street with a teammate and was about to cross the street when the red light atop a fire-alarm box began flashing in the same way the light behind the net does when a team scores. Brimsek froze in his tracks. Staring at the light, almost transfixed, he shouted "Goal! Goal! Goal!" Then he clutched his buddy. "Get me out of here," he muttered.

Gradually, Brimsek regained his net-minding touch. His goals-against average shrunk from an inflated 3.26 his first year back from the service to 2.91 the next year, then 2.82 and 2.72. But tragedy stepped into strike a terrible blow in early 1948. The Brimseks' eleven-month-old son, Frank, Jr., developed bronchial asthma and died. Brimsek seriously considered giving up hockey then and there. He decided to finish out the season with the Bruins, but following the playoffs he said he hoped that Boston would trade him to Chicago so that he could be closer to his Minnesota home.

The Bruins were hesitant, obviously not anxious to surrender a player who had meant so much to their organization. But Brimsek told President Weston Adams and General Manager Art Ross that he would play only one more year of hockey. Reluctantly, they acceded to his request to be traded and sold the goalie to the Black Hawks for twenty-five thousand dollars.

Brimsek stood by his pledge and played just one more season with Chicago. He retired in 1950 at the age of thirty-five after ten NHL seasons. He finished with a 2.94 goals-against average and forty shutouts, one quarter of them in his fabulous rookie season. When he was through, he returned to his native Minnesota.

Hockey a Canadian sport? Don't try to tell that to Frank Brimsek, the Yank who made goaltending history.

Gump Worsley has
been stopping pucks
for more than twenty years
in the NHL,
first with the Rangers,
then the Canadiens and,
since 1969, with the
Minneapolis North Stars.

7
GUMP WORSLEY:
HIS FACE WAS
HIS MASK

Lorne (Gump) Worsley doesn't fit the classical image of the goaltender, the superb physical specimen able to endure the rigors of one of the toughest professions. But the once crewcut net-minder with the pot belly has an important intangible: a "what, me worry?" philosophy.

The pages of hockey history are crammed with goalies whose nerves were stretched tight over the years by the pressures of playing bull's-eye with a bunch of slapshot-happy forwards wearing different-colored uniforms. Eventually, the tension became too much and the net-minder hangs up his pads. Perfectly natural, all things considered. But it never happened to Worsley, who scorned a face mask and shrugged off one-hundred-mile-an-hour shots for almost a quarter of a century as a professional goaltender.

A carefree man, who accepted success and failure with the same so-what shrug, Worsley never let a hockey game get on his nerves. Now an airplane ride might create a few bubbles in his ample stomach, but a hockey game never shook the Gump. And in ten sometimes nightmarish seasons with the then defenseless New York Rangers, it must have taken quite a bit of effort for Worsley to never get shaken. He once was asked about his good humor in the face of the load of shots tossed his way game after game.

"I think too many goalkeepers worry too much about the goals scored against them," said Worsley. "I'd like to work a shutout every game, too, but there's going to be goals scored. And when there are, you can't erase them. So why worry about them? That's my philosophy: Why worry about something you can't do anything about? Once the puck's in the net, there isn't anything you can do about erasing it."

During his decade with the Rangers, Worsley often clashed with Coach Phil Watson and more than once was dispatched to the minors. Gump greeted the demotions with a characteristic shrug. Doreen Worsley became excited every time reports circulated about Gump being sent to Providence or Springfield or some other spot. "Don't worry about it," her goalie husband advised. "If we're in Providence, we're in Providence. Nothing we can do about it."

Worsley's been that way for as long as he can remember, ever since his pygmy proportions landed him in the nets for keeps back in Point St. Charles, a Montreal suburb where he was born. "I was the runt," remembered Gump. "The smallest guy always got the pads, so I was the goalie." Then there was the matter of his first name. "Lorne" just didn't seem to fit him. But Worsley's crewcut with its short, stiff quill look reminded his pals of the comic-strip character Andy Gump. And from then on, he was Lorne to his parents and Doreen, but Gump to everyone else.

Doreen met Worsley early in his hockey career. "She was the first person who ever wanted my autograph," said Gump. He was sixteen and playing junior hockey at the time when a friend came over with a piece of paper and told him to sign it for a girl in the stands. "I thought, This girl I've got to meet," said Gump. Soon afterward, Doreen hopped on the hockey merry-go-round that Worsley rode. "Sometimes I'd play two games a night in those days," said Gump. "I'd play at seven o'clock in Lachine, then take my skates off, jump in a cab, and change my sweater on the way to Verdun for a nine o'clock game. Then I'd walk Doreen home."

Those days prepared Worsley for the shooting galleries he would face in later years with the Rangers. "I remember one game when I played for the Verdun Cyclones, I had 102 shots taken at me," said Gump. "We lost 14–0. My wife remembers that game. She walked in a little late and looked at the scoreboard and it read 1–0. 'Good,' she told one of her friends, 'it's a close game.' Then somebody told her, 'The scoreboard only goes up to 10. This is the second time around. It's 11–0.'" To Doreen's credit, she didn't walk out on the rout. It was good training for life in New

York with Gump and the Rangers.

Worsley first came to the attention of the New York NHL club in 1949 when he showed up with the New York Rovers of the Eastern League. Gump led the league with seven shutouts in forty-seven games and made the first All-Star team with a 2.83 goals-against average. He also developed a very strong distaste for airplanes that year. It happened on a flight home from Milwaukee on one of those prejet four-engine planes. Gump was relaxing when he happened to glance out of the window and saw flames enveloping one of the engines.

The pilot had to do some fancy maneuvering before finding a suitable spot to set down his crippled aircraft. The plane finally made an emergency landing in Pittsburgh, delivering the Rovers and their badly shaken goaltender back to earth. After that harrowing flight, Worsley became a white-knuckles passenger, gripping the armrests of his seat tightly through-out the ride. "It's the one time I don't talk," Gump said once. "I'm too scared to say anything."

Worsley's flight flutters began early. Toe Blake, who coached him for a while during Gump's later days in Montreal, remembers how upset the goalie got. "I can't believe any man could be that frightened in a plane," said Blake. "Even in the waiting room, he's soaked in perspiration. Once he gets on the plane, he clutches at the arm of the seat and shakes the whole time he's up there. It's something you have to see to believe."

After his standout season with the Rovers, Worsley turned pro with the Ranger organization and led the United States Hockey League with a 2.88 average and three shutouts at St. Paul in his first play-for-pay season. He was Rookie of the Year and voted the outstanding goalie as well. That meant a step up in class to the Pacific Coast Hockey League with the Saskatoon Quakers. Again, he led the league in shutouts, the third straight year in three different leagues that he accomplished that feat. The next move was to New York, where the Rangers needed help for aging Chuck Rayner.

Worsley showed up in New York, looking like somebody's kid brother. He was just twenty-three years old, barely five feet, seven inches and maybe weighed one hundred fifty pounds. But he came to play. Gump took over for Rayner when the Ranger regular came up with a charley horse in training camp. And Worsley impressed the New York brass right away. "He's a great prospect," said General Manager Frank Boucher. "He's very cool and sound. Worsley makes no unnecessary moves. He has the ability to make the tough ones look easy." Even after his injury healed, Rayner couldn't dislodge Worsley from the Ranger nets. The Gump had won himself an NHL job and soon he'd won himself an NHL trophy as well. He was voted the Calder Trophy as Rookie of the Year with a 3.06 goals-against average and two shutouts in fifty games.

Rayner retired following that season and the Rangers purchased some goaltending insurance, picking up Johnny Bower from Cleveland. The plan was to have Bower back up Worsley, but nobody told Bower. He went to training camp and beat Worsley out of the Ranger goaltending job. Gump was farmed out to Vancouver of the Western League for the 1953–54 season. "All I can say," muttered Worsley when he heard of the demotion, "is that they're gonna have to go a long way to present that Calder Trophy to me."

Worsley had a sensational season with Vancouver, leading all WHL goaltenders with a 2.40 average and winning the Most Valuable Player award as well. But in the playoffs, he suffered one of the scariest injuries of his career. "We were playing Calgary and Gus Kyle, who used to play for the Rangers, skated right into me. He said he never saw me," said Worsley. After the collision, Gump, who was kayoed, didn't see anything for a while.

When he woke up, Worsley realized that he had no feeling below his waist. "When I fell, it jarred my spinal column. I was paralyzed." Doctors kept plunging needles into the Gump for three days before determining that his injury was a pinched nerve. "I was in the hospital for five days and I got out in time to play the last game of the playoffs. But it was too late. We lost, four games to two. All that summer I had to wear a steel-ribbed corset with the reins in back. It made me sit erect and I wondered every now and then if I was going to lose my mobility because of the injury."

Worsley needn't have worried. He showed up in the Ranger training camp the following fall as good as new and turned the tables on Bower by reclaiming the New York net-minding job he had lost to Johnny. Gump took the switch the same way he had taken it the year before—stoically. "Why get excited?" he said. "The puck is the same size in this league and you still stop it the same way."

Frank Boucher and Muzz Patrick shared the Ranger coaching job in 1954–55, but when the club missed the playoffs for the fifth straight year it was decided that New York needed new bench leadership. The man chosen for the job was an ex-Ranger, Phil Watson. A hot-tempered man who took every game to heart, Watson never hesitated to criticize his players and Worsley was his number-one target.

Never the model physical specimen, Gump found himself being constantly badgered by Watson over his weight. And another thing that bugged Watson was Worsley's carefree attitude. Gump never brooded after a game, regardless of whether he had played well or not.

Now the job of tending goal in the National Hockey League is tough enough without having your boss on your back every night. But Worsley and his thick skin stood up well to Watson's barrage. The coach would stand with reporters in the vacant room next door to the Ranger dressing room and deliver an unfavorable critique of Worsley's work. Then the newsmen would go next door to give Worsley the play-by-play report. "Tell him," Gump would say, "that he's full of baloney."

Once, Watson blew his stack when Worsley surrendered three goals in the third period of a game, allowing Chicago to come from behind and gain a 6–6 tie. Three of the Black Hawk goals belonged to Hec Lalande, who had managed only seven scores in forty games before discovering Worsley. "When a dope like Lalande scores three goals in one game, how good can the goalie be?" stormed Watson.

"You can't play goal with a beer-barrel belly," roared the coach, warming up for his attack on Worsley. "Every time I hop on this fellow, everybody accuses me of attacking him unjustly. But the same guys who go in after a game and pat him on the back are the guys who are buying him beer. Worsley·is the most uncooperative player on the club during practice. He refuses to work, even though he knows he's overweight. He should weigh one hundred sixty-five pounds, but he's over one hundred seventy now. That's all that beer piling up."

Worsley sneered at Watson's explosion. "Beer, huh," grunted the Gump. "That's for peasants. I never drink the stuff and Watson knows it. I'm strictly a whiskey man."

Watson's blood pressure probably climbed a couple of more points when he heard that crack. The coach never quite realized that he was fighting a losing battle with Worsley. He tried needling one of hockey's best needlers. He never had a chance. "For three years, I've been trying to make him care," Watson said once, "and I'm not getting anywhere."

What must have bothered Watson most was Worsley's phlegmatic approach to his job. "I don't take the goaltending home with me at night," Gump once said. "That's a sure way to go crazy. When I'm on the ice, I do my job. When I get off it, I'll be damned if I'm going to worry about it. If you do, it'll make you sick. I'm not going to crack up."

"That man bothers me," said Watson about his goalie. "He's not human. He doesn't worry enough about his job. This is the damndest I-don't-give-a-damn guy in the world. Praise goes to his head. He takes his press clippings too seriously. I'd like him to take practices just as seriously, but I can't get him to do that."

Worsley glided through wind sprints, looking like Carol Heiss in pads. And when another Ranger roared past him, the goalie was not above delivering a well-directed needle. "Gee," he would say as he waltzed through the sprint, "this is fun. I can keep this up all day."

If a teammate tried to trade barbs with the Gumper, he usually wound up on the short end. "You'd better be careful," the goalie once told one of his endless streams of less-than-efficient defensemen. "You can be replaced by half an aspirin." About another long-haired teammate, Worsley remarked, "He gets a haircut twice a year—whether he needs one or not."

Once a young reporter ventured into the Ranger dressing room following another of those shooting-gallery nights Gump experienced so often in the New York nets. The newsman's assignment was an in-depth piece on the goalie. He ambled over to Worsley and began chatting with the Gump. In the course of the conversation, the writer asked Worsley which team gave him the most trouble.

The Gump smiled and motioned the writer closer. Then,

in a voice loud enough to be heard in Watson's office next door, he answered the question. "The Rangers," snapped the Ranger goalie.

At about the same time, Gump opened a restaurant in Montreal. On his menu, he had something called The Ranger Special. A brave diner who ordered it soon discovered that The Ranger Special was salad—chicken salad.

There were occasions during their stormy relationship when Worsley and Watson had a truce. "I just naturally seem to pick on Gump when I can't think of anything else," said Watson in a rational moment one day.

"It's okay with me," answered the Gump. "I don't mind being his whipping boy when he has to let off steam. I never get sore and I don't have to be patted on the back like some guys."

Once, in training camp at Niagara Falls, Watson delivered his first dressing-room speech of the season and floored the goalie. "Every position on this club, bar one, is wide open," the coach said. "I kid you not. Nobody's job is safe except Worsley's. He's my goalie."

Gump's chin nearly hit the floor at that disclosure by Watson, his toughest critic. "That's why we picked Niagara Falls to train in," said the coach. "This is the honeymoon city, isn't it? Well, Gump and I are buddies. It's a beautiful friendship. Why, we even had our picture taken with the Falls as a background."

But the romance was short-lived. As soon as Worsley resembled anything less than the Great Wall of China, Watson was back on his back. Some years later, Worsley reflected on his duels with Watson. "He knows hockey inside out and backwards," said the Gump. "He just couldn't handle men and I was his whipping boy. 'Why me?' I asked him. 'Because you can take it,' he said. I told him, 'Don't do me no favors.' "

Toward the end of Watson's explosive reign as coach of the Rangers, goalies around the NHL were beginning to experiment with face masks. Many wore them in practice although, until November 1, 1959, when Jacques Plante put one on against the Rangers, no net-minder had tried one under game conditions. Practicing in a badly lit rink was sometimes more dangerous than the games and so Worsley decided he'd try the mask for workouts. It was one of the shortest experiments on record.

"I have a mask," Worsley told Watson before one practice. The coach came up with one of his patented harangues.

"You mean you had a mask," he exploded. "Who wants a good-looking goalie? You get hit in the face in practice. You can also get hit in the face in a game or falling down the subway. A mask gives you bad habits. Maybe the next coach of the Rangers will let you wear a mask, but this one won't." And that ended Worsley's experiment with the mask.

Gump was in the Ranger nets at the other end of the ice the night that Plante appeared with the mask in a game for the first time. Gump scorned the idea and continued to for the remainder of his career. When Plante introduced the mask, he was the only goalie wearing one. When Worsley continued to hold out against the protector, he eventually became the only goalie not wearing one.

Worsley's term with the Rangers was a stormy one, even after Watson's ulcers forced him to give up the job. Twice, the Gump was demoted to the minors, spending terms at Providence in 1957–58 and Springfield in 1959–60. The second demotion really teed off the Gump. "I won't come back," he stormed. "I'll stay down there and I won't come back. I still feel I belong with this club. It's not all my fault because we couldn't get going this season. They can leave me down there. I don't care." After fifteen games in the American League, the Rangers summoned Gump back to New York again.

New York's brass often criticized Worsley's style. They said the little round goaltender flopped around too much to be effective. Gump shrugged off the complaints. "When I started to play hockey," he said, "they told me to stop the puck. They didn't care how I stopped it, as long as I didn't let it slide over the goal line. Sure, I go down. There are lots of goalkeepers who go down. The only thing that concerns me is stopping the puck any way I can. If I have to go down to do it, I'll go down."

Worsley had plenty of practice stopping pucks in New York. He faced nightly barrages of forty and fifty shots in the Ranger nets. And he scoffed at goalies with stronger teams, who had more help. There was Plante, for example, winning all kinds of trophies year after year while playing for the Canadiens. "He gets thirty shots on a bad night," chuckled Worsley, shaking his head. "What a piece of cake."

Gump didn't know it, but the cake was to be cut again and he was to get a nice big bite. Montreal, tired of Plante's hypochondriac behavior, offered the goalie around the league. General Manager Frank Selke found a sympathetic ear in New York, where the Rangers were anxious to relieve Montreal of its net-minder. To replace Plante, the Rangers shipped Worsley north. The trade, which started as a simple exchange of goalies, built from there and before they were through Patrick and Selke had assembled a seven-player exchange.

Worsley and three forwards—Dave Balon, Leon Rochefort and Len Ronson—went to the Canadiens in exchange for Plante and forwards Phil Goyette and Donnie Marshall. Switching from New York to Montreal in those days was like moving from the basement to the penthouse. Gump loved it.

"Boy, here they appreciate a hockey player," he said, shortly after being traded to the Canadiens. "If you're in the National Hockey League in Montreal, you're a hero. Don't get me wrong. I like New York. But when you walk down the street here, people know you. Boy, when you're a Canadien, you're something. Inside, I'm still the same. When you play in the NHL, you've got pride. Inside, it doesn't matter if you're with the Rangers or the Canadiens. It's just that people look at you differently."

Worsley arrived in the Montreal training camp in the fall of 1963 with renewed spirits, excited about playing for a team that protected its goalie more zealously than the Rangers had. And Coach Toe Blake, relieved at finally being rid of Plante and his aches and pains, looked forward to having the Gump in Montreal's nets. "We're not going to alternate out goalies this year," said Blake. "Worsley will be our man. We'll carry a spare, of course, but he won't be our second-best goalie." That meant Charlie Hodge, Plante's backup man, was headed back to Montreal's AHL farm club at Quebec City.

Worsley opened the season in the Canadiens' nets and for two weeks, everything was dandy. Then, in a game against his old Ranger pals, Gump threw out his pad to make a save and felt something give in the back of his leg. He finished the game, but his postgame limp was mute testimony to what had happened on the ice. Worsley had pulled a hamstring and Hodge got a hurry-up call to return from Quebec City.

It took a couple of weeks for Gump's injury to heal, but in the meantime, Hodge started playing the best goal of his career. There was no way Blake could lift his hot man from the nets and with Hodge playing Gump would only get stale. There was little alternative for the Canadiens. They shipped Worsley to Quebec City to replace Hodge.

Montreal finished first and Hodge won the Vezina Trophy for the best defensive record in the league. The combination of those factors and the presence of thirty-five candles on Worsley's birthday cake in May 1964 led to the suspicion that Gump's NHL career might be over. Worsley laughed off that kind of talk. "You really want to know the difference between the American League and the NHL?" Gump asked a newsman one day. "I'll tell you the difference. Up there, in the NHL, a goalie doesn't have to stop three-on-nothing breakaways."

Those breakaways kept Worsley sharp and the following season he was ready when Hodge got hurt. Just after Christmas, Montreal called Gump back and he shared the goaltending job with Hodge down the final wekes of the season. Blake wanted both of his goalies sharp as the Canadiens headed for the playoffs. He even went to the extreme of alternating them every five minutes in the meaningless final game of the regular season against Boston. "I didn't do much goaltending that night," grumbled Gump, "but I got in a hell of a lot of skating."

Worsley wasn't thrilled by the two-goalie system that required a team to dress a pair of net-minders. "The ruling is sheer nonsense," he said. "How would you like to sit around doing nothing for half a game and then be asked to take over in the nets? I have nothing against replacing a goaltender, but he shouldn't have to sit around in his uniform all night long. It's impossible for a goalie to go into a game and do well after he's been sitting around in a cramped position. I don't want any part of it."

But the barons of hockey hadn't asked for Gump's opinion and so, when the Canadiens opened their 1965 quest for the Cup, Gump was in uniform, backing up Hodge. Sure enough, Charlie pulled a groin muscle in the second game of the opening series against Toronto and Worsley took over to backstop the Canadiens through the semifinals and into the showdown for the Cup against Chicago. Worsley beat the Black Hawks in the first two games in the final round, then lost game three, 3–1. Warming up for the fourth game, Worsley strained his thigh muscles and Hodge was rushed back into action. The Hawks beat the Canadiens that night to square the series.

Worsley limped badly as he accompanied the Canadiens back to Montreal with the series tied at two games apiece. "It's sore all right," he told reporters with the team. "I'm afraid I'm through for the series. We'll just have to wait and see."

Hodge responded to the challenge by shutting out Chicago in game five. But the Hawks stayed alive, winning game six 2–1. That sent it down to a winner-take-all seventh game— the ultimate showdown between hockey's two best teams with the Stanley Cup at stake. A few hours before the final game, Worsley was relaxing in his hotel room when the phone rang. The voice on the other end belonged to Coach Toc Blake.

"How do you feel?" asked Blake.

"Good," answered Worsley.

"How good?" demanded Blake.

"Perfect," replied the goalie. Then there was a click in Gump's ear. Blake had hung up.

A few hours later, as Worsley waited to meet his wife at a restaurant near the Montreal Forum he received word from trainer Larry Aubut that he would start the seventh game. "I gave the cashier my wife's tickets and then made a dash from the dressing room," said Gump. "I think I shook my way into the pads that night. I was pretty nervous."

When Worsley led the Canadiens onto the ice, the fans were stunned. Hodge had played well in the previous two games and Gump was still nursing his thigh injury. But Blake and Montreal General Manager Sam Pollock had their reasons for starting the Gump.

"We had to make a decision and we looked at it this way," explained Pollock. "If a spectacular game was needed to beat the Hawks, either Worsley or Hodge could do it. But we had to take into account who would be more jittery.

Who was the man with more experience?"

"I went with Gump because I thought he'd be less nervous than Charlie," said Blake. "Remember, Charlie played two good games before that. If it hadn't worked, we'd have looked awful bad." Another factor was Bobby Hull, Chicago's immense scoring threat. "Hull didn't get one shot past Gump during the season or in the playoffs," said Blake. "I figured he'd be more relaxed and would be able to stop Hull's slap shot."

The Hawks discovered early that Blake had guessed right by using Worsley. Montreal grabbed two quick goals for an early lead, but Chicago made menacing gestures in trying to come back midway through the first period. A goal would lift the Hawks and put them back in the game. Then, with Montreal shorthanded, Chicago attacked.

Chicago Defenseman Pierre Pilote, stationed at the blue line, saw little Camille Henry cut out of the corner and head for Worsley's net. Pilote fired the puck perfectly and Henry, breaking for the goal, met the rubber precisely where he wanted to meet it—at the edge of Worsley's crease. Henry got his stick down to deflect it toward the corner, a maneuver at which he was master. Worsley anticipated the move and threw his legs sideways across the net. The deflection skittered off the goalie's skate. Save!

It went like that all night long and when the final siren went off, the Canadiens had won 4–0, and, after years of frustration, Worsley was a Stanley Cup hero. The next day, when the Canadiens were toasted by the city of Montreal in a huge downtown parade, Gump was cheered as loudly as Jean Beliveau. But all of the acclaim didn't really sink in until about a week later when Gump returned to his hometown of Boleil, Quebec, a Montreal suburb with a population of about nine thousand. The town threw a special civic reception for the Worsleys that included a downtown parade with Gump in the motorcade's lead car, waving to the crowd.

"You know," said Gump, "that was the first time the city had a parade for anybody. It was the highlight of my career."

His Stanley Cup success gave Worsley a new lease on National Hockey League life. No longer were there any suggestions that Gump was over the hill. On the contrary, the suspicion was that he might just be beginning to climb it. Gump supported this suspicion the next season when he and Hodge shared Montreal's net-minding job again. The Canadiens finished first during the regular season and they owned the best defensive record in the league. Worsley shared the Vezina Trophy with Hodge.

Now the Vezina is greeted with a so-what shrug by some goalies because it is more a reflection of team efficiency than of an individual goalie. Surrounded by the Rangers, Gump was never a candidate for the goaltending Oscar. But traded to the more defensively competent Canadiens, Gump won it. "I'm the same goalie now that I was then," said Worsley. Winning the Vezina didn't change him, and when President Clarence Campbell made the official presentation, Worsley couldn't help but remember those ten seasons he had spent in the Rangers' shooting gallery while other goalies were collecting the silverware.

In the playoffs, Gump was again given the assignment of leading the Canadiens to another Stanley Cup. Montreal eliminated Toronto in the first round with Worsley playing some dazzling hockey. There was some muttering from the Maple Leafs about Gump being lucky and Worsley bristled at the suggestion.

"I've never seen a rabbit's foot or a four-leaf clover stop a puck yet," he said. "The only two things a goalkeeper has going for him, other than his teammates, are the goalposts. I don't buy that luck jazz."

After finishing off Toronto, the Canadiens moved into the finals against Detroit. And the Red Wings opened fast, stunning Montreal with two straight victories at the Forum. Worsley seemed less than solid, especially in the second game, and the fans got on him with catcalls and boos. Those were the same fans who had cheered him the week before for his play against Toronto.

When the series switched to Detroit, the momentum suddenly switched too. The Canadiens won both games in Detroit and then took the pivotal fifth game as well. Back in Detroit for game six, the Red Wings hopped in front by a couple of goals and Bruce Norris, president of the Detroit club, had a note delivered to David Molson, boss of the Canadiens, suggesting they finalize plans for the seventh game of the series.

But the note was premature. The Canadiens battled back to tie and then with three minutes left to play, it seemed that the note might not be so premature after all. Hockey's greatest scorer, Gordie Howe, got into the clear with the puck and had Worsley's defenseman screening the goalie as he wound up for his shot.

"I couldn't see him," Gump said later, "until he was around the defenseman. That's when I moved." In a flash the confrontation was over. Howe fired and Worsley's leg sprung for the puck, kicking it aside and preserving the tie.

When Henri Richard scored in overtime, the meeting between Norris and Molson became unnecessary. The Canadiens had won the Cup again and Richard was the hero. But it was Worsley's big save on Howe that gave Henri the chance to score the winning goal.

Worsley was on top again and two seasons later, in 1968, he had his name engraved on the Vezina for a second time, sharing the trophy this time with young Rogatien Vachon. Gump played forty games, six of them shutouts. His 1.98 goals-against average was the best he ever posted in the NHL. That was the same year an unfriendly fan in New York conked him with an egg and another admirer tossed a dinner knife at him. It was also the first season of expansion with the six-team NHL doubled in size and spreading all the way to California.

It was the expansion and the increased travel problems it caused that finally caught up with Worsley. Gump never liked airplanes, but when the NHL went no farther west than Chicago, flights seldom lasted more than an hour or so. Now there were five-hour trips to Los Angeles and Oakland and the flights got under Gump's skin. Finally, on a trip to Chicago, Worsley's patience with air pockets and seat belts snapped.

"The flight to Chicago took two hours and fifteen minutes," said the goalie, "and we were strapped to our seats for two hours. I couldn't take any more of it." At the airport in Chicago, Worsley told Coach Claude Ruel he was leaving the club. He called home and told his wife Doreen he was coming back to Montreal—by railroad.

The airplane ride was the straw that broke the camel's back, but it wasn't Worsley's only problem. There were indications that the pressures of his profession might have begun catching up with the placid Gumper. "My nerves are on edge," Worsley admitted. "I'm having trouble sleeping. It's no use playing when you feel that way. After that plane trip to Chicago, I simply got off the plane and said, 'That's it.' You can take just so much of that and, after the rough flight, I didn't want any more of it."

Gump returned home and mulled over the problem with General Manager Sam Pollock, another antiaircraft man. Pollock sent the Gump to a Montreal doctor to try to work out the trouble. The prescription was a month's total rest. No hockey, no skating, nothing but rest for a month. But the doctor didn't place the Forum off limits to the goalie. So Gump was around the club at practices and games. "That way I wasn't away from the team. I'd be in the dressing room every day and we'd talk and kid. If I'd been away for a long time, it would have been hard to go back, embarrassing." Soon the doctor thought Gump might like to skate. The Canadiens made ice time available and the Forum doors were locked, giving Worsley the privacy he needed at this delicate point in his life.

From that Gump advanced to the point where he could put the pads back on and six weeks after he had left the Canadiens, Worsley returned to action. His outlook about flying had mellowed. He still does not enjoy stepping into an airplane, but his visits with the doctor helped him accept flying more rationally. He started riding up front with the pilots and that gave him a bit more confidence, too. "Those pilots are good to me," said Gump. "And you know what? They tell me they get nervous themselves when they sit in the back. It's like being scared when you're riding with a guy who drives his car fast, but not being scared when you're driving yourself."

In January, Gump went back to work and that spring he helped Montreal to another Stanley Cup, the fourth in five years for the club. But Worsley's days with the club were numbered. He and Ruel often clashed over Gump's casual approach to practice. Ruel relied on Vachon to do almost all of Montreal's net-minding and that further diminished Worsley's already limited enthusiasm for practices.

"Hey, if they start paying me for practice, it's a different story, eh," said Worsley. "But otherwise, I'm not about to change. Why waste my energy?"

The conflict between goalie and coach came to a head in

January 1970 when Ruel tried to send Worsley to the American League in order to get him in shape. Nearly forty-one, Gump saw no point to going to the minors. He expressed his feelings to the Canadiens in just two words. "I quit," said Gump.

For three months, Worsley was absent from the NHL scene. He occupied himself making personal appearances and commercial endorsements. There was, for example, a three-day stand at Place Bonaventure where Gump donned a pair of pads for a hockey-stick manufacturing company. "Why not?" reasoned Gump. "The kids have to eat, don't they?"

Meanwhile, in Minnesota, the North Stars had their hands full trying to sneak into Lord Stanley's playoffs. Part of the problem was in goal and General Manager Wren Blair scurried around the NHL, looking for net-minding help. He never thought he'd find it in a stylish Montreal shopping plaza. Worsley! Of course, thought Blair. Worsley!

So the Minnesota GM requested the right to talk with Gump. Montreal gave him the green light and he contacted Worsley. At first Gump turned Blair down. But Wren is a persuasive guy. He was the man who corralled Bobby Orr for the Boston Bruins at the age of fourteen, convincing the young man's parents their boy was old enough to leave home for hockey. He had a reputation of always getting his man and at the moment Worsley was his man.

"Come on, Gump," he said. "At least come out here and take a look around." Worsley agreed and Blair knew he had his goalie. Gump fell in love with the Twin Cities and agreed to join the North Stars for the final month of the 1970 season. He helped the club into the playoffs and derived extra satisfaction when the Canadiens missed the playoffs that season.

"It was the best move I ever made," exulted Worsley. "We love it here. It's quiet and it's clean. The wife and kids love it."

And the Twin Cities loved Worsley. Blair arranged a lucrative contract that paid Gump a bonus every time he played a victory or a tie. Age mellowed Worsley's opinion of the two-goalie system too. He shared the work with Cesare Maniago and both flourished. At forty-one, he was being reborn as an NHL goalie—for the second time.

Montreal Canadiens

Gump became
a Stanley Cup hero
with the Canadiens.

"Kids don't want to play goal much any more," said Gump. "That's why we oldtimers are still around. That and expansion. The kids don't think there's much glamor in tending goal. They feel all the action is in being a forward or a defenseman."

Those forwards and defensemen still gave the old man a workout. Often friends, teammates, and even family suggested that Worsley might put on a mask to protect his profile. He wasn't, after all, as young as he used to be. Gump just laughed off the suggestions. "I'm too old to change my ways," he said. "I couldn't get adjusted to one at my age. My face is my mask."

Soon, Worsley was the only goaltender of any consequence without the mask. "I've got nothing against the idea at all," Gump said once. "If it works for you, great. I just wouldn't feel right wearing one. If I was getting nervous, maybe a mask would add some time to my career. But I'm not. Hell, it's too late to start worrying about preserving this kisser."

Despite Worsley's defiant shunning of the mask, he did try one during preseason games in 1973, and his son, Dean, put one on when he started playing goal in high school. "I left it up to him," said Gump. "I don't help him unless the coach asks me. After all, the coach spends all his time with these kids. Who am I to interfere?"

Gump's oldest son, Lorne, Jr., enlisted in the military when he turned eighteen. What branch? Why the air force, of course. "How about that?" chuckled Gump. "The old man is famous as a white-knuckles passenger, scared to death of flying, and the kid joins the air force. You can see how much influence I've had on him."

Meanwhile, Worsley just rolls along in the NHL. He's tried to retire from the North Stars a couple of times, but Blair always lures him back. "You know," Gump once observed, "if hockey teams traveled by trains like the old days, I might try and play until I'm ninety."

He might just try it, anyway.

It doesn't matter
how you stop the puck,
says Glenn Hall,
making a save for
the St. Louis Blues
against the Canadiens.

UPI

8
GLENN
HALL:
IRON MAN

The pain was in Glenn Hall's lower back. It felt like a toothache—a dull, persistent pain that struck him every so often. If he stood straight up, he was all right; there was no pain. But what goaltender ever spent his whole evening standing straight up? And it was when he made his repertoire of acrobatic moves to block the puck that he felt the pain.

The date was November 7, 1962, and the Chicago Black Hawks were at home against the Boston Bruins for a National Hockey League game. In goal for Chicago was, as usual, Glenn Hall, Mr. Goalie for the Black Hawks. He had played every game in the nets for Chicago since 1957. And before that, he had played every game in Detroit's nets for two full seasons. That added up to 551 consecutive regular-season and playoff games in goal—an incredible streak.

The NHL, in its infinite wisdom, decided that playoff and regular-season accomplishments should be separated. Glenn Henry Hall, the league said, was really playing in his 503rd consecutive game, not his 552. The Black Hawks, nevertheless, had celebrated Hall's half-century mark ten months earlier when his combined regular season and playoff total hit five hundred. Hall thought about that night when the Black Hawks had wheeled a brand-new car out to the center ice, as he stood in front of the Hawks' net again, feeling that throbbing in his lower back and knowing that his streak was nearing its conclusion.

In practice the day before Hall had tried out a new set of goalie pads. The pads were particularly stiff and Glenn had strained his back trying to break them in. He spent a restless night—not an unusual occurrence for him or any other goaltender for that matter—and was stiff the next day. At first, the fear was that he had suffered a pinched nerve, but the conclusion was that it was only a strained back muscle. When Chicago took the ice, Hall, as usual, slid between the pipes to guard the nets.

But during the warmups, the pain became more intense and Glenn, noted for his imperturbable expression, grimaced. As he skated off the ice after the warmups, Coach Rudy Pilous approached his goalie. "You okay, Glenn?" asked Pilous. Hall just nooded his head.

But he was not all right and he knew it. The pain in his back wasn't any better. In the opening minutes of the Boston game, Hall's teammates protected him like a piece of fine china, rarely allowing a difficult shot to reach him. Glenn discovered in those minutes that he could cover the angles of the goal without too much difficulty, but that he couldn't get his legs together without suffering intense pain.

Midway through the first period, Boston's Murray Oliver launched a fifteen-footer that Hall should have gobbled up. Instead, the puck skipped past the goalie and into the Black Hawks' net. The time was ten-twenty and it was at that precise moment that one of the most fantastic iron-man streaks in sports history ended. Hall glided over to the Chicago bench and then went into the Black Hawks' dressing room, ending 33,135 minutes and thirty-three seconds of consecutive NHL goaltending.

"I didn't want to come out of the game even though I knew I wasn't right," said Hall. That's because Glenn had become accustomed to finishing what he started. The last time he had been lifted from a game was some dozen years earlier when he played goal for the Windsor, Ontario, Spitfires. "I got a pretty bad skate cut in the cheek and they took me out in the middle of the second period," he recalled, fingering the scar left by the cut.

Actually, Hall's consecutive-game streak did not end until the Hawks' next game, a Sunday-night date in Montreal. After talking it over with the Chicago club physician, Dr. Myron Tremaine, and trainer Nick Garen, Glenn did not even make the trip to Montreal. It was the first game he had missed in over seven seasons and Hall was modest. "It's not a bad average, I guess," he said.

Not bad at all. In the slap-shot, screened-shot world of net-minding, the law is a Darwinian survival of the fittest. And no man proved fitter than this baby-faced native of Humboldt, Saskatchewan, who brought a bubbly stomach and fierce determination to the game. Night after night, Hall's job made him sick to his stomach—so sick that he couldn't keep his pregame meal down. "I never believed the stories about him and his stomach," said Ed Giacomin, another member of the goaltending union. "Then at an All-Star Game, I saw him have the dry heaves in the dressing room." That was a regular ritual for Glenn, whose stomach never quite accepted his dangerous occupation. "When they elect him to the Hall of Fame," an ex-teammate once said, "they ought to send his bucket along too."

If he had known the particular hell he was letting himself in for in future years, it's a cinch Glenn would have found some other job on the hockey team when he started playing the game. Humboldt was an icebox town that had long winters and plenty of ice for the local citizens to practice their skating. Hall took advantage of all the ice to play hockey throughout the winter and by the time he was eleven, he had migrated to the nets—through necessity, not choice.

"I was captain of our local team. Our goalie—I think his name was Wilson—quit. No one else wanted to play goal. I didn't either, I guess, but it was up to me. So I became a goalie," said Glenn.

"You know how it is with kids," he continued. "Everybody wants the glory jobs. In baseball they all want to be the pitcher and the quarterback in football. Well, it's the same in hockey. But I found out quick I'd never be able to skate well enough to go anywhere as a forward or even a defenseman for that matter."

So Hall spent his time in the nets and for the next few years played juvenile and junior hockey around Humboldt. Along the way, he attracted the attention of Fred Pinckney, a scout for the Detroit Red Wings, whose territory included Saskatchewan's prairie country. Some years earlier, Pinckney had brushed the hay out of the hair of another young man from that province and directed him toward Detroit. After their success with Gordie Howe, the Red

Wings paid close attention to all of Pinckney's finds.

Pinckney invited Hall to try out for the Red Wings' farm club in Windsor, Ontario, and although he didn't make the Spitfires in his first try, he returned a year later. This time, he stayed. The year was 1948 and Hall won the number-one goaltending job for the Spitfires, who were coached by Jimmy Skinner. Glenn spent the next two years with Windsor and was named the league's Most Valuable Player in his last season of junior hockey. "I learned a lot about goaltending under Jimmy," said Hall. "He taught me all about the angles and how to keep a mental book on the opposing forwards."

Windsor is a mere tunnel ride from Detroit and the Red Wing organization made good use of the proximity of the two cities. "When we had an off day and the Red Wings were home, Jimmy would take us over to the Olympia," said Glenn. "We didn't have seats and I used to stand behind the goalies and watch them very closely."

The Detroit goalies that Glenn watched were Harry Lumley, the resident net-minder, and his backup man, Terry Sawchuk. "They were great and it was an education to watch them," said Hall. The following year, the Red Wings signed Hall for their Indianapolis farm club in the old United States Hockey League. Indianapolis needed a goalie because their regular man, Sawchuk, had moved up to the Red Wings for good, replacing Lumley, who had been swapped to Chicago in a huge nine-player trade. The Red Wings had won the Stanley Cup the previous spring, but General Manager Jack Adams was no stand-pat guy and so he made the deal that made Sawchuk Detroit's goalie and Hall Indianapolis's net-minder.

Hall winces when he recalls his first season of professional hockey. It was a nightmarish year for him. Surrounded by an awful team, Hall surrendered an average of four goals per game and the team dipped to the bottom of the USHL standings. Often during the season, Hall got the feeling his net was located at the bottom of a steep hill. He faced a shower of rubber and that winter of discontent helped him formulate his philosophy for tending goal.

"Only 10 percent of the goals scored are the fault of the goalkeeper," said Hall. "The rest are the result of mistakes up the ice that let a guy get through to take a shot.

The goalkeeper either makes the last mistake or makes the great save that wipes out the other mistakes."

In Indianapolis, there were more mistakes than Hall could handle. "Don't talk about that year," he said. "We didn't have such a good club. I think we finished last or next to last."

There was one good thing about that season. Hall established himself as the number-two goalie in the Detroit organization and when Sawchuk was injured the next year Glenn got the call to mind goal for the Red Wings. Armed with major-league teammates, Glenn turned in four victories and a tie in six games. Included was his first National Hockey League shutout. His debut was a 2–2 tie in Montreal that, as one might expect, stuck vividly in Glenn's mind. "I was so nervous, I thought I'd never be able to tie my pads on in time to play," he said. "My stomach was pretty jumpy."

Tommy Ivan was the Red Wing coach that year and he remembered Hall's debut for another reason.

"Like most kids, and particularly goaltenders, Glenn was nervous about being in the National League," said Ivan. "The first period was rough and Hall was a bit unsteady. Gordie Howe got in a fight with a Montreal player just before the period ended. He should have been plenty riled up as we went to the dressing room."

As Ivan sat next to his young goalie, trying to calm him, trainer Lefty Wilson passed out tea to the players, a tradition for the Detroit club. Then Ivan noticed Howe.

"A baggage truck separated Howe from Wilson," said Ivan. "Instead of rising to reach for the paper cup of tea, the big guy turned the blade of his stick flat and had Wilson put the cup on it. Then, nonchalantly as you please, he pulled the stick toward him without spilling a drop."

"Mind you, Howe wasn't showing off," Ivan continued. "He was just letting the guys know they had to show they weren't worried about Sawchuk not being in the nets so that Hall would have that much more confidence in himself. It did more to help Glenn than any words I could have said to him. The boys came back and tied the Canadiens and Glenn played very well."

That season and for the next two, Glenn did most of his goaltending for Bud Poile's Edmonton Flyers in the

Western Hockey League. In his first two years in the WHL, his goals-against average was well above 3.00, but in his third year he chopped it to an impressive 2.83. Each September he began in the Red Wing training camp and each October found him back with Edmonton. He wasn't surprised or disappointed, either.

"When I went to Detroit's camp those years, I knew that Sawchuk had the job sewed up. I was happy to play in Edmonton. To be perfectly honest, I hated to leave I liked it so much. But the money is in playing for a National League club and, naturally, it was my goal to make the grade."

There had been an additional two-game fill-in for Sawchuk during the 1954–55 season and Glenn allowed just two goals. That meant that in eight NHL games, he had only given up twelve goals and many observers suggested that the curly haired youngster was ready for the big league. But Sawchuk blocked his way. Terry had led the league with a 1.94 goals-against average and twelve shutouts in 1954–55 and the Wings had won the regular-season championship for a seventh straight year. Detroit also took the Stanley Cup, beating Montreal in seven games.

With that kind of record, one would think Detroit would stand pat. But not Jack Adams. He thought Sawchuk's nerves might be getting the best of him and, with Hall waiting in the wings, the Detroit general manager dealt his goalie to Boston in a nine-player trade that rocked the hockey world. Now Hall had his chance.

"The first I heard of the trade was when a reporter called me at home in Humboldt and asked me how I felt about becoming the first-string goalie for the Stanley Cup champions," said Hall. "I told him I was glad he was so sure I had the job locked up because I wasn't. After all, Detroit had a lot of fine goalies in their organization. Fellows like Gilles Boisvert and Dennis Riggin. And besides, I knew I'd have to win the job when I got to training and I never seem to go good in the preseason training camp."

Regardless of whether Hall wanted to accept the fact or not, he was the man the Red Wings expected to fill Sawchuk's pads. "We had to make a decision between Sawchuk and Hall," explained Adams. "We decided to go with Hall and it was no snap decision. Glenn had played eight games with us in the past. He has shown us enough to prove he belongs in this league. He was more advanced at that time than Sawchuk was when he joined us."

Hall, as he expected, had a less than outstanding training camp. As the exhibition season drew closed, the Red Wings, as Stanley Cup champions, were scheduled to play the NHL All-Stars in the annual game. Nowadays the game is a mid-season affair matching the stars of the two divisions, but back in the 1950s it was played before the start of the regular season and matched the Cup champs with a squad of All-Stars from the other five teams in the league. It was not the very best of circumstances for a rookie goaltender —especially one like Glenn Hall.

"I'm always nervous," admitted Hall, "and early in that game I thought my pads would shake off." There was the small matter of a twenty-five-game home-ice unbeaten streak for the Red Wings to protect. Detroit had finished the 1954–55 season with nineteen victories and six ties at home. But the goalie in those games was Terry Sawchuk, and now he was at the other end of the ice, playing for the All-Stars, and a skinny, somewhat scared rookie was in the Red Wing nets.

It also didn't help matters that the All-Stars kept buzzing the Red Wing nets. All-Stars like Jean Believeau, Maurice Richard, and Bernie Geoffrion of Montreal, Sid Smith of Toronto, Ed Litzenberger of Chicago, Danny Lewicki of the Rangers, and Leo Labine of Boston headed a host of sharp-shooting forwards.

The Stars had Hall bouncing around pretty well and the goalie's stomach turned flip-flops of its own. Early in the second period, Gordie Howe scored the game's first goal, giving Detroit the lead. The Stars stormed back trying to get even. Doug Harvey, the great Montreal defenseman, stick-handled over the center red line and sidestepped a check from Red Wing defenseman Red Kelly. Once inside the blue line, Harvey pulled up to let the Stars' attack get organized.

Hall set himself in the Detroit net. His pads formed an inverted Y, giving Harvey an inviting target to fire at. But Doug wasn't shooting. Instead, he located Lewicki cruising across the ice. As the New York forward cut for the net, Harvey hit him with a perfect pass. Now Lewicki was in position, bearing down on the Red Wings' net with only Hall between him and the goal. The first thing he saw was the gap between the goalie's pads. It was too inviting to pass up. Lewicki snapped his wrists and the puck flew at the net, headed directly for the empty space. Instantly, Hall clamped his pads together, so quickly it was blurred to anyone watching the goalie. Thump, Lewicki's shot banged off the leather of Hall's pads. Save!

Time and again, the same thing happened and soon the shakiness disappeared from Glenn Hall's knees. "I felt all right after handling a couple of shots. I didn't feel like a fill-in—not with that team in front of me."

Dutch Reibel added two goals for the Red Wings—the second one into an empty All-Star net and Detroit won the game 3–1, extending its home-ice streak to twenty-six unbeaten games and doing a lot to settle its young goalie. Red Wing coach Jimmy Skinner, Glenn's old friend from his junior days at Hamilton, helped too.

"He kept me going," said Hall. "He gave me a lot of confidence. I knew I looked bad before the season started, but Jimmy told me not to worry and things seemed to work out all right."

Hall was better than all right as far as Skinner was concerned. "He's the guy who kept us in there in the first part of the season when we couldn't beat any goalie," said Skinner. "We weren't too concerned with Hall. We wouldn't have traded Sawchuk if we were, would we? We knew what Hall could do and that was enough for us."

Even Hall's pregame jitters, which he could never quite shake, didn't bother Skinner. "That's the mark of a pro," the coach said. "No real pro, in any sport, is worth his salt if he doesn't get those butterflies in his stomach before a game. But once Hall's on the ice, he's awful tough to beat. Wait'll you see him in a few years."

The Red Wings had problems early in Hall's rookie season. They started in the very first game on October 6—just three days after the goalie's twenty-fourth birthday. The game was in The Olympia where, four nights earlier, Hall had backstopped the Wings to their victory over the All-Stars. Now the home-ice streak was at twenty-six games and the opposition was Chicago, a team that had won just thirteen of seventy games the year before. The Red Wing fans were confident that the Cup champs could handle the Black Hawks. "Sure, I remember that game opening that season," said Hall. "The score was tied 2–2 going into the last period and, at about the six-minute mark, Nick Mikoski scooted around Marcel Pronovost to come barging in on me. He fired a low shot from about fifteen feet into the right-hand corner of the net." Final score: Chicago 3, Detroit 2.

The fans weren't thrilled with the outcome and, as usual, blamed the goalie. And they kept right on blaming him as Detroit got off to a stumbling start. The problem for the Red Wings was offense, not defense, but Hall was a handy target. He stood out like a sore thumb—a stand-up goalie completely opposite in style to the deep crouch Sawchuk favored. Hall took the criticism in stride. He just came back, game after game, blocking shot after shot. "He's a good boy," said Jack Adams, smiling. "He never blames anybody else when the other team scores on him. He just says, 'It was just an act of God.'" Most of the fans never blamed anybody else, either.

Despite the charges of nonchalance—his bubbling stomach was guilty of anything but that—Hall prospered. He turned in a sparkling 2.11 goals-against average, led the league with twelve shutouts and was named the NHL's top rookie. His dozen blankings were the most ever recorded by a first-year goalie in the NHL and only one short of Harry Lumley's record of thirteen. It wasn't a bad debut for the pale, rail-thin net-minder who rarely kept his pre-game meal down.

But while it was a successful year for Hall, it was not so successful for Detroit. The Wings' string of regular-season titles ended at seven when Montreal beat them out of first place. Then, just to prove it was no accident, the Canadiens beat Detroit in the Stanley Cup finals as well.

The next year it was time for a turnabout. Hall's shutout total dropped from twelve as a rookie to only four and his goals-against average was up from 2.11 to 2.24. But the Red Wings finished first and all was well again for GM Jack Adams. Now it was time for the playoffs and Detroit's revenge on Montreal and reclaiming of the Cup from the Canadiens—or, at least, that's what Adams figured would happen. But he never counted on the Boston Bruins. The fourth-place Bruins battled doggedly, forcing the semifinal series to a decisive seventh game. Then, just when it seemed the Red Wings would finish them off, Boston erupted for three goals in the third period of the final game to elimi-nate Detroit.

Adams was enraged. His championship team knocked off by a fourth-place club! In the last period of the series by a trio of goals in the final twenty minutes! Somebody's head would roll because of this and the leading candidate seemed to be the man who had made the last mistake on those goals. Adams blasted Hall's net-minding, holding him re-sponsible for the loss to the Bruins. Two months later, Hall was gone, traded to Chicago in another of Adams's mam-moth player swaps. It was no surprise to Glenn when it happened.

"I felt sure I wouldn't be back with Detroit when I was so severely criticized in public print for my play against Boston in the Stanley Cup playoffs," the goalie said.

"I didn't think I played that badly," Hall continued. "I wasn't as sharp as I might have been, I'll admit. But there were other factors that might have been considered too." Obviously, Glenn was thinking of the 90 percent of goals scored because of the mistakes made someplace else on the ice. Adams didn't want to hear about them and when he started offering his young goalie around, he had little trouble finding a taker. Was Chicago interested? You bet.

The Black Hawks needed help in the worst way. The team had finished last four straight times, seven times in eight years, and nine times in eleven seasons. Offered a goalie who had finished second in the Vezina Trophy race in each of his two NHL seasons and who had been a second-team All-Star as a rookie and then a first-team All-Star in his sophomore season, the Black Hawks grabbed him.

When Hall got to the Hawks' training camp, his old friend Tommy Ivan, who had preceded him to Chicago, had a sur-prise in store. He had assigned Glenn's goaltending rivals, Al Rollins and Harry Lumley, to minor-league affiliates. Hall would be the Black Hawk goalie.

"I had anticipated a three-man battle for the Chicago job," admitted Hall. "I was surprised to learn that Al wasn't even coming East and that Harry had been placed with Buffalo. It gives you a bit of a lift when your boss shows obvious confidence in you. We are all always out to win. But when a fellow has other capable men and still entrusts the job to you, you just want to do that much better in appreciation."

It would be nice to be able to report that the acquisition of Hall turned the Black Hawks from have-nots to champions overnight. But it just didn't happen that way. The transition took four years and in 1960–61 Chicago won its first Stanley Cup in twenty-three seasons. The hero was Hall, who had two shutouts and a playoff-leading 2.10 goals-against average for twelve games.

Glenn was the model of consistency in Chicago. He had identical records in 1959–60 and 1960–61, leading the NHL with six shutouts in each of those seasons and allowing 2.57 goals-against per game. The next season, his average moved up to 2.65, but so did his shutouts. He led the league with nine whitewashings. What's more, Hall was in the nets, night in and night out. He never missed a game and in Chicago, the fans labeled him "Mr. Goalie." But Hall never was a relaxed, happy-go-lucky guy during those glory years with the Black Hawks.

"Playing goal is a winter of torture for me," he said. "Plenty of times, I've been tempted to climb into the car and head for home. Don't get the idea I'm knocking the business. It has provided a high standard of living for me. But here's the kind of profession it is. We're riding on a plane. I doze off. Suddenly, I wake myself up by kicking one leg. When John McKenzie was with the club, he usually rode with me. He'd grin and ask whether I'd stopped that shot."

As if the nightly pressure of playing bulls-eye for a frozen hunk of rubber wasn't enough, Hall almost yearly got into tight battles for top goalie honors. Five times he finished second in the race for the Vezina Trophy, twice losing the prized award on the final night of the season. That kind of thing can knot any man's stomach.

A friend once asked Hall to describe his job. Glenn gave him his best sad-eyed expression and said, "Oh, it's an hour or so of hell." But Hall endured his own personal hell without relief for game after agonizing game and soon he had assembled his impressive record for consecutive games played. As he drew closer to five hundred straight games without relief, the Chicago club planned a special night for him.

The night was January 17, 1962, and Montreal was in town to play the Black Hawks. As usual, Hall was the first player up the staircase that leads from the Chicago dressing room to the ice. The fans gave him a standing ovation. Then, after the national anthem was played, both teams lined up at the blue lines. The glass partitions at one end of the ice parted and out glided a brand new car. Hall was flabbergasted.

"I knew it was my night and I thought there might be some little gift or something like that," the goalie said. "But this really floored me. Cars and things like that are for the big boys. I'm just a journeyman hockey player doing his job."

On this particular night, the Canadiens did a job on Hall, blasting seven shots past Mr. Goalie. "I never fought the puck so hard before in my life," he said. "I just couldn't make the right moves."

The next year, Hall's streak ended because of his back injury. And ironically, after his streak was snapped, Glenn came back stronger than ever and captured the Vezina Trophy for the best defensive record in the league. For the fourth straight season, he led the NHL in shutouts as well. Coach Rudy Pilous thought the end of the streak helped Hall.

"I think all of us would have to agree that the business of going in game after game finally got to him," said Pilous. "Maybe he was playing at times when he should have been resting an injury. Let's just say he needed a rest, and his injury finally forced him to take one. He missed three games and apparently it's done wonders for him."

The man who filled in for Hall was Denis DeJordy, a promising goalie who had been waiting in the wings at Chicago's American League farm club in Buffalo. Most teams around the NHL had adopted the two-goalie system, carrying a pair of net-minders who shared the work load. But Hall was an iron man and so there was no need for DeJordy. Once the consecutive-game streak ended, though, the Hawks decided that DeJordy would spell Hall. "At one time I don't think I'd have approved," said Glenn. "I guess maybe I've mellowed. Anyway, it seems like a pretty good idea now, particularly in view of the pressure we're under these days as one of the top teams. I hope we'll change quite a bit. Seventy games is a long grind and he plays well."

The Hawks changed goalies, but not often. Hall missed

only four games the year that his streak ended and only five of seventy games the next season. He relished those nights out of the shooting gallery. "When I found out this afternoon I wasn't playing," he said while sitting out a game in Detroit, "I skipped my nap because I wanted to enjoy every minute of it."

A night off was a gift to be relished and savored. "I often look at those guys who can whistle and laugh before a game," said Hall. "I never have been one of them. You'd think they didn't have a care in the world. Me? I'm plain miserable."

Why did he go on then? Why didn't he just turn his back and walk away from it all? It was a simple matter of economics. Hall always dreamed of the day that he could retire to a farm in Alberta's prairie country. "Give me a place where I can walk into a field by myself," he once said, "and yell, 'to hell with you,' and hear the 'you, you, you' echo across the field. But every time I save a dollar, the price of farms goes up two."

Finally, in 1966, Hall decided that he had absorbed all the rubber he could take. He sent a letter to General Manager Tommy Ivan saying that he was retiring. The return address was Stoney Plain, Alberta, where Hall had purchased one hundred fifty-five acres of land. The goalie's idea was to develop the land and farm it profitably. Until then he would work in nearby Edmonton to support his family. It all sounded perfect. But he couldn't find a job.

"I simply couldn't get a job in Edmonton," he said. "I wasn't looking for an executive's job. I'd have settled for one hundred dollars a week. There simply wasn't anything available." Hall worked on his farm, painting the barn and doing other chores, while the Black Hawks gathered for training camp. Ivan called once or twice and must have detected a twinge in Hall's voice.

"Since nothing was developing, I suppose the thought kept coming up in my mind: 'Where can I earn the kind of money the Hawks will pay me?' Soon I was asking myself: 'Where can I earn anything?' "

The answer was in the nets in Chicago and, sure enough, Hall wound up there again. He returned for a fourteenth professional season, although he wasn't enthusiastic. "Don't get me wrong," he said. "I think hockey is a great game.

It's tremendous for spectators and it's great to play when you're a kid. But for me, it's just a job that I don't like having to do."

Hall did his job well enough in 1966–67 to share the Vezina Trophy with DeJordy. His work load was only thirty-two games—less than half the number he played in earlier years. But he was also thirty-five years old and when the NHL expanded from six to twelve teams the next summer, Hall's name was on the list of available goaltenders. St. Louis snatched him. Now the question was whether the reluctant goalie would report.

"I had made up my mind to play for whichever expansion team drafted me—provided the price was right," said Hall. "Just say I'm another moonlighting farmer. This farmer will be able to afford a few luxuries which other farmers may not have."

Hall reported to the Blues and led the expansion team into the final round of the Stanley Cup playoffs against the power-laden Montreal Canadiens. It would, of course, be no match. The Canadiens expected to win in four straight against the expansionists. Montreal did, too. But because of Hall, it was some match! All four games were decided by one goal and two games stretched into overtime, thanks mainly to the spectacular net-minding of Hall. When it was over, Glenn was awarded the Conn Smythe Trophy as the Most Valuable Player of the playoffs.

The next year the Blues had a treat for Hall. They added old pro Jacques Plante, and the goalie partnership flourished. Together, they turned in thirteen shutouts, a league-leading eight by Hall. And together they shared the Vezina Trophy, the third time Glenn's name was inscribed on the award.

In November, teammate Red Berenson, like Hall a deep-thinking hockey player, approached the goalie. "Can you give me a good reason for your not wearing a mask?" said the forward. "If it isn't perfect protection, it's better than nothing."

Hall, one of the last of the bare-faced goalie brigade, looked at Berenson for a moment. Then he said, "You know, I can't."

The next night, Hall showed up at Madison Square Garden with his face covered for the first time. He was as shaky as ever, maybe even more so. Early in the game, Vic

The Iron Man's
consecutive game record
of 502 is likely to
stand forever.

Hadfield lofted a seventy-five-footer past him, a situation that hardly helped Hall's disposition. Moments later, Referee Vern Buffey whistled a debatable delay-of-game penalty on defenseman Noel Picard. Enraged, Hall rushed the referee and bumped Buffey. That was all for Mr. Goalie. He was invited to watch the rest of the game from the press box. "See that," he said to Berenson later. "Every time I wear a mask I get thrown out of a game."

The next year, Hall retired again. "I've been playing goal for a livelihood for twenty-three years," he said. "I've played major-league and minor-league and junior hockey and pee-wee league, and if you add it all together, gosh, I must be one hundred and five years old."

In November, the Blues invited Hall to St. Louis to formally accept the Vezina he had earned with Plante the year before. And before he knew it, Glenn signed another two-year contract. "I had definitely decided before coming to visit St. Louis that I would not play," he said. "I had purchased many new pieces of equipment for the farm and I had my mind made up. But the reception from the St. Louis fans, the genuine warmness of my teammates, and the sincerity of the St. Louis management and ownership made it impossible for me to refuse."

Hall played two more years, passing the nine-hundred-game plateau for his career, second only to Terry Sawchuk's career total of 971. Then he finally moved to Alberta for keeps. There was a brief turn as a coach with the World Hockey Association Edmonton Oilers, but for the most part Glenn was a gentleman farmer. He finished with sixteen NHL seasons and when he was asked the most important asset for a goalie, he answered quickly.

"I think it's a matter of confidence," he said. "That's half the battle with goalkeepers. When you're having trouble and figure you can't stop a football, you've had it. When I'm moving right, I'm stopping the puck. When you figure you can stop it, you go out there and just eat the puck."

The problem for a man with a stomach like Hall's would be keeping it down.

UPI

Bernie Parent's
first stint with the
Philadelphia Flyers began
in 1967; two teams
and another league later,
he's a Flyer again.

9
BERNIE PARENT:
TALE OF TWO LEAGUES

The bumper sticker is like most bumper stickers, designed with a smile and a message. It says simply: "Only The Lord Saves More Than Bernie Parent."

How true. And if you don't believe it, ask the Philadelphia Flyers, who watched Parent's miracle-making in the nets lead them to the 1974 championship—first to the National Hockey League's West Division and finally to the Stanley Cup. Or you might ask the Atlanta Flames, New York Rangers, or Boston Bruins—all victims of Parent's spectacular net-minding in the playoffs.

The Flames were snuffed out in four straight games, the Rangers hung on for seven, and the Bruins bowed in six. And on Sunday, May 19, 1974, the Philadelphia Flyers became the first expansion team to win the Stanley Cup. Mostly, the Flyers won the Cup because of Parent, a well-traveled goalie who, W. C. Fields notwithstanding, prefers Philadelphia to other places.

It was Parent's desire to be in Philadelphia that led to one of the most remarkable episodes in hockey history—the first jump from the established National League to the fledgling World Hockey Association.

The date was February 28, 1972, and there, grinning out of the morning newspapers, Toronto hockey fans found smiling Bernie Parent, proudly displaying a uniform jersey decorated with an eagle perched on a hockey stick. Parent had just signed a lucrative contract to tend goal for the

Miami Screaming Eagles of the World Hockey Association.

Now this wouldn't have been earth-shattering news except for one small detail: Bernie Parent at the time was employed by the Toronto Maple Leafs of the National Hockey League. And, understandably, the Toronto Maple Leafs and their fans weren't thrilled with the idea of their goalie forsaking the Leafs.

Parent was unveiled with a sense of history. He was the first player from the NHL to cash in his chips and switch to the fledgling WHA. He gave the new league credibility, an established name on which to hang its hat. Others would follow, but history will note that Parent was the first to go. He also turned out to be the first to return, but this is getting ahead of his odyssey.

As Bernard Marcel Parent grew up in Montreal's East End, he no more thought of turning his back on the NHL than of letting a day go by without playing hockey. The puck was a tennis ball in those days. The net was two well-packed mounds of snow. The sideboards were also long lines of piled-up snow. It was impromptu and crude, but for Bernie Parent and his friends it was a miniature Montreal Forum. "We didn't care about a thing," said Parent. "We used to play when it was twenty below."

Parent and his friends galumphed around in heavy galoshes as a substitute for skates in the deep snow. Bernie was always the goalie for no legitimate reason other than that his hero was Jacques Plante, who was at the time the nonpareil goaltender of the NHL Montreal Canadiens. "I can't remember ever playing any other position," claimed Parent.

Bernie never got to see the Canadiens play at the Forum because tickets to Montreal games were not that readily available. "Of course, I listened to every Montreal game on the radio," he said. "Plante was my hero all right." And the fact that Plante's sister lived next door to Bernie's family reinforced the hero worship of the young goalie for the Canadiens' star.

Once, Plante visited his sister and Parent had advance word of his hero's arrival. Bernie hid in some bushes, afraid to approach Plante and lacking the nerve to request an autograph. He huddled there and watched his hero from closer than he'd ever thought he'd get to Plante.

Parent graduated from galoshes to ice skates when he was eleven, and to rinks with real nets instead of mounds of snow and real pucks instead of tennis balls. His talent as goalkeeper blossomed. He was playing for a team in Rosemount, Quebec, when he came within a whisker of recognizing his boyhood ambition to be affiliated with the Montreal Canadiens.

At the time, NHL clubs locked up young prospects by sponsoring the teams for which they played. Junior players were not drafted in those days. If an NHL team liked a player, his team would be sponsored and he would be a chattel of that NHL club. While Parent performed for Rosemount, the Canadiens considered whether to sponsor the club or another club from Verdun, Quebec. The Canadiens eventually chose the other team and the Boston Bruins hopped in to sponsor Rosemount.

Among the players Boston acquired in the sponsorship, of course, was Parent, and the first time Leighton "Hap" Emms set eyes on the young goalie, he knew the Bruins had stumbled onto something big. Emms, a former NHL player, ran the Bruins' Niagara Falls farm club in the Ontario Hockey Association and later became general manager of the Bruins. He whisked Parent out of Rosemount to play OHA hockey at Niagara Falls. He wasn't sorry.

"He had the best record in at least thirty years in the junior OHA," said Emms. "He had a 2.7 goals-against average in the regular season and a 1.5 average in the playoffs." Those numbers and Emms's subsequent arrival as GM in Boston meant that Parent could not be far behind. Emms promoted the young goalie to the Bruins in 1965. Bernie was just twenty years old, and he realized then that the Canadiens' decision to sponsor Verdun instead of Rosemount had hastened his arrival into the NHL.

"Actually, at the time there wasn't much chance of making the Montreal team," Parent said. "They had some pretty good goalies playing for them—Gump Worsley, for example. I didn't mind going to the Boston organization and I would have to say that Hap Emms was like a father to me."

The Boston Bruins of 1965 were not exactly the world's best hockey team and it was a tough setting in which to throw a twenty-year-old goalie. Parent, however, somehow survived. Sometimes he wasn't sure that he would. Once, in

Madison Square Garden, he was beating the Rangers, leaving New York's fans in an ugly mood. When Referee John Ashley called a penalty against the home team, the fans showered the ice with debris, much of the mess landing near Parent. The goalie finally took a prudent step; he crouched down and crept into his net for shelter from the missiles. It is entirely reasonable to suspect that while in his net, Parent wondered what he was doing there.

Parent spent half of the 1965–66 season with the Bruins, producing an inflated 3.69 goals-against average. He had eighteen more games with them the following season for a 3.64 goals-against average. When he wasn't needed in Boston, the Bruins shipped him to their Oklahoma City farm club in the Central Hockey League. There Bernie posted four shutouts, leading all CHL net-minders in that department despite playing only fourteen games for the farm club.

Parent's partner at Oklahoma City was happy-go-lucky Doug Favell. The Bruins also owned two other goalies—Ed Johnston and Gerry Cheevers—and with the NHL expanding from six to twelve teams in 1967, the club had to decide who it would protect from the expansion draft. The decision was made to keep the more experienced Johnston and Cheevers, thus exposing both Parent and Favell. Philadelphia grabbed both goalies, Parent on the first round and Favell on the second.

The draft was held in Montreal, Parent's hometown, but Bernie was absent from the expansion meeting when Bud Poile, general manager of the Flyers, selected him. Parent had gone out to have a sixteen-pound pike mounted and then he stopped at a local driving range to practice his golf shots. It was there he heard of the draft.

"All I can say about being drafted is that they [the Flyers] have certainly proven their confidence in me. They could have chosen an older, more experienced player instead of me. I'm only twenty-two. All I can say is I will do my best to prove they made the right choice."

Poile had available to him a host of more familiar goaltending names than Parent's. Available, and picked by other expansion teams, were Glenn Hall, Terry Sawchuk, Cesare Maniago, Charlie Hodge, and Roy Edwards, among others. But the Flyers decided to cast their lot with youth, selecting Parent and Favell. The noisy buzz of excitement in the crowded room where Poile announced his selection must have pleased the Flyer GM. It was the expected reaction when one of the better names available in the draft was plucked. And Parent, despite his youth and relative inexperience, was considered better indeed. Scouts liked his quick stick and aggressive style in the nets; he had been marked as a definite NHL prospect.

In training camp, both Parent and Favell proved that Poile had made a couple of wise selections. The two goalies had excellent sessions and Coach Keith Allen found little or no difference between the two net-minders. So he didn't choose. The Flyers would not have a number-one goalie. Parent and Favell would share the job and split the work right down the middle.

Some goaltenders don't like the idea of dividing the net-minding chores. But Parent had a different view. "Let me give you an example," he said. "I like to hunt rabbits. If I have two beagles, I have a much better chance to get them than with one beagle."

So Parent and Favell embarked on their first Flyer season. Halfway through the campaign, they had allowed fewer goals than any other team in the league. Each delivered four shut-outs and Philadelphia won the West Division title. The Flyers were in a life-and-death struggle with Los Angeles in the final weeks of the season, completing their final Western swing with a stop at Oakland. It was Parent's turn in goal and Philadelphia needed a victory.

Early in the first period with the game scoreless, the Seals broke away from their end of the ice and headed for Philadelphia's zone. Some nifty passing sent Billy Hicke in on goal and Parent came out to meet the charge. Hicke, a swift skater, broke over the blue line and shifted the puck to his backhand as he cut sharply in front of the Flyer net.

Parent, faked to his knees by Hicke's move, lunged for the puck as the Oakland forward fired it. The rubber thumped into Bernie's pad, deflected out of danger.

The Flyers won the game, 5–1, and that went a long way toward nailing down the West flag by a slim one-point margin over Los Angeles. Parent finished with a 2.49 goals-against average in thirty-nine games and in the playoffs his 1.35 average for five games was the best mark turned in by any goalie that season.

The year was big for Parent. Not only did he justify Philadelphia's faith in him, but he also went to a Christmas party at the Spectrum. It turned out to be the most important party he ever attended. There he met Carol Wilson, a front-office employee. One word led to another, and before long Parent discovered that he and the attractive young lady lived in the same suburban-Philadelphia apartment complex. They dated each other and an engagement followed. In the summer of 1969, Carol and Bernie were married. They settled in Cherry Hill, New Jersey, an attractive residential community a short drive from the Spectrum. Their nine-room house was to play an important role in Parent's hockey future.

For the next two seasons, Parent was an iron man in Philadelphia's net. Injuries hampered Favell and Bernie found himself handling the bulk of the work. He flourished under the heavy schedule. "I like to play a lot," he said. "Once in a while, it's nice to have a rest. You get tired . . . not physically, but mentally. There's a lot of pressure in being a goaltender. You're the last man. On the day of a game, I take a nap and I sleep good. But as soon as I get up, I begin to feel the pressure. And I feel it all the way to the end of the game."

Parent tries to conceal his nervousness behind a smile. But it doesn't always work. His old coach, Vic Stasiuk, saw right through the grin. "Bernie jokes around," said Stasiuk. "He tries to come across as an outgoing, carefree person. But he isn't fooling anybody who knows him. He's plenty nervous. Why, hell, he's the last outpost. After the puck gets by him, why there's the game, right there. You'll see him on the ice. He fiddles with some loose equipment to ease the pressure, especially when they're heavy around his net. He'll come back to the bench for some water. His hands will be shaking."

The goalie admitted that his coach was right. "Yeah," he said. "I'm out there shaking the whole time, afraid of making a mistake. But nothing can beat the feeling you get when your team comes back to tie the game after you let in a goal. That's beautiful. No money could buy that feeling."

There was another feeling that bugged Parent—the rubber he felt in his knees every time he climbed aboard an airplane for a road trip. A couple of shaky flights had scarred Bernie's psyche. The number-one Flyer became a most reluctant flier. Then he suffered through another particularly unsettling flight between Philadelphia and Detroit and when the plane hit the ground, Parent swore off aircraft. "No more flying," he said. "Never again."

Some teammates calmed Bernie down sufficiently for him to climb aboard the return flight to Philadelphia. When the plane landed, Parent headed straight for a doctor to discuss his aerophobia. "The doctor already had read the newspaper story about how I couldn't stand flying," said the goalie. "I asked him if he could help me and he gave me some pills to take before we fly. I don't know exactly what they are, but whatever it is, it helps keep me calm. I still hate to fly, but at least I can live with it this way."

Parent and his pills played 120 games for the Flyers in the next two seasons and he became a fixture in Philadelphia. The fans adopted him as their favorite Flyer. And that's no small accomplishment for an athlete in Philadelphia, where the fans have been known to boo everything and everybody in sight, including the hot-dog vendors.

Bernie always worked hard at perfecting his craft. "I don't have great reflexes," he said, "so I work at cutting down the angle on shots, at being an angle goalie. I try to analyze the goals scored against me and why they were scored. I believe what I do in practice is what I do in a game. In practice, I work on myself, on different moves. I won't say I enjoy practicing, but I know I've got to work."

Parent got his share of work during those two seasons with the Flyers. "I was just like a machine out there," he said of his grueling schedule. With two weeks to go in the 1969–70 season, the Flyers were challenging for second place. Then they suffered six consecutive losses, the last two by 1–0 scores. The season ended on a dismal note when defenseman Barry Gibbs of Minnesota, who had scored just two goals all season, whistled a sixty-foot shot past Parent for the winning goal in the final game—the goal that cost Philadelphia a playoff berth.

"Something happened to the machine," said Parent, sighing, "and the puck went in. I couldn't tell what happened. I just didn't see it. I guess I took my eye off the puck."

The memory of that goal is etched deeply in Bernie's memory. He knows, firsthand, that a momentary lapse of concentration by the goaltender can be most costly. When the puck is at the other end of the ice, Parent once told a reporter, he is occupied with analyzing his opponents' last attack. "It's like an instant replay of the shots they tried and of what I did to try and stop them. But all of this takes place in only a fraction of a second, because, I'll tell you, if you lose your concentration for longer than that, even while it may look safe, it is going to cost you some goals."

During these years with the Flyers, other coaches expressed great respect for Parent. "He's the best young goalie in the NHL," said Scotty Bowman, then boss of the St. Louis Blues, "and when Glenn Hall and Jacques Plante retire, he'll be the best in the game. He's perhaps the quickest goalie with his hands in the league. And he's playing under pressure all the time. Philadelphia has been having trouble scoring goals. That's always pretty tough on the goalie."

The Flyer scoring problems weren't lost on Parent. "It would be nice if the team could score a few goals for me," he said, "but my job is to stop shots, not score with them." Vic Stasiuk, his coach, acknowledged the problem. "It's a strange thing," said Stasiuk, "but most of the time they just don't score for him. They seem to figure, 'What the hell, Bernie's in there and he'll hold us up.'"

After the playoff berth disappointment of 1970, the Flyers were determined not to let a lack of offense cost them a post-season spot again in 1971. With Doug Favell recovered and sharing the Philly goaltending job again, the Flyers decided they could afford to trade one of their net-minders for scoring punch. The Flyers were especially interested in young Rick MacLeish, who played for Boston's Oklahoma City farm club in the Central League. But at the time the Bruins were perfectly satisfied with their goaltending tandem of Gerry Cheevers and Ed Johnston. Now if Philadelphia could offer something more interesting, someone like Mike Walton, the Bruins might listen.

Walton at the time was on the trading block in Toronto. So Keith Allen, general manager of the Flyers, called his opposite number in Toronto, Jim Gregory. After a bit of haggling, the deal was arranged. The Flyers would get journeyman goalie Bruce Gamble, Walton, and a draft choice from Toronto in exchange for Parent and another draft choice. Then Walton would move on to Boston for MacLeish and another young forward, Danny Schock—and shock was the way Parent greeted the trade.

Unlike W. C. Fields, Bernie had been happy in Philadelphia. He had married a local girl and bought a handsome house. Weeks of shopping had been climaxed by the purchase of several thousand dollars' worth of furniture, which was scheduled for delivery, ironically, the very week he was traded to Toronto. There was one good thing about the move. Toronto's other goalie was Jacques Plante, Parent's boyhood hero. Bernie was thrilled to be a teammate of Plante's. The Leafs were thrilled, too.

"Parent could solve our goaltending problems for ten years," said King Clancy, Toronto's assistant general manager. "We have been trying to get him for years. He's a good size, stands up and plays the angles well. And he'll learn a lot here from Jacques Plante, the best goaltender in the world, and Johnny Bower."

Parent was smart enough to realize that Clancy was right about the gold mine of net-minding knowledge available in Toronto from Plante and ex-Leaf goalie Bower, then an assistant coach with the club. "When Ernie Wakely went to St. Louis, he was just another goalkeeper," said Parent. "After working with Plante for a season, he became a West All-Star. I'll take everything Plante tells me, you'd better believe it. I need to work on my play with the goalstick. Plante is fantastic at fielding and passing pucks. And Bower has the great poke check. I hope I can learn that from him. I intend to listen and I know they'll teach me. Both are great with young goaltenders. It is a big break for me."

Plante's influence rubbed off on Parent immediately. Bernie quickly adopted the Plante face mask, an improved model developed by the goalie who had introduced the first one to modern hockey twelve years before when Parent was still playing midget hockey. Bernie quickly shed his old mask in favor of the new Plante model and this mask became the center of a loud controversy during the first-round playoffs against the New York Rangers.

Parent was in goal for Toronto when a fight broke out in the corner. Bernie violated the goalie's creed by skating over to the bout. He shoved his mask atop his head. In the middle of the squabble, a Ranger grabbed for Bernie's hair and came up with the mask instead. He flipped it over the Madison Square Garden dasher boards, in among the fans, and that was the last Bernie saw of his mask that night.

Plante's masks are custom-made and Bernie did not have a spare. A plea was made to the crowd to return the mask. It was greeted with a round of long, loud boos, for the Leafs were beating the Rangers. Without the mask, there was no way Bernie would return to the net. Plante replaced him for the remainder of the game while Bernie sat, melancholy and bare-faced, on the Toronto bench.

After the game, Plante issued an SOS to his mask company in Magog, Quebec, where Parent's mold was on file. The workers went on overtime to manufacture a new one and it arrived at Maple Leaf Gardens in time for the next game of the series. Parent's original mask finally showed up, too, six months later, when the Ranger fan who had wound up with it had second thoughts and shipped it back to the Leafs.

Parent quickly became as popular in Toronto as he had been in Philadelphia. "Sometimes as many as twenty kids knock on my door in a day," the goalie said. "They ask for autographs or pictures, and a few just stand and look. The word soon got around where I lived. One kid found out and got an autographed picture. That was the same as lighting a match to one corner of a big pile of dry hay. Everything spread quickly from there. They don't bother me. Most are very polite. Besides, I really like kids."

Parent shared Toronto's goaltending with Plante for the 1971–72 season and produced a 2.56 goals-against average and a smile on the face of Leaf General Manager Jim Gregory. "He's the best young goalie in hockey," said Gregory, who was also convinced that in Plante he had the best old goalie as well. "He is a sound, consistent goalie who will continue to get better. We expect him to be on top for at least ten years. He's very durable. He's the guy we're forming a team around."

Little did Gregory know that Parent was also one of the keys to the infant World Hockey Association. In the fall of 1971, the ambitious WHA plans were revealed. A twelve-team league would begin operations in October 1972 with players culled from amateur and professional ranks. Amateur ranks meant the same junior leagues that for years had fed its graduates into the NHL. Professional ranks meant the NHL and affiliated minor leagues.

For five months, from October 1971 until February 1972, the WHA was little more than a lot of talk. The league lacked one important element; it had no players. Not even one professional player had announced his intention to perform in the new league. Some did mention it in guarded, hushed tones, but no player came right out and took a stand. Then, in February 1972, rumors spread throughout Toronto that Parent was WHA-bound. The goalie was noncommittal, but his attorney, Howard Casper of Philadelphia, was not. It was Casper's contention that Parent did not have a legal contract with the Maple Leafs and that his man was entitled to negotiate elsewhere, the NHL's reserve clause notwithstanding. Elsewhere led Casper to the WHA and sunny Miami, where a team with the engaging name, the Screaming Eagles, was being formed.

Parent had been drafted by the WHA's Calgary franchise, but indicated he'd be more willing to listen to offers from a city with a more reasonable climate, a city like, say, Miami. So the Alberta team transferred its rights in Parent to the Screaming Eagles. And, in mid-February, Casper and the Miami team reached agreement on a contract that was worth about one million dollars. Bernie thus became the first WHA-created millionaire.

A press conference was arranged for Sunday, February 28. The night before, the Maple Leafs had played at home in Toronto. Harold Ballard, boss of the team, was asked about the Parent situation following the game. "I don't think Bernie will be in Miami Sunday," said Ballard. "He's got more loyalty to the Leafs than many people think."

The next morning, Carol and Bernie Parent were on a Florida-bound airplane. On the same flight, ironically, was John McLellan, the Maple Leafs' ailing coach, who had been ordered south to rest his ulcer. The sight of Parent on the plane did little to settle McLellan's bubbling stomach.

Parent was presented at a press conference, complete with the Screaming Eagles' jersey, which made quite a picture in Monday's Toronto newspapers. And the goalie, silent through most of negotiations, spoke out boldly on his move to the new league. "I know other NHL players who have signed with the WHA," he said. "I think the WHA is the best thing that ever happened to hockey players. It means we are finally going to get the money we are looking for. Up till now, I think the Leafs have looked on me going to the WHA as a joke. Well, for a joke, it's gone pretty far."

Parent had jumped for some big numbers—something like $750,000 over five years. "Anyone would be stupid if he'd get an offer like this and turn it down," said the goalie. "At my present salary [$40,000], it would take me ten to fifteen years to make the kind of money I'm going to make with Miami. Even if this new league doesn't get started, I'm going to get my money and that's all I care about."

Clarence Campbell, president of the NHL, greeted the news of Parent's departure with some skepticism. "I'll be impressed when he gets the dough," said Campbell.. "Never mind when he signs a contract with them. That still doesn't mean he's got the money." Campbell said that NHL teams could take individual legal action to prevent jumpers from going to the WHA. But the Leafs said they would not pursue Parent through the courts. "Nobody ever won anything in court," said Harold Ballard.

Ballard might have added that nobody ever played a hockey game on Biscayne Bay. The Miami caper was perfect in every respect for Parent and the WHA, except for one detail—the club didn't have a building and the city was in no great hurry to build one for the Screaming Eagles. So, before the first eagle could scream, Miami's WHA franchise quietly folded and disappeared into the Everglades. Where, one might wonder, did that leave Parent and his fat contract? Right back where he started in the city of Philadelphia.

When Miami was unable to satisfy its franchise responsibility, it was shown the WHA door. Good-bye Miami, hello Philadelphia. To replace the Screaming Eagles, the WHA granted a franchise in Philadelphia to James L. Cooper and Bernard Brown. Parent was delighted to be back as was his wife, who had never adjusted to Toronto and was uncertain she would feel at home in Miami, either.

The return to Philadelphia, however, wasn't without its problems. First, the ice at the Civic Center refused to freeze properly, causing cancellation of the Blazers' first two home games. Then, early in the season, Parent turned his skate to block a shot and broke his foot.

The injury kept Parent and his flamboyant jersey, numbered 00—what could be a better number for a goaltender?

—on the sidelines for a while. Player-coach Johnny McKenzie was also injured and the club was then coached by Phil Watson. Watson soured on Parent in November. It happened in the Blazers' dressing room.

"I told them they were going to make the playoffs," said Watson, recalling a talk he had delivered to the dejected club. "I heard Parent make a joking statement to a teammate. 'I don't need the [extra] $3,000,' he said. 'I'll just give it to the government, anyway.'"

Watson pretended he hadn't heard the crack, but filed it away for future reference. With Parent hurt, the Blazers floundered. They used elderly Marcel Paille, who was too old, and youthful Yves Archambault, who was too young to replace the goalie. Neither fill-in's performance matched Parent's net-minding. When Bernie recovered, Watson rushed him into the nets. And he kept him there, game after game, with no nights off.

When Parent's consecutive-game streak reached fifty, he revealed that he had been having talks with his brother, a psychiatrist, once a week. Were the pressures of tending goal continuously that great? "Well actually," confessed Parent, "he calls me. You know, you can go bananas in that job."

Philadelphia survived a neck-and-neck four-way struggle to finish third in the WHA's Eastern Division. Then, in the midst of the playoffs against Cleveland, Parent's plush contract caused problems. Involved was the deposit of a one-hundred-thousand-dollar guarantee that attorney Casper claimed had not been made. And until the situation was rectified, announced Casper, the Blazers would get along without Parent.

"He will not lift a finger for the Blazers unless they live up to their end of the agreement," declared Casper. "If the situation is not resolved, . . . he'll be wearing a different-colored uniform next year. I've tried everything I could to resolve it. . . . I called them six times and I haven't had the courtesy of a return call. What other goalie would play in fifty-five straight games and not bitch about it? . . . Bernie went out and played in every damn game and carried the team on his back. This is the reward he gets. Hell, we'll negotiate with the NHL."

The Blazers, understandably, were furious over Parent's

walkout. They were forced to use Archambault in the final three games of the playoffs and the twenty-year-old, who had just recovered from a bout with mononucleosis was no match for Cleveland. Johnny McKenzie, Philadelphia's coach, seethed as he discussed Parent.

"I never say a word against any player as long as he comes to play," said McKenzie. "He got all his money as of April 2 [a week before the walkout]. If he had some other problem, he has all summer to work it out. He's selfish and a baby. This isn't a Ping-Pong game where you depend on yourself. There are eighteen other guys involved here, and another eighteen or more in Roanoke City, where we had to take Archambault from in the middle of their play-offs."

McKenzie said that perhaps Parent's inflated salary had caused him to forsake teammates earning considerably less than the goalie. "I guess he doesn't need another six thousand dollars," said McKenzie. "These other guys need that extra six."

When he left the team, McKenzie and owner Bernie Brown pledged that Parent would never play for the Blazers again. And shortly after moving their franchise to Vancouver, they made sure of it by trading Bernie's WHA rights to the New York Golden Blades. At about the same time, Toronto swapped Parent's NHL rights back to Philadelphia in a deal that also involved a couple of draft choices.

Now Parent had his choice. He could stay in the WHA and play in New York or return to the NHL and perform with his old friends, the Philadelphia Flyers. The big house in Cherry Hill, New Jersey, and his wife's affection for the Philadelphia area helped Parent decide. Casper hammered out a five-year contract with the Flyers and Bernie was back home again.

When Parent agreed to join Philadelphia, the Flyers had to compensate Toronto with another player. That extra player would only go to the Leafs if Parent signed and, when he did, Toronto claimed Parent's goaltending buddy, Doug Favell, to complete the deal.

That left Parent as the main cog in the Flyers' goaltending wheel—the same situation he enjoyed from 1968 to 1970 with Philadelphia.

Parent responded brilliantly to the challenge, missing just

five games all season. He turned in twelve shutouts and a spectacular 1.89 goals-against average. He shared the Vezina Trophy with Chicago's Tony Esposito and led the Flyers, first, to the West Division crown, and then to the treasured Stanley Cup. He started the season with a 2–0 shutout against Toronto and, ninety-five games later, he finished it with a 1–0 shutout against Boston that clinched the Cup.

The goalie was a popular choice for the Conn Smythe Trophy as the playoffs' Most Valuable Player. In a year in which he set marks for the most games played and the most games won by a goalie, Bernie capped it all off by drinking champagne from the Stanley Cup. And when he finished swigging the bubbly, Bernie smiled and, in the typical enigmatic tradition of goalies, said, "I can't wait to get to training camp."

Toronto Maple Leafs

Bernie surprised the natives when he turned in his Toronto Maple Leaf uniform for one with the Miami Screaming Eagles, a team that never got on ice.

**Turk Broda's
entire NHL career
was with the Maple Leafs.**

10
TURK
BRODA:
WEIGHT
WATCHER

Glenn Hall once called tending goal in the National Hockey League "an hour or so of hell." Tony Esposito says, "It's torture, pure torture." Bill Durnan termed it "agony." The roster of brave men who've tried their pads at this hazardous position usually have similar thoughts about the job. It is an assignment not designed for the faint-hearted. And it often leaves those who try it uptight. That, of course, is understandable, considering the risks involved.

There was, however, one goalie who never was bothered by the pressures of his job. Walter "Turk" Broda was completely at ease in the nets, a man as relaxed as he might be in the hammock in his backyard. Broda was unflappable, as cool as man could be under less than favorable conditions for the preservation of life and limb. And he was also a pretty good goaltender.

One theory about Broda's happy-go-lucky disposition was that he had been a goalie all his life and was used to the pressures of the occupation. It is true that Broda never played anywhere else but in the nets. But that was not by choice . . . just chance.

Born in Brandon, Manitoba, Broda was a solidly built youngster whose favorite times of the day were breakfast, lunch, and dinner, although not necessarily in that order. When he wasn't eating, Broda cavorted on Manitoba's frozen ponds with his boyhood friends. "I was of Polish extraction and none of the other kids ever thought of calling me Walter," Broda once explained, tracing the acquisition of his nickname in those days. "I had a lot of freckles. When the boys kidded me about this, my face and neck became so red they said I looked like a turkey-gobbler. This was later abbreviated to Turk and it just stuck with me."

In school, Broda was still Walter to the principal, who one day announced the formation of a hockey team. Turk came out for the squad, determined to be a defenseman. But his bulk and timing both worked against him. He wasn't the most agile skater in the world and he showed up late for tryouts as well. "I'm sorry," the principal told him, "we have all the defensemen we need."

Young Broda turned to leave, but then the principal had an idea. "Wait a minute, Walter," he said. "We need a goaltender. Get into the goal." So Walter got into the goal and that was the beginning of one of the finest goalies ever to block a shot. Broda never again played any other position and rarely, if ever, did people ever again call him Walter. From then on, he was Turk Broda, goaltender.

The Turk bounced around Brandon bantam and juvenile hockey teams and moved on to Winnipeg to play his junior hockey for that city's Monarchs. In those days, the Detroit Red Wing organization collared most of the good young hockey players developed in Canada's Western prairie land because, if for no other reason, they had the region thoroughly scouted. When young Broda showed some talent for puck-stopping, the Red Wings signed him for their organization and assigned him to their International League farm club, the Detroit Olympias. With Broda in goal, they were good enough to win the IHL championship in 1934–35.

Now, at just about that time, Conn Smythe, the shrewd operator of the Toronto Maple Leafs, decided that he'd better start looking for a replacement for goalie George Hainsworth. He got that idea in the 1936 Stanley Cup series between his Leafs and Detroit when the Red Wings poured nine goals past the forty-year-old Hainsworth. When that happened, there had been extreme pressure on Smythe to lift Hainsworth and substitute a younger man. The churlish boss of the Leafs rebelled at the idea.

"No one wants to win the Stanley Cup more than I do," said Smythe, "but that does not justify my benching Hainsworth at this time after his honorable career in hockey. There is more to the sport than the actual winning of games."

Hainsworth was allowed to go out gracefully and after the playoff series was over Smythe hunted for a new goaltender. He had heard that the Red Wings had a good one playing with the minor-league Windsor Bull Dogs. So Smythe went to take a firsthand look at Earl Robertson. It was Robertson's misfortune to have a nightmarish game in the nets with Smythe looking on. He was beaten for eight goals and Detroit major-domo Jack Adams, hoping for a sale, kept pointing out the shortcomings of Robertson's defensemen and telling Smythe that the young man really did have big-league credentials.

"Maybe so," rasped Smythe, "but I like the fat kid at the other end better. I'll take him." The fat kid was Turk Broda. Smythe and Adams agreed on a purchase price of eight thousand dollars for Robertson and Toronto sent that amount to Detroit. But in return the Maple Leafs got Broda instead of Robertson. Adams turned around after making that sale and sold Robertson to the New York Americans.

Smythe was unconcerned. He had his man and introduced the twenty-two-year-old Broda at the Leafs' training camp the following fall. Hainsworth was back, but it was no match. The youngster clearly had the goaltending edge and early in the 1936–37 season Smythe dealt Hainsworth to the Montreal Canadiens and Broda became the regular goalie for Toronto. It was a move Smythe never regretted.

From the day Broda became Toronto's regular goalie he was an iron man. Despite the hazards of his profession, the Turk played every scheduled game for Toronto for seven years before service in World War II interrupted his string. In those days, though, it was easier to be an iron man. There were only forty-eight games to a season when Broda graduated to the NHL, and in addition to playing thirty fewer games than teams today the travel schedule was easier, too. There were eight teams then, compared with today's eighteen, and none of them further West than Chicago, making travel schedules easier than the coast-to-coast hops modern players endure.

Broda was a happy-go-lucky guy who loved a joke, whether he was on the receiving end or not. He never reflected the tensions of his job; he just went out night after night and frustrated the other team. He enjoyed some of his greatest successes, ironically, against Detroit, causing a few sleepless nights for Jack Adams, the man who traded him away. "He hasn't a nerve in his body," raged Adams, after his Wings had suffered through one particularly galling defeat at Broda's ends. "He could tend goal in a tornado and never blink an eye."

Very often, it seemed that Broda did exactly that. Take, for example, the 1942 playoff series against Detroit with the Stanley Cup at stake. Toronto had finished second during the regular season, but then turned around and upset the first-place New York Rangers in the opening round of the playoffs. That set up a championship series between the Maple Leafs and Adams's Red Wings.

Detroit shocked the Leafs by winning the first three games of the series, two of them in Toronto. Before the next game, Billy Taylor of the Leafs, perhaps trying to relieve some of the tension of a team on the verge of elimination, kiddingly told newsmen, "Don't worry about us, we'll beat them four straight."

Even Broda couldn't laugh at that crack—not the way things had been going for the Maple Leafs. Toronto did take game four and repeated in game five, so the Red Wings went for the knockout punch again in game six. Midway through the second period of that game, the Red Wings had a chance to get the drop on Toronto. Don Grosso, cruising in front of Broda's net, took a pass from the boards and had the goalie at his mercy.

"He was about eight feet from me, all alone," said Broda, many years later. "I was about to dive and then I didn't. I figured that's what he wanted. So I waited for him to make his move. I waited and he waited and, what do you know, he blew it." Grosso lost the war of nerves and his wrist shot was sticked aside by Broda.

The Maple Leafs won the game 3–0, squaring the series at three games apiece. That sent it down to a decisive seventh contest and by then Taylor's prophecy rang in the ear of every player on the ice. And it came true, too. Again, Broda came up with a magnificent effort in goal and the Leafs won 3–1, becoming the only team in Stanley Cup history to wipe out a three-game deficit to win the Cup.

The year before his Stanley Cup heroics, Broda moved into the final week of the season with a comfortable seven-goal edge in the battle for the Vezina Trophy. With only four games remaining on the schedule, Broda seemed a cinch to win the award. Then Broda's Vezina express ran afoul of the New York Rangers. Everything seemed to go wrong and when it was over the Rangers had hung eight goals on the scoreboard turning the seven-goal Vezina advantage into a one-goal disadvantage. Suddenly Detroit's Johnny Mowers, who had been out of the Vezina picture, led the race for the cherished trophy.

For the next two games, Mowers maintained his one-goal lead. On the final night of the season for Toronto, Broda pulled out all the stops and shut out the Black Hawks. After the game, the Leafs left for Boston to open the first round of the playoffs. They got there in time to catch the Bruins' final game, which just happened to be against Detroit and Mowers.

Turk and his teammates went to the game and while most of the Leafs relaxed, Broda was tense as he watched Mowers. Only when the Bruins slipped their second goal of the game past the Detroit goalie did Turk relax, knowing that the Vezina was his. The postgame beers were on Broda.

World War II took its toll on National League players with many stars leaving hockey to serve in the armed forces. After the heroic 1942 Stanley Cup turnaround, Broda joined them. That seems like a simple enough matter but not for Broda, who became a cause célèbre before it was over.

Turk received his draft notice in October 1943 and decided instead to enlist in a Montreal-based outfit, where he could continue his hockey playing for the service team. A Montreal staff sergeant was dispatched to Toronto to accompany Broda by train to Montreal. His job, obviously, was to see that the goalie got where he was going without interruption. The sergeant failed.

The Quebec-bound train was halted by no less an authority than the Royal Canadian Mounted Police. The Mounties boarded the train and took Broda into custody, returning him to Toronto where another army unit had been seeking his goaltending services. The intraservice squabble caused a considerable stir in amateur hockey and federal political circles.

Broda lost two full seasons and most of a third one in the service and did not return to the Maple Leafs until 1946. While most of the returning NHL players found that the interruption had eroded their hockey skills, Broda was unaffected. He was every bit as sharp after the war as he had been before it. And he was every bit as funny, too.

Once, he shut out Adams's Red Wings and his teammates rushed around the Turk to congratulate him. But he was having none of that. He kept shoving the other players away. The reason? He was too busy scooping up a handful of cigars that an appreciative customer had tossed to him when the game ended.

Broda's standout goaltending led the Leafs to a second-place finish in 1946–47. But he was worried about the commotion his teammates made over him. "I wish they'd stop complimenting me," noted Broda. "It makes me nervous. Every time I read those nice things about me I get a nasty hunch that Smythe's getting ready to sell me to Chicago."

The Black Hawks in those days were a sorry team and Chicago was the Siberia of hockey. Broda knew it.

"I don't carry enough life insurance to play for Chicago," cracked the goalie. "I'll just have to go out and play a bad game so that the boys will pan me and Smythe will be forced to keep me around for a couple of years."

Broda, of course, could do that. He'd go out and have an absolutely terrible game. Then he'd come right back the next night and look sensational, blocking everything in sight. During the 1946–47 semifinals against Detroit, the Red Wings hit Broda for nine goals in the second game. He came right back and limited the Red Wings to one goal in each of the next three games as Toronto won the series and eventually the Stanley Cup. A few years later, he surrendered nine goals in the last game of the regular season against Detroit. The Red Wings, who were to face Toronto in the first round of the playoffs, rubbed their hands gleefully. They couldn't wait to get at Broda again. But in the playoffs Turk was a different goalie. He blanked the Wings twice and permitted just ten Detroit goals in the seven-game series.

Observers often called Broda the greatest playoff goalie ever. Asked to explain his playoff prowess, Broda just grinned. "I always needed the money," he said. Turk got the reputation of being a clutch goalie and his teammates termed him "Old Eagle Eyes."

After the Maple Leafs had swept to the Stanley Cup in Broda's first full year back from the service, Old Eagle

Eyes set his sights on the Vezina Trophy in 1947–48. He had plenty of competition, most of it from Detroit's Harry Lumley. With two weeks to go, it appeared that Lumley had won the battle. He held a five-goal bulge over Broda. But the Turk remembered how his seven-goal Vezina margin had melted in one game a couple of years before and he bore down. The fact that the Leafs and Red Wings were neck and neck in the race for first place kept the pressure on both goalies, too.

The pennant race and Vezina battle came down to the final two games of the season, a home-and-home series between the Leafs and the Wings. Toronto held first place by one point and Broda and Lumley were in a flatfooted tie for the Vezina Award, each having allowed 138 goals.

The Leafs knew they could wrap up the title by winning at home on Saturday night and they came from behind twice to overtake the Wings, 5–3. With the matter settled, Toronto turned to the problem of nailing down the Vezina for Broda. "We're playing the second game [of that series] for Turk," said defenseman Gus Mortson. "He's been great for us all season."

With his teammates concentrating on checking, Broda thwarted the Red Wings 5–2, to clinch the Vezina Trophy for the second time in his career. His momentum and that of the Maple Leafs carried right into the playoffs. Toronto needed just nine games to wrap up another Stanley Cup. Broda surrendered only twenty goals in the series and after the season he sat atop the hockey world. That lasted only as long as it took Coach Hap Day to decide that his goalie had let his success go to his waist.

Day spied Broda partaking of a distinctly unathletic menu and decided his goalie's silhouette was too plump. The coach cracked down on his goalie. In practice, he took away Broda's stick, forcing Turk to use his gloves to block shots and snatch pucks out of the air. When the Leafs weighed in, the scales betrayed Broda. Day lowered the boom.

"Get that weight down in three days," stormed the coach, "or it will cost you." Broda got it down and his wallet escaped intact. That was the first, but not the last, of his weight squabbles with Toronto's front office.

In 1948–49, Toronto slipped to fourth place during the regular season but in the playoffs Broda stood tall again.

Turk backstopped the Leafs to their third straight Stanley Cup, posting a sparkling 1.67 goals-against average. He allowed only fifteen goals in nine playoff games and, in the finals against Detroit, Toronto swept the Wings in four consecutive games with Broda surrendering only one goal in each of those games. "That was some record for a Stanley Cup final," said his boss, Conn Smythe, "and against players such as Marcel Pronovost, Red Kelly, Ted Lindsay, Sid Abel, Gordie Howe. . . ."

But Broda and Smythe were on a collision course and the cause of the problem was Turk's affinity for the good life and three square meals—and maybe a little snack in between—each day. The Leafs had won the Stanley Cup three years in a row, but when they stumbled at the start of the 1949–50 season Smythe decided upon drastic action. He diagnosed the problem as a severe case of excess poundage being toted around by some of his players, most notably his goaltender.

Turk at the time weighed 197 pounds, which was seven more than Smythe thought appropriate. His solution was a seat on the end of the bench for Broda, who had never missed a game in goal for Toronto except for his two and a half years in the army. "I'm taking Broda out of the nets," announced Smythe, "and he's not going back until he shows some common sense. Two seasons ago, he weighed one hundred eighty-five. Last season he went up to one hundred ninety. Now this. A goalie has to have fast reflexes and you can't move when you're overweight."

If Broda thought Smythe didn't mean business, the Leaf boss proved it by calling up Gil Mayer from Toronto's Pittsburgh farm team in the American Hockey League. "We're starting Mayer in our next game," announced Smythe, "and he'll stay in there even if the score is five hundred to one against the Leafs—and I don't think it will be."

Smythe's weight-watching crusade sent Broda scurrying to the diet charts. The goalie frequented steambaths and munched fruit instead of ice cream in an effort to roll away the pounds.

"It seems to me I've been eating nothing but apples," moaned Turk midway through his battle with the scales. "I'm killing my thirst with oranges. For my evening meal I have a lean steak and spinach. No potatoes, no bread. And a cup of tea. No cream, no sugar."

One day of dieting melted four pounds off Broda. Good, but not good enough for Smythe. "If Turk makes one hundred ninety pounds and makes the team, he can play," announced Smythe. And then he announced that he was shipping five players and a bundle of cash to Cleveland for a young goalie named Al Rollins. This was clearly getting serious.

Broda's battle became front-page news in Toronto. Advice poured in as fans offered sure-fire diets to the beleaguered goaltender. But as dieters before and since have discovered, the best cure for a man trying to drop a few pounds is a stiff arm used to push himself away from the table. Finally, it was time for Broda to weigh in. Turk stepped up to the scale in the Toronto dressing room, took a deep breath, and got on. The weights were at 197, Broda's poundage when the waistline war began. Mercifully, they did not balance. Trainer Tim Daley moved the weights down, first to 195. Still, they did not balance. Now Daley adjusted them to 193 and then 191. Still no balance. At 190, the adjusting stopped. A grin crossed Broda's face and the afternoon Toronto newspapers carried the happy news on page one in giant letters—"Turk Hits 190."

That night, the New York Rangers were in Toronto to play the Leafs. A crowd of better than thirteen thousand packed Maple Leaf Gardens and let out a huge roar when the Leafs took the ice, led by their now-svelte goaltender. The band, sensing the history of the moment, greeted Broda with a serenade of the popular and certainly appropriate "Too Fat Polka." Broda grinned from ear to ear. Then he proceeded to set the Rangers on their ears, shutting out New York, 1–0. The crisis of an eight-game Toronto winless streak was over and the band noted it by playing "Happy Days Are Here Again," as Broda was mobbed by his happy teammates.

Smythe, of course, was delighted. Even before the game, the Toronto boss was smiling. His ultimatum had worked and that's all that counted for him. "There may be better goalies around somewhere," he said, "but there's no greater sportsman than the Turkey. If the Rangers score on him tonight, I should walk out and hand him a malted milk, just to show I'm not trying to starve him to death."

That, of course, was unnecessary, since Broda produced the shutout. Afterward, Broda joked about it all. "Someday," he said, "I'm going to write my memoirs and I'll write the real reason why I got my weight down below one hundred ninety pounds. The real reason is that I was afraid that if I didn't get down to one hundred ninety pounds, Coach Day would have made me sleep in an upper berth on the road trips."

Broda, his lower berth assured, went on to post a 2.45 goals-against average and had a career-high nine shutouts. But by the time the playoffs ended, he was thirty-six years old and it was obvious that the Maple Leafs had to break in a successor. The obvious candidate was Rollins, the rookie imported to peer over Broda's shoulder during the previous season's pound crisis.

The switch was not as immediate as Broda's own takeover from George Hainsworth had been fourteen seasons earlier. Instead of Rollins moving in to carry the work load alone, the Leafs divided the goaltending burden between the young goalie and Broda. Rollins played thirty-nine games and Broda thirty-one and the duo allowed less goals than any other team in the league. It meant another Vezina Trophy for Toronto, but league regulations in those days permitted only one name to be engraved on the trophy. So the NHL lists only Rollins's name as winning the Vezina for 1950–51 season, but it's a fact that Broda's 2.19 goals-against average and six shutouts contributed heavily to the winning of the award.

When it came time for the playoffs, though, Broda's reputation as a clutch performer and his greater experience caused the Leafs to depend on him more than they had during the regular season. And the Turk didn't let them down. In eight games, he permitted just nine goals for a sparkling 1.12 goals-against average as the Leafs nailed down the Stanley Cup again.

The next season, Broda retired, or at least almost retired. Rollins was the full-time goalie and Turk handled only practice chores for the Maple Leafs. In December, Conn Smythe relaxed a rigid policy against honoring individual players with special nights at Maple Leaf Gardens. Broda was given his own night complete with a huge assortment of gifts from his fans. When Smythe stepped forward to speak to the crowd, he noted that Broda had played in ninety-nine playoff games. "We'll see to it that you get number one hundred," said the Leafs' boss, nodding at the old goalie.

That might have been a shock for the Turk, but it was nothing compared to the one he got at a private party after the pregame celebration. A couple of Toronto press people and Leaf personnel were doing a gag radio broadcast that was interrupted by an "urgent" message. A six-day-old infant had been abandoned and a collection would be taken among the crowd to buy the orphan some clothing. The suggestion was also made that if any benevolent person in the Broda party felt charitable enough to offer a permanent home for the tyke, he should stand up.

A couple of the pranksters had hooked up Broda's chair with some wires leading to a couple of dry-cell batteries. At that precise moment, the juice was turned on, ejecting the Turk from his chair. As soon as he stood up, an attendant rushed up to place the needy infant—a baby piglet—in Broda's broad arms. Turk broke up. And he even had the last laugh because, when he sprang out of his seat, he knocked over a considerable amount of the table's refreshments, splattering many of the conspirators in the process.

Smythe kept his playoff promise to Broda. When Toronto lost the first game of the playoffs to Detroit, the Leafs' boss rushed Turk in, hoping to inspire his club. Broda, who had played in only one game all year, put on an heroic show, surrendering only a first-period goal to Johnny Wilson. But that was all Detroit and goalie Terry Sawchuk needed to beat the Leafs, 1–0. Broda played one more game in the series before hanging up his pads for good. When he finished, he had played in a record 101 Stanley Cup games, turning in a remarkable 2.09 goals-against average and a record 12 shutouts. In regular-season play, his goals-against average was a fatter 2.56 for 13 seasons. He also had 61 regular season shutouts.

After retiring, Broda turned to coaching and enjoyed considerable success behind the bench at the minor-league level. He won consecutive Ontario Hockey Association titles with the Toronto Marlboros in 1955 and 1956 and also had stints with the Quebec Aces of the American Hockey League and Charlotte Checkers of the Eastern League. He liked the work because it enabled him to help young players.

"Kids today have a great future," he said. "When I played, there were one hundred twenty players in the National Hockey League. But with expansion there will be more and more clubs. The opportunities for the kids are fantastic." But coaching had its drawbacks, too. "As a goalie, I had only one job to worry about," Broda said. "But as a coach, I have to worry about the efforts of fifteen boys. It presents plenty of problems, too, but I like working with the kids."

Broda always realized how important the youngsters he worked with were to the future of big-league hockey. In fact, he may have realized it before big-league hockey did. "The clubs in the NHL who want to be successful have to pay attention to the juniors," the old goalie said at a time when little attention was being paid to that farm system. "That's the lifeline these days. I can't understand why so many minor pro clubs waste their time by hiring veterans as drawing attractions when they should be trying to develop youngsters. I know I could have had a dozen jobs [playing hockey] after I quit the Leafs."

The Turk's popularity followed him throughout his coaching days and into other sports as well. He had considerable interest in horse racing and a friend, Marc Cavotti, named a horse for the old goalie. In September 1972 with most of the country glued to television sets watching the pulsating final moments of Team Canada's international hockey showdown with Russia, Broda was in the winner's circle at Toronto's Woodbine Race Track to congratulate his four-legged namesake on a big victory. "Only a horse could get Turk away from a hockey game," noted one observer.

Scarcely two weeks later, Broda was dead at the age of fifty-eight. His old boss, Conn Smythe, who nominated him for election to the Hall of Fame in 1967 eulogized: "I am sure nobody ever had the flair that Turk did."

And very few, Smythe might have added, tended goal as well as Old Eagle Eyes, either.

Terry Sawchuk, in
a Red Wing uniform,
was a Ranger when he
met an untimely death.

11
TERRY SAWCHUK:
TALLEST IN THE CROUCH

Off in a corner of the Detroit Red Wing dressing room, the goaltender sat, slumped in front of his locker. Terry Sawchuk's uniform was soaked with the perspiration of another night's work—thirty-nine saves and a 3–0 victory over the Montreal Canadiens. The goalie was almost too tired to begin unlacing the bulky pads that covered his legs. And the crowd buzzing around the dressing room wasn't making Sawchuk's postgame recuperation any easier. It was November 10, 1963, and the Detroit dressing room was lined wall-to-wall with writers. It looked like Grand Central Station.

The center of attention was across the room from Sawchuk, over in the cubicle where the Red Wings' Gordie Howe was accepting congratulations. Howe had scored one of the three Detroit goals that night, but it was not just another goal for the big right winger. This was number five hundred forty-five—the goal that moved Howe ahead of the retired Maurice Richard and made him the highest scorer in the history of hockey. Now, if one considers the excitement Hank Aaron's home-run chase of Babe Ruth created in baseball, there is a parallel significance to Howe's record.

Howe was the hero; over and over he detailed the historic goal for the swarm of writers who had trailed him, waiting for him to score it. Sawchuk chuckled to himself over all the attention Gordie was getting. That's because Terry's shutout wasn't just another shutout either. Lost in the tumult of Howe's record-shattering goal was Sawchuk's ninety-fourth career shutout, which tied the goalie with George

Hainsworth's all-time net-minding record. And any goalie will tell you that ninety-four shutouts is every bit as tough to accomplish as five hundred forty-five goals. But one would never have known it from the absence of excitement in Sawchuk's corner of the room that night.

Two months after Sawchuk reached Hainsworth's record, he broke the mark, again blanking the Canadiens. That gave him ninety-five and he eventually added eight more shutouts for an all-time record of 103—a measure of goaltending excellence that likely will stand forever. Sawchuk once was asked how he felt about the shutout mark.

"Certainly I'm proud of it and I feel it means a lot," he said. "After all, for shutouts you're not allowed to make one mistake. The big scorers can make a dozen mistakes and still get a goal toward a record. A goalie makes a single goof and he has to wait until the next game to start all over."

It seemed that throughout his life Terry Sawchuk was always starting over. The deck always appeared stacked against him, but he overcame huge odds to become the most successful goalie in modern hockey history. He survived a series of crippling injuries that would have finished a lesser man. But he always came bouncing back, starting over again.

It started for Terry on the frigid outdoor rinks of his native Winnipeg, Manitoba, where Bob Kinnear discovered his hockey potential. "I was running a hockey program in Winnipeg," said Kinnear, who later became a Red Wing scout. "Terry was one of a hundred or more boys who were around my outdoor rink. He was about eleven or twelve, husky and chubby. I remember he was a defenseman with his school team. We always needed equipment for the rink and I recall Terry telling me that he had a pair of pads at home. I told him to bring them on down and I think I suggested, 'You try them.' Anyway, he did and it was apparent from the first that Terry was a natural in goal."

But there was tragedy in the pads that Terry brought to Kinnear's rink. They had belonged to Terry's older brother, Mitch, who had died at the age of seventeen from a heart attack. Terry had worshipped his brother and those pads were his legacy from Mitch. When Terry climbed into them, he was playing for two goalies—himself and his brother.

When Kinnear was hired by the Red Wings, he called General Manager Jack Adams's attention to the young goalie, who had developed so well in the Winnipeg Recreational League. Adams was interested and pursued Sawchuk. But at the same time, Terry pursued other sports. He was a red-hot baseball prospect, good enough to be scouted and offered a professional contract by the St. Louis Cardinals. And he also played football, much to the displeasure of his parents.

Finally, his mother put her foot down, ruling out football for young Sawchuk. But Terry snuck in a few games anyway, and in one of them he was injured, banging up his right arm. He was afraid to tell his parents what happened, so he said nothing, enduring the pain instead. Subsequently, his mother noticed a lump on Terry's elbow and took him to the doctor. By then it was too late to do anything about it and the injury, a dislocation of the elbow, left one of his arms a couple of inches shorter than the other and produced a career-long problem with bone chips.

Kinnear took Sawchuk to his first Red Wing training camp in 1946, riding the train from Winnipeg to Detroit. Terry showed enough promise for Adams to enroll him with Detroit's junior affiliate at Galt, Ontario. He had one season of junior hockey at Galt and that was enough to convince Detroit officials that the young goalie had legitimate professional potential. After three games with another junior team —the Windsor, Ontario, Spitfires, in 1947—the Wings turned Terry pro and sent him to Omaha of the United States Hockey League. "I've never seen a young goalie with more ability," said Tommy Ivan, Detroit's coach. "All he needs to rank right at the top of the list is experience."

Sawchuk got all sorts of experience with Omaha, most of it good, some bad. He played for the Knights in Houston on December 28, 1947—his eighteenth birthday—when he experienced a brush with tragedy. It came on a pileup in front of the Omaha net with players sprawled everywhere. Terry was watching the puck and turned his head—only to have a swinging stick catch him squarely in the right eye.

The goalie fell to the ice as if pole-axed. The stabbing pain ripped through his eyeball, deep into his brain. He was helped to the dressing room, then taken to the hospital. Sawchuk remembered those terrible hours vividly.

"When I got to the dressing room, the doctor said something about losing the eye," he said. "I broke down and cried. I didn't want to lose an eye much less give up my hockey career." The doctors took three stitches in Saw-chuk's eyeball that night. "I didn't sleep a wink," the goalie said. "I was worried about what I might do for a living." The next morning, the doctors examined his eye and the news was better. He would need a couple of weeks off, but his sight had been saved. He could play hockey again. "I'll never forget that doctor," said the goalie. "Dr. Schultz was his name."

By late January, Sawchuk was back in action for Omaha, playing every bit as well as he had before the injury. He was the United States League's top goalie and was named Rookie of the Year in his first professional season. The Red Wings rewarded him with a promotion to Indianapolis of the American League the next year. His coach there was Ott Heller, a long-time NHL defenseman. He worked long and hard with Sawchuk.

"We had a pact, Ott and I," the goalie said. "When I used to fall, he'd always stand by me and yell for me to get up on my feet. We worked that over and over again, me starting to fall and him hollering for me to stand up. That's a very important thing because when a guy is coming in on you, you have to try and stand up as long as possible and keep him guessing. That way you might be able to confuse him or get him to commit himself too early or too late."

Heller's work with Terry was a replay for the goalie. Mud Bruneteau, his coach at Omaha, had also devoted long prac-tice hours to developing Sawchuk's goaltending ability. "Bruneteau taught me how to block angles better. He would take shots and I would attempt to save and this went on until I had it down pat," said Terry.

Indianapolis and the AHL was only one step away from Detroit and the NHL and Sawchuk knew it. Terry played well for the Caps and for the second time in as many pro seasons he was chosen the top rookie of his league. But the path to Detroit was blocked by another good goalie—Harry Lumley.

The next season, 1949–50, Sawchuk was back at In-dianapolis and Lumley back in Detroit. Then, in mid-season, Terry got his chance to play for the Red Wings. Lumley had been injured in an exhibition game while clowning around as a forward. Lum tripped and fell awkwardly to the ice, twisting his ankle. The crowd roared in laughter, thinking it was part of the act. But his telltale limp off the ice brought no smiles to the face of GM Jack Adams, who put in the hurry-up call to Sawchuk.

Terry reported on January 8, 1950, barely a week past his twentieth birthday. Facing the Wings that night were the Boston Bruins and Sawchuk looked scared when he took the ice at the Detroit Olympia for the first time, squeezed into Lumley's uniform. "I was scared out there," Terry confessed later, "but it wasn't like my opening pro game in Dallas. I was so tense then that I let the first shot on goal go in without making a single move, right in the first forty seconds." Sawchuk won that game 5–1, but his Detroit debut didn't have such a happy ending.

The Wings, trying hard to protect their young goalie, gave Sawchuk more trouble than the Bruins. Twice, defenseman Clare Martin tried to intercept passes in front of the Red Wing nets and both times wound up deflecting the puck past the startled Sawchuk. Another Bruin shot caromed off a Red Wing skate and into the net. Final score: Boston 4, Detroit 3.

The first player waiting for Sawchuk when he left the ice that night was Lumley. "Don't worry about it, kid," the goalie said. "I couldn't have done any better myself."

The Wings kept Sawchuk for six more games and one of those was a 1–0 shutout against the New York Rangers. When Lumley's ankle had healed, Terry returned to Indianapolis. But a 2.28 goals-against average in that seven-game trial convinced Adams that Sawchuk was ready for the NHL.

Lynn Patrick, coach of the Rangers, was talking about goalies at the time. "There are only three big-league goalies around right now," said Lynn, "and one of them is in the minors." The Wings knew who Patrick meant, too.

"We knew Lynn was right," said a Detroit official, "but we had to wait for an opportunity to move Terry in. When the time came to make a deal with Chicago, they wanted a goalie thrown in."

The deal was a mammoth one with nine players changing clubs. Ironically, when the Black Hawks asked for a goalie, the Red Wings offered Sawchuk, hoping Chicago would turn that down and demand Lumley instead. That's just what happened. "It was a gamble, but it worked," said Adams.

The Black Hawk thinking was simple. Lumley was a proven

big-league goalie and Sawchuk was not. Detroit felt that Sawchuk could step right into the NHL and Adams was convinced that whichever goalie he offered Chicago in the trade, the Black Hawks would want the other. He decided to offer Sawchuk, fully prepared to ship Lumley to Chicago when the Hawks demanded him instead.

The Detroit club's confidence in Sawchuk was complete. The goalie's confidence in himself, however, was not. First, there was the matter of his troublesome elbow. Doctors removed several chips from it in the summer of 1950. "The two weeks I was in the hospital and the weeks after that I spent recuperating—just laying around, taking it easy—made a fat man out of me. My weight went up to 217 and I felt like a balloon. With all that fat on me, I thought I'd be too slow to play well enough in a big-league goal. And I wasn't sure about my elbow, either.

Terry need not have worried. He not only made it in the NHL that first season, but he made it big. He turned in eleven shutouts in seventy games for a 1.98 goals-against average. He won the Calder Trophy as Rookie of the Year, marking the first time any player had swept rookie honors in three different leagues. It was a goaltender's hat trick and, speaking of hats, Terry kept his teammates outfitted with them. Sawchuk never wore one, but a Detroit hat dealer had a promotion gimmick, awarding one for every three-goal game or shutout enjoyed by a Red Wing player. Whenever Sawchuk worked a shutout, the hat man delivered a certificate for a free chapeau. Terry passed the first one on to trainer Lefty Wilson. Then the next five went to his defenseman. The seventh went to Sid Abel, a veteran center. "I figured it was time to give the forwards a break," said Sawchuk, laughing.

Sawchuk practiced a unique style in the nets. It was something the NHL had never seen until he arrived on the scene. He crouched low in his net, bent so deeply that his padded knees almost touched his chin. "I get low because I can follow the puck better looking through the legs than I can trying to peek over shoulders and around those big backs," the goalie explained. "My reflexes are better that way. It's an easier way to get hurt, I guess, but nothing's happened so far."

The Red Wings in Sawchuk's rookie year were a powerful

club. They proved it by copping their third consecutive regular-season championship. Often their defense protected the goalie so well that he'd have little or no work to do. One night, the Wings bottled up their opponents and Sawchuk wasn't bothered with a shot for a full twenty-two minutes. It was almost as if the ice was inclined with Terry protecting the goal at the top of it. That situation sounds like a goaltender's Shangri-la, but it didn't thrill Sawchuk.

"The funny thing about it," said the goalie, "is I wasn't comfortable at all during that time. I was more scared in those twenty-two minutes than at any other time during the game. You get the nervous heebie-jeebies expecting someone to break loose on you at any minute, and when he doesn't you get more nervous than ever. I could really feel it, just looking down at the other end and watching that clock move so slowly. I got cold, too. Just standing on a big chunk of ice so long without moving is no fun."

More than one rookie sensation has turned into a sophomore dud and Detroit wondered if Sawchuk would prove a flash in the pan as the Red Wings approached the 1951–52 season. The talk didn't last long though, because Terry opened the season as sensationally as he had in his rookie year. He started with a 1–0 shutout against Boston and two games later he blanked Rocket Richard and the Montreal Canadiens. He permitted four goals in his first four games, a stingy 1.00 goals-against average per game. Naturally, Terry couldn't keep it up. His average was sure to go up as the season went on and, of course, it did. All the way to 1.94. He had twelve more shutouts, giving him twenty-three in two seasons, and people started calling him the new Mr. Zero.

The regular season is one element in hockey and it's nice to finish first the way the Red Wings did again that year. But the Stanley Cup is what the season is all about. Vivid in Sawchuk's mind was the fact that the Red Wings had won the Cup two years earlier with Harry Lumley in goal, but had been eliminated the previous season with Terry Sawchuk in the nets. Sawchuk vowed to make up for that failure.

Detroit opened the 1952 Stanley Cup playoffs against Toronto and Sawchuk shut out the Maple Leafs in the first game of the semifinal series. In game two, Detroit was protecting a narrow 1–0 lead when two Red Wings went to

the penalty box just a few moments apart. That meant the
Leafs would have hockey's best scoring opportunity—a two-
man power play. Sawchuk girded for the assault on Detroit's net.

The Leafs sent Max Bentley out to play the point on the
power play and, sure enough, the faceoff came to the shifty
Bentley. He sidestepped a check and broke for the net with
Sid Smith, another good scorer. Sawchuk's brain clicked like
a high-powered computer.

"I figured Max would try to deke [fake] me," said Terry.
"I made up my mind not to move. Bentley faked me, then
passed across to Smith, who let a shot go. It was really
labeled, but I managed to kick in time to stop it with my
foot."

"That was Toronto's big threat," Sawchuk continued. "Our
men got back before they could do any damage and we won
1–0 to take a two-game lead in the series."

Detroit won the next two games as well, eliminating the
Maple Leafs in four straight. Next it was Montreal's turn,
and again Sawchuk stood tall. He backstopped the Wings to
victories in the first two games in Montreal and then finished
the Canadiens with two more shutouts. The Red Wings had
won the Stanley Cup in the minimum eight games and
Sawchuk had turned in a phenomenal four shutouts. He had
permitted five goals in eight games for an unbelievable 0.62
goals-against average. And when the Red Wings sipped
champagne from the Stanley Cup, no player deserved his
drink more than their crew-cut goaltender, who played goal
like a man on a holy mission.

The young man's performance impressed some of hockey's
oldtimers—men who had watched and played against the
Vezinas, the Benedicts, and other past greats of the art of
goaltending. Frank Boucher, general manager of the Rangers, was one of those who believed that Sawchuk was better
than any of them.

"Terry Sawchuk is the greatest goalie in the history of
big-league hockey," said Boucher. "I know the real test of
greatness is achievement over a long period of years and
Sawchuk is just a kid. But what a kid! Rookie of the Year
in three different leagues and an average under two goals
per game in both of his NHL seasons. He has introduced a
new technique with that low crouch of his and you'll see a

lot of youngsters copying that style now. He's already down to block the low shots which others have to drop to cover. Terry can cover those without leaving his net unprotected and when he does go down he has such quick reflexes that he can bounce right back into position."

Sawchuk played goal compulsively. His aim was perfection. He never wanted anything to get past him. Not just pucks, but anything. Old teammate Vic Stasiuk remembered how meticulous Terry was about his goal area.

"He couldn't stand anything going into his net," said Stasiuk. "You know how fans throw things on the ice . . . gum wrappers, peanut shells, and things like that. Players have a habit of picking them up and tossing them in the back of the net. You couldn't do that with Terry. He'd get mad as hell. He certainly kept that goal area clean. He was always sweeping it with his stick. What concentration! What dedication! But then, all great athletes are artists and this takes concentration and dedication. And Terry was an artist."

After his 1952 Stanley Cup heroics, Sawchuk's troublesome football elbow started acting up again. The Red Wings sent him to the hospital and Dr. Donald Sheets decided to clean the joint out once and for all. "He really did a job," said Sawchuk. "He removed over 60 pieces of bone, taking everything he thought might break off and cause trouble later on. I haven't had any trouble with the elbow since and for the first time in over ten years, I'm able to have complete movement of my arm."

With full mobility restored, Sawchuk came back in 1952–53 and won his second straight Vezina Trophy, lowering his goals-against average to a dazzling 1.90. There were nine more shutouts for the Red Wings' hefty goalie, who packed quite a bit of excess poundage. "I stopped so many shots," he joked, "because there was so much of me in the nets."

But GM Jack Adams wasn't laughing. He ordered his goalie on a strict diet and Sawchuk began shedding pounds. When he got down to the weight Adams wanted him to carry, Terry didn't stop losing pounds. He had no appetite and the Wings became concerned about his health. Again he was ordered to the hospital for a checkup. That's when they discovered the young goalie's infected appendix with its poison spreading through his system.

A year later, there was an auto crash in which Sawchuk suffered three broken ribs and a collapsed lung. And in 1955, when he won his third Vezina Trophy with a 1.94 average, his back acted up. He walked almost bent over because of his swayed back. Technically, the condition was called lorbosis. Actually, it was a case of goaltender's back.

"I am the kind of guy," said Sawchuk after one of his frequent stays in the hospital, "who makes health insurance popular."

Ironically, Sawchuk's 1955 Vezina came just a year after he missed the goalie trophy by the barest of margins—a single goal. Old friend Harry Lumley won it in 1954, allowing 128 goals to Sawchuk's 129. The margin came in the final game of the season when Detroit whipped Toronto, 6–1. The only Leaf goal—the one that beat Sawchuk for the trophy and prevented Terry from winning it for four consecutive years—was a long-range blooper launched by Toronto defenseman Jim Thomson. It was a one-thousand-dollar goal because that's how much the Vezina was worth and NHL President Clarence Campbell had said both goalies would get the bonus if they finished tied.

Late in the 1955 season, Sawchuk slumped. He surrendered ten goals in two games, prompting Adams to announce that he would give his goalie a couple of days off. "We're giving Terry a rest," said Adams, "nothing more." Summoned from Detroit's Edmonton farm club was young Glenn Hall as Sawchuk sat out three games. Hall played well and the rookie's performance planted an idea in Adams's mind, just as Sawchuk's fill-in job for Lumley six years earlier had done. Hall was ready for the NHL and Adams decided that Sawchuk, despite his outstanding record, was expendable.

Rumors spread that the goalie would be traded. Sawchuk shrugged them off. "A year ago the reports had me going to Chicago or New York," he said. "Believe me, I had the jitters over them. I was really upset. Now they've got me on the trading block again. This time I don't care. It doesn't bother me a bit. If I'm traded, I'm traded."

The best rumor was that Sawchuk was headed for the Bruins. General Manager Lynn Patrick laughed off that talk. "If there were any truth to it, I'd be very happy," said Patrick. "But there isn't. We wouldn't approach Detroit for Sawchuk because we know it would be fruitless."

Then the Bruins turned around and approached the Red Wings for Sawchuk and—surprise!—it wasn't fruitless. Adams was in a trading mood, even though the Red Wings had won their seventh consecutive regular-season crown and second consecutive Stanley Cup. He exchanged four Red Wing players for four Chicago players and less than a week later, he completed a nine-player exchange with Boston, terming it "a million-dollar deal." Sawchuk and three forwards, Vic Stasiuk, Marcel Bonin, and Lorne Davis, went to the Bruins in exchange for forwards Ed Sandford, Real Chevrefils, and Norm Corcoran, defenseman Warren Godfrey and rookie goalie Gilles Boisvert. Patrick was ecstatic over the trade.

"We needed a top goalie in the worst way," he said. "Last year we had twenty-one tie games and I believe if we had Sawchuk, we might have won ten or eleven of them," the Boston GM added.

And a top goalie was what Patrick was getting in Sawchuk. Terry in five seasons with the Red Wings totaled fifty-seven shutouts and his highest goals-against average with Detroit was 1.98. The goalie accepted the trade philosophically, just as he said he would. "You don't play with a group of fellows for so many years and then take being traded off without being shocked," he said. "I live in Detroit now and I have a great number of friends there. However, the Bruins have been swell to me and I'm anxious to play for them. I'm going to play just a little bit harder against Detroit, I think. But I'm not mad at being dealt off. That's just the way it goes. When you're with Detroit and that salary goes up too high, you can figure you'll be going because they have somebody right behind you all of the time."

Sawchuk's stay with the Bruins was short and stormy. His 2.66 average in 1955–56 was the highest he had ever posted in the NHL and instead of zooming toward the top of the standings with Terry in goal, the Bruins sagged to fifth place, finishing out of playoff contention. The next season, Sawchuk regained his touch. The Bruins moved up near the top of the league and things seemed to be straightening out for Sawchuk. At least on the ice. But the goalie didn't feel well; he was weak all of the time.

"It was getting so that I couldn't eat and I couldn't sleep," he said. "I was awfully tired, but I'd lie there all night and smoke and couldn't go to sleep. Then I'd get up but I wouldn't have any appetite. I thought I was getting lazy because I wanted to lie down all the time. I thought maybe I'd become too complacent mentally too. But we were winning and in first place and I kept getting by even though I could hardly wait for each game to end because my legs were so tired."

The goalie was kayoed in a game at Montreal and when the doctor examined him, he discovered swollen glands in Sawchuk's neck. It was the first clue that the goalie was suffering from mononucleosis, a blood disease. Asked to describe the ailment, Sawchuk said, "It feels like the red and white blood corpuscles have chosen up sides and are playing a game of hockey in your veins."

The only cure for the disease is total rest, usually for about two months. Sawchuk rested for two weeks before returning to the Bruins, pronounced fit again. But the goalie wasn't fit. A couple of weeks later, he was named the NHL's All-Star goalie for the first half of the 1956–57 season. The next day, Terry left the club, declaring that he "was through with hockey."

The announcement caused almost as much excitement in Boston as Paul Revere's ride had some two centuries before. The word used most often was "quitter," an unfair slur on one of the sport's great competitors. Newsmen harassed Sawchuk both in Boston and, after he returned to his family, in Detroit as well. The goalie was troubled by all the attention his announcement received. "Can't a guy give up the game?" he said. "Won't you leave me alone? I'm not going to say anything.". There was one ugly scene when an over-zealous reporter backed off after Sawchuk whirled on him over that "quitter" term and said: "All you'll get is a punch in the nose."

Sawchuk, never a great fan of journalism, also threatened to take some critical writers to court over their published theories on why he had departed the Bruins. "I'm mad," he said. "I'm not talking. I wasn't hiding out. I was locked up in my room and didn't answer the door or the telephone. And I've got news for you. I'm going to sue four Boston newspapers for what they said about me."

A week after he left the Bruins, Sawchuk held a news conference to explain what he called "the toughest decision of my life." He said he simply could no longer take the goaltending grind.

"Since my illness in December, I certainly have not felt in the right frame of mind, though I have tried to adjust myself to continue playing for the Bruins. I haven't been getting the proper sleep. I've lost my appetite. My nerves are shot. And I'm just edgy and nervous all the time.

"I'm still under contract to the Boston hockey club. They have always treated me very well. But my health, for my family's sake, is certainly more important than any monetary consideration." So Sawchuk turned his back on his sixteen-thousand-dollar salary, highest for any NHL goalie, and retired from hockey. The decision stood for six months.

In Detroit, GM Jack Adams had become disenchanted with Glenn Hall, especially after an early playoff elimination. He decided that the perfect replacement was right there, in Detroit, doing nothing. Terry Sawchuk, of course. Adams contacted the Bruins, who had suspended Sawchuk for life, pledging the goalie would never again play for Boston. The Boston club gave Adams the green light to contact the goalie and Sawchuk said, yes, he would consider playing hockey again, but only for Detroit. The Red Wings shipped Johnny Bucyk to the Bruins for Sawchuk and cleared the decks for his return by shipping Hall off to Chicago in another five-player deal.

"I wouldn't have gone back to Boston," said Sawchuk. "I had decided I didn't want to play for any club, unless it might be the Red Wings. When Mr. Adams got permission from the Bruins to contact me last April, I was surprised and happy. It's wonderful to be back with the Red Wings. I have established my roots in the Detroit area. I have an outside business and my family is here. Playing in Detroit, I can be close to both of them."

And what of his health?

"I've been thoroughly examined by the doctors, and they say the blood infection is completely gone," said Sawchuk. "I feel the best I have in four years. I weigh about one hundred ninety, which is my best playing weight, and I'm fit to play hockey."

That was good enough for Adams.

"Glenn Hall is a fine goalie," said the Red Wing boss. "But as I have often said, when Terry Sawchuk is on his game, he's the best goalie in the world. That's why I dealt with Boston to get him back."

Was Sawchuk afraid about his return?

"If you were really afraid, you wouldn't be out there in the first place," the goalie said. "In the back of your mind, you know you can be hurt, but in the heat of action you forget it."

Skeptics doubted that Sawchuk's second stay with the Red Wings would last very long. But they were wrong. Although he never approached the goaltending excellence he had demonstrated in those sensational first five seasons of his NHL career, Sawchuk did make a successful comeback. He provided the Wings with solid net-minding, despite a continuing string of troublesome injuries. There was, for example, the time Toronto's Bob Pulford sliced his hand open. Sawchuk remembered the episode vividly.

"A pass came out in front of the net," the goalie said. "Pulford slapped at it. I got the puck. The whistle blew. I put my hand back to get my balance and my arm gave way. That's when Pulford accidentally stepped on it. I took my hand out of my glove. It looked like a little cut at first. Then it opened up and I could see the knuckle bones. Funny thing, it hurt very little.

"I tried to open my hand as I was going off the ice. But the fingers snapped right under. In the first-aid room they just wrapped it up and sent me to Toronto East General. I watched the rest of the game on television, waiting for the doctor.

"I was in the operating room about two hours. Dr. James Murray operated. I think he did a perfect job. They had to gore my arm to get the tendons. I asked him how many stitches he took. He said he stopped counting after fifty, but I think it was something like seventy-eight." That was nothing new. Stitches were routine for the gritty goalie. He had better than four hundred of them sewn into his face alone throughout his career.

Sawchuk's second stint with Detroit lasted seven seasons and he reached and passed George Hainsworth's shutout record for goalies. It was a monumental achievement for the old goalie. But hockey doesn't operate on nostalgia. It's strictly a case of what have you done lately? And Sawchuk was being crowded out of Detroit by a younger goalie,

Roger Crozier. In June 1964, Terry's name showed up on the list of available names at the NHL's summer draft meetings. He was thirty-four at the time, but Toronto boss Punch Imlach never let age scare him away from a hockey player. Imlach believed Sawchuk had some good hockey left in his aging body and gambled the thirty-thousand-dollar draft price. As usual, Punch was right.

Teamed with another ancient goalie, Johnny Bower, Sawchuk flourished. Together, Bower and Sawchuk allowed less goals than any other team in the league and won the Vezina Trophy. It marked both the first time that the Vezina had gone to a goaltending tandem and the true introduction of the two-goalie system.

The next season, Sawchuk slumped. He couldn't figure out what was wrong until Marcel Pronovost, a Toronto defenseman and the goalie's longtime roommate at Detroit, solved the puzzle. Pronovost was sitting out a knee injury, watching Sawchuk struggle in the nets when the goalie's problem hit the old defenseman. After the game, Pronovost went to his friend.

"Terry, you invented the crouch for goalies and did your best goaltending out of that position," Pronovost told him. "Now you're standing upright. Why?"

Sawchuk had no answer. Pronovost was right. "The crouch seems to give me better balance and spring action when I have to move fast. If I have several bad games in a row, it's usually because I've unconsciously straightened up. When I go back to the crouch, I improve."

It could be that Sawchuk had started standing up in the nets to relieve the pain in his back. For five years, he thought he had arthritis. He slept fitfully, sometimes for no more than two hours a night because of the throbbing pain. Finally, at the end of the 1966 season, the goalie's left side went numb. "I thought I had suffered a stroke," he said.

When he went to the hospital, the doctors diagnosed the problem as two herniated discs in his back. Surgery threatened his hockey career, but had to be performed. The doctors operated and the old goalie made a remarkable recovery. A week after the operation he was swimming. A month later he was walking eight miles a day and by the time training camp arrived he was playing thirty-six holes of golf.

"I'm pretty thankful I can walk, let alone skate," he said

as training camp opened. But the old goalie seemed a shell of his former self. Easy shots went in and it looked as if he had reached the end of the hockey trail. "I was tired and discouraged," he said. "There seemed no point in staying around any longer." He was ready to pack it in, but the Leafs wouldn't let him do it. "Punch Imlach and King Clancy both told me that, if the season were opening the next day, I would be their goalie. That made me reconsider. Gradually my reflexes and timing came back."

So Sawchuk stuck around and it was a good thing he did. On March 4, 1967, more than four years after he had broken George Hainsworth's shutout record, he recorded his one hundredth career shutout, blanking the Chicago Black Hawks for the big one. "That was my centennial project," he said later, while accepting congratulations on the feat. "I was beginning to think I'd never make it."

In the playoffs, Sawchuk was scintillating. He replaced Bower in the fifth game of the semifinal round against Chicago and backstopped the Leafs to victories in that game and the clinching sixth one as well. Then he starred in the final round against Montreal.

The Leafs led the series three games to two, and held a slim one-goal lead in game six against the Canadiens. Montreal, battling to avoid elimination, swarmed around Sawchuk like bees at a honey comb. But the old goalie refused to give an inch. He darted in every direction, blocking their shots. Finally Montreal lifted its goalie for an extra attacker in the final minute. A Toronto shooter reached the gaping net and the Leafs were champions with Sawchuk making forty-one saves in the final game.

In the happy dressing room, the Maple Leafs celebrated wildly. Sawchuk did not. He sat at his cubicle, sipping a Coke, too exhausted to strip off his sweat-soaked uniform. It was the last game he ever played for Toronto. A few months later, he was drafted by the expansionist Los Angeles Kings, one of six new teams added to the league in 1967. He spent one year there and another back in Detroit as a seldom-used backup goalie. Then he moved on to the New York Rangers for his twentieth NHL season, then a longevity record for a goalie.

It was with the Rangers that he hung up his final career shutout—number 103. That came on February 1, 1970. Four months later, he was dead. Injured in some horseplay on his front lawn, he endured three major stomach operations in four weeks. Finally, his huge heart gave out and he died on May 31, 1970. A year later, he was inducted into the Hockey Hall of Fame where his accomplishments are permanently enshrined.

Ed Giacomin,
no "boy wonder,"
took a while
before he made it
to the big league.

Paul Bereswill

12
ED GIACOMIN:
THE KID FROM SUDBURY

The first time Ed Giacomin stepped in front of a goaltender's net, it was strictly to keep him out of the way of the other kids in Sudbury, Ontario. He wore borrowed equipment and carried a borrowed stick, but he found a home between the goalposts.

Giacomin grew up in Sudbury, a town described by a former resident as "a stretch of blacktop outside of Toronto." Tony and Cecile Giacomin had emigrated from Northern Italy and settled in the small Canadian town where Ed was born in June 1939. The Giacomins found no easy life in Canada and hockey equipment did not top the list of necessities.

It was that the Giacomin brothers—Jiggs, Rollie, and Ed —took turns in the single set of hockey gear they owned. When Jiggs outgrew it, the equipment was passed on to Rollie, who was six years older than Eddie. And, like any other kid brother, Eddie waited impatiently for his turn. "The kids would gather for games every day after school and all day on Saturday and Sunday," recalled Ed. "Nobody had to have an excuse to play hockey. It was just the thing to do." Occasionally, when Rollie wasn't playing, he'd lend the equipment to Eddie. At other times, the younger Giacomin wandered over to the rink and borrowed some gear.

"I usually just hung around and watched," he said. "If one side needed a goalie, I'd borrow a stick from somebody and get into the game. They made a goalie out of me just to get me out of the way. Most of the kids wanted to score. I was happy just to play."

There were other sports in Eddie's life too. He was a better than average outfielder for the semipro Cooper Cliff Redmen and a fine quarterback for the Sudbury Hardrocks. But hockey was the game he liked best. Unfortunately, it was not the game he played best. Most promising young hockey players join Canada's vast network of junior leagues, where future major-league talent is refined and developed. Junior A is the top level. Junior B is a cut below the best, but still promising. Young Ed Giacomin barely made Junior C. "I was never good enough for the better leagues," said Giacomin.

Nonetheless, around Sudbury the word was that if you needed a goalie for a pickup game the Giacomin house was the place to go. Ed was ambitious enough about his hockey to go to the training camp of the Hamilton Red Wings, Detroit's affiliate in the prestigious Ontario Hockey Association, the cream of the junior-hockey leagues. The Hamilton people thanked him for his interest and sent him back to Sudbury, preferring two other goalies—Carl Wetzel and Dennis Jordan.

The sad-eyed Giacomin was discouraged, but not defeated. He got a job as an apprentice electrician and played in a commercial league. He tended goal for the Bell Telephone team in the Sudbury Industrial League, a level of hockey that is the last place one would expect to find a potential major leaguer. "I was nineteen, and I had to pay to play hockey while others were getting paid to play," he said.

Then, all at once, Giacomin's hockey playing career almost ended completely. One morning he was upstairs in the family house when he and Rollie noticed smoke filtering into the bedroom. The brothers rushed down the staircase into the kitchen. Almost at the moment they arrived, the stove exploded in front of them. The brothers managed to extinguish the fire, but Eddie's legs—perhaps a goaltender's most important asset—were covered with second- and third-degree burns.

"It was tremendously painful," recalled Giacomin, who spent a long period in the hospital undergoing delicate skin grafts. "The doctors told me I'd never be able to play hockey again. They said I'd have to wear bandages around my legs all year."

But medical science didn't take into account the size of a

man's determination. Eddie Giacomin wasn't giving up hockey that easily and before long he was back on the ice. The Industrial League played its games at 11:00 P.M., because that was the only time the ice was available. And the players chipped in two dollars apiece for the privilege of using the rink. Sometimes, when money was a problem, the games were held on outdoor rinks with the temperatures dipping to as low as fifteen degrees below zero. In goal, his legs still bandaged, stood Giacomin. "My feet would get so cold," he said, "that I'd have to throw snow on the toes to thaw them out."

Once, not long after the accident at home, Giacomin played in a beer-league game. He was unsure of how much mobility the burns on his legs had taken away from his netminding. Then, early in the game, a puck fell loose at center ice and one of the other players picked it up and swooped down like a giant bird on Eddie's net. As he came over the blue line, Giacomin moved out to meet the charge and cut the angle the way Rollie Giacomin would do it. Rollie was Eddie's goaltending teacher. "I learned to play goal by watching him," said Giacomin. "He sure had the moves."

The puck carrier faked Giacomin one way, dropping his shoulder neatly. Eddie went for the move, but suddenly the puck wasn't there. The attacking forward had pulled it on Eddie to backhand it into the vacant net. Giacomin, realizing what had happened, swung his body quickly and threw out his legs—those burned legs which had yet to be tested since his return to the nets. Miraculously, Eddie got his padded leg up high enough and the puck plunked off it harmlessly. Save! This proved the flames that had licked at his legs had not robbed him of the mobility so essential to tending goal.

There was family opposition to Eddie's pursuit of goaltending. Jiggs, the oldest brother, had broken his collarbone three times playing hockey. Rollie had absorbed the usual bumps and bruises. Still, Eddie was adamant. He enjoyed the sport too much to give it up. And he kept playing in the commercial league at night while working during the day.

Meanwhile, in Washington, D.C., a crisis developed in that city's Eastern Hockey League franchise. The problem was in goal. Washington's regular man had been injured and the Lions desperately needed a net-minder. Then somebody remembered Rollie Giacomin up in Sudbury, Ontario. Rollie once had an offer to play in the Montreal organization, but turned it down to help support his family. Surely, if he earned an offer from the Canadiens, he was good enough for the Eastern Hockey League.

The Lions wired Rollie Giacomin, offering him a couple of weeks as goaltender. When the telegram reached the Giacomin house in Sudbury, the most excited member of the family wasn't Rollie, but Eddie. Rollie was lukewarm about the offer, especially since it would interfere with his job. "Stick to your job at the plant," advised his father. "You've got two years' seniority." Rollie decided that if he couldn't go maybe Eddie could. It took some convincing, because the trip from Sudbury to Washington was by plane and Eddie had never flown before. The lure of the shot with Washington was too much to turn down, however, and Eddie agreed. He went in Rollie's place.

Eddie flew to Washington and entered the arena on somewhat wobbly legs, still recovering from his first airplane ride. He introduced himself to Andy Brandigan, coach of the Lions.

"Oh, you're Rollie Giacomin," said Brandigan.

"No, sir," replied the young goalie, "I'm Eddie, his brother. Rollie works the night shift and couldn't get away from his job."

Brandigan was less than thrilled by Eddie's explanation. He hadn't been happy with the idea of playing an untested goalie in the first place and now the untested goalie had been replaced by his kid brother. Washington had no margin for error: the Lions had nine games to play and had to win them all to qualify for the playoffs. Brandigan did not want to place his team's fate in the hands of a commercial-league goalie. He used another net-minder instead, while Eddie sat and watched, just as he sat and watched Rollie play when both were growing up in Sudbury.

The Lions lost three straight games with the other goalie and were out of the EHL playoff picture when Brandigan decided to let Eddie get his skates wet. Giacomin played the last six games of the season and Washington won them all, causing Brandigan to wonder what might have happened had he used the beer-league goalie when he showed up.

The Washington franchise was owned by Lou Pieri, who operated the American Hockey League's Providence fran-

chise as well. Pieri and his general manager, Ken Reardon,
watched Giacomin. They liked what they saw and decided
to offer the young man, a tryout the following season. Despite
his love for hockey, Giacomin hesitated when Reardon
called to invite him to the Providence training camp in
1959.

After his brief fling with Washington, Eddie had returned
to Sudbury baseball and football. Cam Church, coach of the
football club Eddie quarterbacked, set up an athletic scholarship for his signal-caller at San Fernando State College in
California. It required the completion of a final year of high
school and was an excellent opportunity for the goalie. Giacomin weighed the two offers. It was not an easy decision,
but Eddie decided once and for all to find out if he could
play professional hockey. He told Reardon that he would
come to the Providence camp. His bonus for signing was
a skimpy five hundred dollars.

When Giacomin arrived in Providence, he found a prob-
lem named Bruce Gamble. Winner of the Western Hockey
League's Rookie of the Year award the year before—a long
way from the Sudbury Commercial League—Gamble beat
Giacomin out of the goalie's job at Providence. The Reds
decided that the jump from the commercial league to the
American Hockey League was too steep for Giacomin.
They assigned him to the Eastern League.

The Eastern Hockey League was a unique circuit that
stretched as far north as Clinton, New York, and as far south
as Jacksonville, Florida, with stops in-between at such di-
verse points as Commack, Long Island, Johnstown, Pennsyl-
vania, Charlotte, North Carolina, and other metropolises. The
league was linked by buses and anyone who bussed from
Clinton to Jacksonville never forgot the experience. The Sudbury Commercial League with its primitive conditions was
the perfect training ground for a year in the EHL.

Giacomin spent the 1959–60 season in Clinton and out on
Long Island with the New York Rovers. He played a total of
fifty-one games and surrendered 206 goals for a sad average
of 4.04 goals-against per game. When you consider the bus
rides, it's a wonder that an EHL goalie kept his average under
five goals per game. The league's defensemen were about as
much in evidence as doctors making house calls at 3:00 A.M.

Providence called Eddie up for the final game of the

season and he beat Buffalo 5–4, blocking forty-one shots in his pro-hockey debut. The next season, Eddie was back in the Rovers' shooting gallery on Long Island. Then lady luck smiled. The Boston Bruins, Providence's National Hockey League affiliate, needed goaltending help and plucked Gamble out of the AHL. His replacement was veteran Don Simmons, but fifty-one goals in ten games convinced Providence Coach Phil Watson that he was not the answer. The Reds sent out a distress call for Giacomin. Eddie had left a favorable impression in his only AHL game the year before and now he got a chance to win a full-time job. Coach Watson handed him the assignment.

"Watson gave me my first big break," said Giacomin. "He told me the job was mine." Eddie did a creditable job too, averaging thirty-six saves per game for the Reds in his first full professional season. He displayed remarkable reflexes and a willingness to work on his weaknesses. The beer-league goalie displayed an insatiable thirst for work and would have played every minute of every game if the Reds had let him.

His first year with Providence seemed to give Giacomin the confidence he needed. For the next two seasons, he shared the Providence nets with journeyman Gil Mayer, a veteran professional playing since 1949. In both of these seasons Giacomin stopped better than 90 percent of the shots hit at him and lowered his goals-against average from 4.26 his first year to 3.60 and then to 2.62 in 1962–63 when he led Providence to the AHL's Eastern Division title. Coach Fern Flaman gave him the bulk of the credit for the Reds' victory. "Eddie had to work for everything he has," said Flaman. "When I first saw him play he showed promise, but his ability had limitations. Through hard work and extra practice, he's made himself one of the finest young goaltenders in hockey today."

' This fact wasn't lost on a handful of National Hockey League club executives either. They were attracted to the Providence goalie with the slender, drawn face and the salt-and-pepper-streaked hair. Giacomin spent two more seasons in Providence, burdened by a less than notable defense that caused his goals-against average to balloon. But he still displayed a knack for solid, dependable goaltending.

In 1963–64, he led the AHL in shutouts with six. A Providence clothier decided to reward the net-minder with a new pair of slacks for each whitewashing he turned in. Giacomin collected the first pair and then, one by one, dispatched his five defensemen to cash in after the succeeding shutouts. "I couldn't have gotten those shutouts without those fellows," he said. "Remember, a goalie is only as good as his defense."

Providence's defense in those days would never be mistaken for one of major-league caliber, but Eddie stood up under the barrage of rubber he faced night after night. In back-to-back games against Baltimore, he blocked a total of 108 shots. He faced an average of close to forty shots per game with the Reds, but never wilted and was voted Providence's Most Valuable Player in 1964–65, his fifth full season with the AHL team.

Eddie began to believe that he would spend the rest of his career with the Reds. His career 3.55 goals-against average didn't raise many NHL eyebrows and every time a club demonstrated some interest in Eddie, Pieri's asking price was considered out of line. But there were important things happening in New York—important for the NHL Rangers and for Giacomin. Emile Francis, an energetic former goalie, had been hired as general manager of the New York club and given the task of rebuilding the Rangers from the farm system to the major-league club. He greatly expanded the Ranger scouting staff and kept close tabs on promising talent that might have been overlooked before. Consistently the best reports to cross Francis's desk were on Eddie Giacomin. He was steady in the nets. "We've watched him for several years," said Francis. "I've seen him play behind good teams and behind bad teams and I've been impressed."

Also eying Giacomin were the Detroit Red Wings, shopping for backup help for Roger Crozier, who had been named Rookie of the Year in 1964–65. Toronto also expressed a more than passing interest in the goalie. Now Pieri sat pretty; he had a commodity and was entertaining bids for it.

Toronto dropped out of the bidding early and that left the Rangers and Red Wings. New York's need was more pressing, since Detroit already had Crozier. The Rangers, meanwhile, had surrendered 246 goals the previous season compared to just 175 for Detroit's champions. Obviously, New York needed help in goal more than Detroit did and would pay more for it than the Red Wings might.

Pieri set the ground rules. "First of all," he said, "Giacomin is not for sale. If we do make a deal, it will be for players, not money. Our club has to rebuild for next season and you can't build a winner with money. You need players."

Francis made a date to see Pieri and flew to Providence the night before. Coming back from dinner, he met a Detroit front-office man in the hotel elevator. The Ranger GM guessed correctly that the Red Wing man hadn't stopped in Providence on vacation. He was there to make Detroit's firm offer for Giacomin—seventy thousand dollars and a couple of hockey players. The package was tempting, but not quite tempting enough. The problem was the player part of the offer. "We felt only one of the players they offered was acceptable for our needs," said Pieri.

Now it was New York's turn to bid. Francis knew Pieri needed bodies and the Ranger boss assembled a four-man package—goalie Marcel Paille, defenseman Aldo Guidolin, and forwards Sandy McGregor and Jim Mikol. He called it a one-hundred-thousand-dollar offer and Pieri agreed. They shook hands and the deal was made. Ed Giacomin now belonged to the New York Rangers.

"It was, at the time, one of the greatest things that ever happened to me—until I finally played my first game in the NHL," said Giacomin. The plan had been for Giacomin to be eased into the NHL by old pro Jacques Plante, the Rangers' resident goaltender. But Jake the Snake announced his retirement shortly after New York acquired Giacomin, putting Eddie squarely on the Madison Square Garden spot. In training camp, the Rangers had Giacomin, Cesare Maniago, Gilles Villemure, and veteran Don Simmons as goaltending candidates. Giacomin, because of the expensive price paid for him, had the inside track and won the first-string job with Simmons selected to back him up. Maniago and Villemure were dispatched to the minors.

Giacomin broke into the NHL with back-to-back contests against Montreal's powerful Canadiens. It is not the recommended way for a rookie goaltender to be introduced to the NHL. The Canadiens edged the Rangers 4–3 in both games, but Giacomin played well enough in the New York nets and he stayed there. A couple of weeks later, Giacomin ran into the Canadiens again. He had surrendered twelve goals in his last three games and then Montreal blitzed him for nine more. Afterward, the two hockey clubs both were at the railroad station to catch midnight trains. Alone at one end of the platform was Giacomin, sagging as he remembered the load of rubber that had found its way past him. Suddenly, he felt a hand on his shoulder.

Eddie looked up to find Gump Worsley, Montreal's goalie. Worsley had spent a decade in the Ranger nets, facing the same barrage that now inundated Giacomin. He was rescued by a trade to the Canadiens and he was now on his way to sharing the Vezina Trophy with teammate Charlie Hodge. But he had a long memory and the sight of Giacomin, downcast over what had happened to him, caused the Gump to approach the Ranger goalie. "I know what it's like in New York," said Worsley sympathetically. "Don't let it get you down."

That was more easily said than done. Giacomin struggled through half of the season. There were a couple of six-goal games and an eight-goal nightmare in the thirty-six games he played with the Rangers that year. He surrendered 128 goals —an average of more than three and a half per game. "It wasn't anything to win the Vezina with," he said. What made matters worse was Giacomin's style. He roamed far and wide from his net to cut off the puck—a style first popularized by Jacques Plante. But Plante was doing it for the Canadiens, who covered for him. The Rangers of Giacomin's rookie season could not be mistaken for Montreal's powerhouse. Eddie got trapped out of position and the puck wound up in the net. The fans blamed the goalie, booing him unmercifully and finally driving him back to Baltimore in the American Hockey League. His replacement was the gangly Cesare Maniago, greeted by the Garden gallery with chants of "Hail Cesare." His average was not much better than Eddie's had been, but his style was more to the crowd's liking.

When Giacomin was sent to the AHL, Francis admitted that the goalie's failure had shaken the Rangers. "He was," said the general manager, "a disappointment. A major disappointment." And yet there were those in the New York camp who believed that Giacomin wasn't all that bad a goaltender. "He's a good goalie," insisted Rod Gilbert, New York's top scorer. "You wait and see. He'll be back and he'll be an

All-Star. I know he's good because in practice he stops my best shots. I don't let up on him like some guys do in practice. And he stops everything I throw at him."

Nothing came easily to Giacomin and he determined not to give up on making it in the NHL. He came to New York's training camp the following season determined to erase the bad memories of the year before. Maniago won the starting job with a dazzling performance in the exhibitions and Giacomin was relegated to stand-by status. Then, in the last preseason game, Maniago injured his back and Giacomin stood in the nets when the Rangers opened the season. Chicago welcomed Eddie like an old friend, blasting him for a 6–3 victory.

Maniago had recovered sufficiently to start the second game of the season. But he got hurt in the second period and Giacomin took over, surrendering Toronto's last goal in a 4–4 tie. Eddie blanked the Maple Leafs 1–0, in New York's next game, but dropped three of his next four starts. Then he was victimized for a couple of late goals, forcing the Rangers to settle for a 3–3 tie against Toronto. That caused Francis to switch back to Maniago. Cesare was in goal when Boston came to the Garden on November 9, 1966, a date that is etched indelibly on Giacomin's brain.

The Rangers took a 2–1 lead in the first period, but Maniago was kayoed when he stopped a Bruin shot with his chin. Giacomin took over in the Ranger nets and another New York goal made it 3–1 as the teams headed into the final period. Giacomin played well and the Rangers seemed home-free with their two-goal edge with less than two minutes to play. Suddenly, Johnny Bucyk broke over mid-ice, dashed in on Giacomin, and scored. The crowd hardly had a chance to hoot when the referee disallowed the goal. Bucyk had been offside and the two-goal lead was still intact. But not for long.

Incredibly, just a few moments later, the Ranger defense surrendered the puck at center ice to Ron Murphy on an almost identical play. Murphy wheeled in and scored, cutting the deficit to 3–2 with eighty-nine seconds left to play. The Bruins needed just fifty-five of those seconds to score the tying goal. Boston lifted goalie Gerry Cheevers for an extra attacker. The sixth skater was Wayne Connelly, who zoomed in to beat Giacomin for the tying goal.

The booing began upstairs in the Garden's cheapest seats and cascaded down, section by section, settling all around the beleaguered Giacomin. Then one of the goalie's critics decided to throw an orange peel at Eddie. The first piece of debris led to a second and the second to a third. Soon Eddie Giacomin stood in the middle of an awful mess. They threw eggs, coins, programs . . . anything not nailed down. "It's happened before," said Giacomin, of the shower of garbage heaved at him, "but never like that."

In the Ranger dressing room, Francis was livid. Losing what seemed like a certain victory was only half of it. Watching his goaltender subjected to that kind of abuse in his own building left the New York boss seething. "I thought it was wicked," he snapped. Then he went to Giacomin. "Look," he said, "if they ever throw garbage at you again, you pick it up and throw it right back at them. You're my goalie and nothing they do is going to change that."

The conversation was a cut below Knute Rockne's "Win-one-for-the-Gipper" speech, but it had the desired results. Francis had committed himself to Giacomin. He went with Eddie in the nets, no matter what. By the end of the season, the same fans who had heaved garbage at him in November showered praise instead.

"The next game was in Montreal on Saturday night," recalled Giacomin. "I expected Emile would switch to Maniago, but he stuck with me and we won, 6–3." By the end of the month, he had posted consecutive 5–0 shutouts over Toronto and Chicago to pull the Rangers into the thick of the NHL race. Suddenly, Ed Giacomin led the league in shutouts and goals-against average. Now he was a big-league goalie. And the credit, he said, belonged to Francis. "He showed me that he had confidence in me," said Eddie. "Confidence is half the battle, too. You can only get it from experience and from knowing someone has faith in you. For the first time in my career, I had a former goaltender coaching me. I'd have to say that the number-one difference in my play was Emile. He really worked with me in practice. Most non-goalies wouldn't even realize what I was doing wrong. But Emile gave me concentrated attention and work I never got before. If he saw me doing something wrong, he'd stop the whole drill to correct it."

One of Giacomin's most flagrant indiscretions was leaving

his net to chase down the puck and then being caught out of position. He had done the same thing throughout his minor-league career and it had made him a hero in Providence. In New York, he was a goat because of the wandering. Francis cut down his goaltender's trips. "Right now, I'm more or less restricted in the nets by Emile," Giacomin said. "The thing he pointed out to me was that when I did my roving, I was going into the corners. And when I was rushing to get back to the nets, I couldn't concentrate on where the puck was. He doesn't stop me roving behind the nets or racing to the blue line to get the puck. But his advice about the corners really paid off.

"In the past, I always played for coaches who were either forwards or defensemen," Eddie continued. "They didn't know anything about goaltending and always thought that I was great and that I was helping the club, whatever I did."

Giacomin went to Francis with a request of his own. Hockey players have traditionally gone easy on their goaltenders in practice, figuring the net-minder faced enough tough shots and hard rubber during regular games. Eddie felt this hurt his work in the Ranger nets. He asked Francis to take the wraps off the Rangers. The players were told to throw their best stuff at the goalie during workouts. That, of course, was nothing new for Rod Gilbert, who had been doing just that for some time. "If I can't stop my own teammates in practice," said Eddie, "how am I going to stop the other clubs in games?"

Practice is relaxing for many goalies, but not Giacomin. One of his favorite drills is to throw away his big goaltending stick and have two forwards attack him at once. He always is one of the last players off the ice, taking extra shots in an effort to refine his net-minding skills. He works every bit as hard in practice as during games. "I have to," he said. "They're firing bullets and if I didn't try in practice, I'd get hurt more. I tell them to shoot as hard as they want. When we play Montreal, I have to have hard shots to be ready."

Slowly but surely, the tide turned. Giacomin began stopping shots that had been passing him. Soon the fans were in his corner, cheering his saves. "It's a good feeling," said the goalie, laughing. "Certainly better than having them throw things at me." And Eddie gave them plenty to yell about. He led the league with nine shutouts and was named the All-

Star goalie—the first Ranger net-minder in twenty-eight years to achieve that honor. He was second in the race for Most Valuable Player, trailing only scoring champion Stan Mikita of Chicago. He spearheaded New York's rise from the cellar to fourth place and the Rangers' first playoff berth in five seasons. "We couldn't have gone as far as we did without him," said Francis. "If there was one single factor that contributed most to our success, it would have to be Eddie's outstanding play in goal."

One vignette that season demonstrated the kind of intestinal fortitude Giacomin brought with him each time he skated into the Ranger nets. It was during a game in Toronto and Frank Mahovlich, then with the Maple Leafs, zoomed in on Eddie and pulled the trigger on one of hockey's hardest shots from no more than twenty feet away. The puck took off and crunched into Giacomin's jaw, decking him. Francis rushed to his goalie's side and, after looking at the welt, the New York boss wanted to lift Eddie. "When I asked him to go out," recalled Francis, "he told me, 'I don't care if my jaw is broken. I want to stay.'" So he stayed and completed a 1–1 tie against the Maple Leafs.

Surprisingly, the breakaway like the one Mahovlich had against him is not Giacomin's biggest worry. "The hardest thing for myself, and for any goaltender," he said, "is the screen shot. You have to anticipate and sometimes you make the wrong move. Should you go to the right or to the left? You know where the puck's coming from, but you don't see it. Sometimes, all you see are legs, skates, and sticks. Before you know it, there's a blur and the puck is in the net. It looks easy to stop the shot from where the fans sit. It would be, too, if everybody wasn't in your way."

Breakaways are a different problem. "When a player skates in on me alone," said Giacomin, "I feel I have a good chance of beating him. He has four corners of the cage to shoot at—upper and lower left and upper and lower right. By skating out to meet him, I cut down his scoring angle, eliminating the lower two corners. I try to stand as long as possible. I hope he tries to deke [fake] me out of position. If I can stay with his deke and then force him to shoot, I should be able to keep the puck out."

For the next three seasons, Giacomin was a second team All-Star and an iron man in the Ranger nets. In an era when almost every NHL team had introduced the two-goalie system, the Rangers stuck almost exclusively with Giacomin. In four seasons, he never played fewer than sixty-six games and in each of the years in which he was a second-team All-Star, his goals-against average was lower than the 2.61 he posted in 1966–67 when he was named to the top All-Star team. He insisted that he wanted to play every game and for a while he seemed to thrive on the heavy goaltending load. But he slumped near the end of each season and by the time the playoffs rolled around, the Rangers were playing with a worn-out net-minder. The answer, it seemed, was someone to share the goaltending load with Giacomin. Francis had the perfect candidate in little Gilles Villemure, a veteran minor leaguer, who had bounced around the New York organization for the better part of a decade. Villemure was promoted to the varsity in 1970 to share the load with Giacomin.

At first, Eddie was not thrilled with the idea of dividing the work. He felt that to stay sharp he had to play as often as he could. But before long the benefits seemed obvious. There was less pressure on him and Villemure proved a more than adequate NHL goalie. Giacomin, his load lightened, flourished. In the midst of the season, steady Eddie turned in two straight shutouts and a stretch of scoreless hockey that covered 151 minutes, 27 seconds. When he finally surrendered a goal against Detroit in Madison Square Garden, the home fans greeted the score with cheers. For a moment, there was an incongruous sound of Ranger fans cheering a Red Wing goal. Then it became obvious that what they were cheering was not the Red Wing goal but rather the sensational job of airtight goaltending that Giacomin had delivered until then. "I couldn't believe it at first," recalled Eddie. "When I heard them cheering, I didn't quite know what to do."

It was that same season that Giacomin, one of the NHL's last bare-faced holdouts, finally converted to a mask. Eddie had hesitated about using one and even his wife, Marg, had given up on his ever putting one on. Then he came home one day and simply announced that from then on he would wear a mask. "You're kidding," his wife said.

Wearing the mask was only one of the changes Giacomin introduced in 1970. Another was his little black book, a

New York Rangers

**Eddie's only NHL team
has been the
New York Rangers.**

careful listing of every goal he surrendered, updated after every game he played. "Sure, I keep a book on them," said Giacomin. "Every time a guy scores against me, I write it down with a description of how the goal came. I don't want it to be a guessing game when a guy is coming in on me. If I can get any kind of edge, I'm going to take it."

The book worked well for Giacomin, but it wasn't infallible. "Sometimes there are surprises," said Eddie. "Take Ralph Backstrom. He always has shot low at me, ever since I've been in the league. I had him pegged that way. Then one time he came in on me. I got set for the low shot and he put a high one over my shoulder." Giacomin figured out what had happened. "You know," he said, "that guy must keep a book on the goalies."

With book, mask, and Villemure, Giacomin again was named to the number-one All-Star team in 1970. His goals-against average was a miserly 2.15 and his eight shutouts led the league. The last one came on the final night of the regular season and clinched, for Giacomin and Villemure, the Vezina Trophy. It was the first time that NHL award had gone to the Rangers since 1939–40. The Ranger goalie in those days was Davey Kerr, who set a club shutout record with forty whitewashings. It was a mark that stood up for three decades despite a parade of Ranger goalies that included Hall of Famer Chuck Rayner and Gump Worsley. That record fell during the 1972–73 season, when Giacomin turned in four shutouts and raised his career total to forty-three. He had five more in 1973–74, reaching forty-eight for his NHL career.

He's been an All-Star and has won the Vezina Trophy. He's had more shutouts than any goalie in Ranger history, but there is still one achievement Giacomin is anxious to add to his collection. He wants to be the first NHL goalie to score a goal. He's come close a couple of times, missing one by an eyelash in the playoffs a few years ago. "It requires a special situation," said Eddie. "First of all, the other team has to have pulled its goalie for an extra skater in the last few minutes of the game. And we have to draw a penalty, so that I can shoot the puck the length of the ice without risking an icing penalty."

Those conditions make it a long shot for Giacomin, but Eddie has faced long odds before. After all, how many NHL players have come out of the Sudbury Commercial League?

The stitches
on his mask
are part of the
Gerry Cheevers legend.

UPI

13
GERRY CHEEVERS:
KEEP 'EM IN STITCHES

There was a time not so many years ago when the Boston Bruins were hardly the National Hockey League powerhouse they are today. In one eight-year stretch during the early part of the 1960s, the Bruins finished last six times and fifth twice. Personnel were shuffled in and out of Boston in a desperate attempt to make the Bruins competitive with the rest of the then six-team National League. The front-office shuffle was just as frantic. Coaches and general managers moved in and out with little success.

One of the GMs the Bruins tried was Leighton "Hap" Emms, who had run Boston's Niagara Falls farm club for some time. It was Emms's bad luck to be the Bruins' boss in the days before Bobby Orr developed into the hockey super-player who led the franchise out of the doldrums. Orr's rookie year was 1966–67—Boston's last rendezvous with the NHL basement. Another Bruin freshman that season was goaltender Gerry Cheevers and, as any Boston net-minder of the previous decade could tell you, there were nights when it seemed he was posted at the bottom of a steep hill, wearing a bull's-eye instead of a hockey jersey. Cheevers, however, had a happy-go-lucky mood, ideal for the job of minding goal for that edition of the Boston Bruins. Emms, however, did not share his goalie's cheerful nature.

There was one game in rickety old Boston Garden that saw Chicago absolutely blitz the Bruins. Every time Cheevers looked up, it seemed, another sortie of Black Hawks headed his way. And every time Emms looked up, it seemed, the puck landed in the Bruins' net. This situation did not please the Bruin fans, who, history tells us, can become rather impatient when their team loses by eight goals, the case on this particular night. Seeing Emms in the stands, the fans began blistering the GM with a variety of unpleasant remarks that left his neck a deep shade of red by the time the game ended. As the fans departed the building, drowning their sorrows, Emms headed for the Boston dressing room, ready to drown a few Bruins.

He stormed through the door, fire in his eyes. His team sat around the room on the wooden benches, too exhausted to even begin stripping off their sweat-soaked uniforms. In the corner sat Cheevers, his bulky pads still strapped on his legs. Emms stood in the doorway for a moment and then located his goalie. He made a beeline for Cheevers. Standing in front of the goalie, his fedora firmly in place, Emms looked down at Cheevers and asked, "Gerry, for crying out loud, what the hell happened out there tonight?"

Cheevers, who by this time had begun to loosen his pads, looked up at the GM with an innocent little-boy look, a trace of a smile on his round face. His voice, unlike the GM's, was totally calm.

"It's very simple, Hap," said Cheevers. "Roses are red. Violets are blue. They got ten. We got two."

At that moment Gerry Cheevers produced the credentials necessary to make him an integral member of hockey's Gashouse Gang—the Boston Bruins who would win two East Division pennants, miss another by an eyelash, and capture two Stanley Cups over a three-year period. And even though Cheevers left Boston for a lucrative one-million-dollar contract with the Cleveland Crusaders of the new World Hockey Association in 1972, it's natural to identify the Bruins with this goalie and his thinning blond hair, ready smile, and quick tongue.

There is, for example, the story he likes to tell about his father, who made Canada's lacrosse hall of fame and served as a hockey scout for the Toronto Maple Leafs in St. Catharines, Ontario, where the Cheevers family lived. Joe Cheevers coached the local Catholic Youth Organization team and one day the goalie did not show up. Father turned to son and pointed young Gerry toward the net. "He didn't have the nerve to ask anybody else to play goal," remembered the younger Cheevers. "So he put me in there and we got beat, 17–0." Undaunted by the shaky beginning. Gerry nevertheless remained in the nets. "The other goalie didn't show up for games after that—we had a pretty lousy team—so my dad kept me in there."

By the time he was eight years old, the young goalie had better luck in keeping the puck out of the net. "We played twelve games," he said, "and I won the first eleven by shut-outs. When you're eight, there aren't too many Bobby Hulls drilling 'em at you. I finally allowed a goal in the twelfth game. I haven't had as good a year since." Joe Cheevers encouraged his young son and Gerry weaved his way through kid hockey and one day found himself playing for St. Michael's School, at that time a Junior A hockey affiliate of the Maple Leafs. The senior Cheevers, of course, was a Toronto scout. "I think they fired him," recalled Gerry, laughing, "when they found out I was the only guy he scouted for them."

Cheevers has always had an unorthodox goaltending style. "I'm not a stand-up type and I'm not a flopper," he said. "I might do either one in a particular situation. It's impossible for a forward to guess my move because I honestly don't know myself how I'm going to play it. It's pure reflex. I don't try to outthink the puck carrier. I just go for the puck." Cheevers also does his share of roaming, often wandering far away from his net to clear a loose puck—a rather unsettling sight for a coach to watch and one coach decided he had seen enough of Cheevers's adventures away from the net. If Gerry wanted to do some skating, he decided, the best place for him to do it would be as a forward.

It happened toward the end of Cheevers's junior career at St. Michael's. "They had another goalie, younger than me, and they were grooming him to be my successor," said Cheevers. "They promised him he would play twelve games of Junior A that season. It was around Christmastime and a lot of the players, who came from all over Canada, went home on vacation." That created the opening his coach had waited for. He moved the other goalie—Dave Dryden—into the nets and informed Cheevers that since he liked to skate so much he would get his share of it on left wing.

"I almost got killed," said Gerry. "All the guys on the other teams who were mad at me, maybe because I took a goal away from them, started to take runs at me. I'm lucky

I survived."

There was one memorable experience for Cheevers in his stint up front. It was his breakaway chance—an opportunity for the goalie to score a goal. The net-minder on the receiving end was Roger Crozier who, like Cheevers and Dryden, later made his mark in the NHL. His job in this instance was to avoid the embarrassment of surrendering a goal to a guy who, until then, had spent most of his time stopping shots instead of taking them. "You'd think," said Cheevers, "if anyone knew how to beat a goalie, it would be a goalie." Gerry found the puck on his blade and nothing between him and Crozier but a lot of ice. He cradled the puck on his stick and took off.

As Cheevers reached the blue line, Crozier came out and cut down the angle. By this time, though, Cheevers had other problems. "I was in such a hurry I didn't take the time to think," he said. The goalie wound up and shot at the goalie. "I shot straight into his pads." Save! "I only wish everyone played forward like I did," said Cheevers. "I'd never be scored on."

Cheevers returned to the nets, perhaps a bit more appreciative of the problems forwards have. But his term up front did not alter his net-minding style. He continued to take little side trips away from the net whenever the urge and opportunity came along. Occasionally, the wandering backfired and the puck found its way into his team's net while Cheevers was otherwise occupied. The goalie developed a formula for handling what would seem to be that most embarrassing situation. "The thing you try to do when something like that happens is act nonchalant as hell. The roof is coming down. The fans are screaming. You just try to give the impression that you were beaten on a tough shot and you have to try to wipe it from your mind. The worst thing you can do is blow another one worrying about the last one."

Gerry couldn't have blown too many in the St. Michael's nets because the team won the Memorial Cup, emblematic of Canada's junior-hockey championship, in 1961. St. Mike's wiped out Edmonton in five games and when the series was over, Murray Armstrong, a former NHL player who had moved into the coaching ranks at Denver University, offered Cheevers a four-year scholarship. Gerry now had to choose between playing college hockey or turning professional with

Toronto. The Maple Leafs won.

"I thought seriously about going to school in Colorado," said Cheevers. But the Maple Leafs had lost two young goaltenders, Cesare Maniago and Jerry McNamara, in the draft that summer and they offered me what I considered a damn good contract to turn pro." The numbers that lured Cheevers? A four-thousand-dollar bonus to sign, six thousand dollars for his first professional season, and sixty-five hundred dollars for the second. Today, no self-respecting junior hockey player would even consider those figures. But in 1961, it was more than enough to get Cheevers's autograph on a pro contract.

Gerry went to training camp with the Maple Leafs that fall. He remembers it well. "You have no idea how hard National Leaguers can shoot that puck until you've been hit a few times," he said. "It comes as a great shock." The Leafs had their share of hard shooters and Cheevers, trying hard to make an impression, stood right up to them. "The first time Frank Mahovlich hit my shoulder with a shot," he said, "I staggered back and my shoulders banged into the crossbar. It was as much from surprise as the force of the shot. I just hadn't expected a puck could feel like that."

It was as if Mahovlich was tendering his own personal welcome to the NHL to the young goalie from St. Michael's. A few days later, Cheevers played in his first exhibition game and discovered that the Big M's greeting was a pleasant little how-do-you-do compared to what other teams had in store for him.

In the first game against the Bruins Cheevers was understandably nervous. His knees were rubbery as he skated out to defend the Toronto net. But that uneasy feeling disappeared fast. He never had time to think about it; he was too busy wiping the blood away from his eye. Burly Leo Boivin unloaded a wicked slap shot and the puck grazed defenseman Tim Horton on the way toward the Maple Leaf net, deflected high, and crashed into the young goalie's eyebrow. Welcome to the National Hockey League, Gerry. It took ten stitches to close the wound.

Cheevers did the bulk of the Maple Leafs' goaltending during the exhibition season as Punch Imlach, then Toronto's general manager-coach, gave his regular man, elderly Johnny Bower, all the time he might need to get ready. That was one of the privileges of age and Bower took full advantage of it. He was not unaware, however, of young Cheevers's good work in the nets. Neither, for that matter, was Imlach.

"Gerry played very adequately with us this fall," said Imlach. "Any game we lost wasn't his fault. In fact, I'm rather high on the kid. He's going to be a very good goalie." But in those days there were only six NHL goaltending jobs and none of them belonged to twenty-year-old rookies just out of junior hockey. It was clear that Cheevers would be farmed out. Bower hoped that the youngster's traveling papers could be delayed. "I'd like to have him stay with us for a couple of months," said the old Toronto goalie. "I'd make a heck of a goalie out of him. He has the stuff and for a kid just coming out of junior, he knows a lot. He has a good set of hands and he clears the puck well. I'm not going to last forever."

Bower was thirty-seven then and for a while it seemed that he would last forever. He fooled Father Time, playing so well in the Toronto nets year in and year out that Cheevers always found himself working in the minor leagues. Each fall, Gerry came to the Toronto camp full of hope and each year he wound up in Rochester or Sudbury or Sault Ste. Marie. Imlach began to worry about Bower's advancing years when John hit forty in 1964. He shopped for a younger man and came away from the NHL's 1964 summer draft with Terry Sawchuk, a mere thirty-five. The following season, the two graybeards split the Toronto goaltending almost down the middle and shared the Vezina Trophy. Cheevers, meanwhile, did his third term at Rochester, leading the league with five shutouts and being named the American Hockey League's best goaltender. He was impatient with what was going on in Toronto. "Bower was playing very well for them and then they picked up Sawchuk. I knew there was no way I was going to win a job from a pair of greats like that."

What Cheevers also knew, however, was that Imlach would be allowed to protect only two goalies in the summer draft and that Punch had three net-minders to choose from. Simple mathematics says that somebody is going to have to be exposed to the thirty-thousand-dollar draft price. But Imlach wasn't surrendering that easily. Punch had a reputation as one of the NHL's wiliest operators—and he didn't get it through sitting by idly while other teams plucked away his players. When he submitted his list of protected players to the draft meetings, he had Bower and Sawchuk listed as his protected goalies. Cheevers? Oh, he was protected too. As a left-winger.

The rest of the general managers were amused by Imlach's fertile mind, but in no mood to let Punch escape with that ploy. "That, Mr. Imlach," he was told by President Clarence Campbell, "is not acceptable." Punch argued briefly that Cheevers had, after all, played left wing in junior hockey, but he knew he wasn't going to win. He had to make a final choice on his goalies. Pick two and leave the third one available to the draft. Cheevers figured he knew which two Punch would protect.

"You know how Punch thinks," said Gerry. "He'd never leave himself with only one NHL veteran. So any chance he'd protect me instead of Terry Sawchuk was gone. Besides, Johnny Bower and Sawchuk had just won the Vezina Trophy. I was gone."

The goalie was right. Boston, hurting for a goalie, chose Cheevers on the opening round of the intraleague draft. If the Bruins hadn't grabbed him, some other club would have. There was no way Imlach could've sneaked him through that draft. "Sure, I was disappointed," said Cheevers. "It's tough to leave a team you've been with since you were fifteen. But, in a way, I was glad. After all, now I was in the NHL."

Well, not quite. When Cheevers arrived at Boston's training camp, he found holdover Ed Johnston and a young rookie named Bernie Parent also competing for the net-minding job. Those two had valuable assets going for them in the three-way battle. Johnston had been there first and Parent was a favorite of Hap Emms, for whom he had played at Boston's Niagara Falls affiliate. Emms just happened to be the general manager of the Bruins. It all added up to a ticket to Oklahoma City to play for the Bruins' Central League farm team. It would be another minor-league season for Cheevers. There was no way it would produce the kind of memories he derived from his last minor-league season in the Toronto organization at Rochester.

The Amerks had played one Saturday night game in Springfield and bussed back to Rochester for Sunday's game against Quebec. When he came home, Cheevers discovered his wife had gone to the hospital to give birth to their first child—two months prematurely. Cheevers went straight to the hospital and stayed there until time to leave for the rink. When he took the ice, Gerry had not been to bed in thirty-six hours.

Early in the first period, he stopped a backhander by Red Berenson with his upper lip. "It knocked out three upper front teeth and three lower front teeth," said Cheevers. "It was a mess. I was spitting blood and teeth as they led me to the infirmary. I can still see a couple of those teeth landing in my glove."

Experiences like this inspired Cheevers to experiment with a mask. After washing out in his first trial with the Bruins, Gerry was more concerned with his goaltending career than in finding a mask that suited his needs. A training-camp knee injury hastened his departure from Boston and when he got to Oklahoma City, he was a dejected young man. He found help in the form of the Central League team's playing coach, Harry Sinden.

"He was a bit down on himself for not having stuck with the Bruins," recalled Sinden. "But I figured we could straighten him out at Oklahoma, and we did. The team seemed to rally in front of him, and we went on to win our first title in the playoffs and the Jack Adams Trophy." The performance earned a promotion to Boston—for Sinden, not Cheevers. Gerry was the shuttle goalie, coming up from Oklahoma City when an injury hit either Johnston or Parent.

"I was covering more ground than some stewardesses," quipped Cheevers. "For a while there, I had to look down at my uniform to see what team I was playing for. All the towns and the arenas looked the same. The human yo-yo was at home anywhere." Cheevers spent enough of his time in Oklahoma City to win the CHL's leading goaltender award in 1966–67, a year in which the Bruins finished last and surrendered 253 goals, the highest total in the NHL.

It began to appear that Cheevers was stuck on the same kind of treadmill in the Boston organization as he had been on earlier with Toronto, but the NHL's majordomos rescued him. Two years earlier, the Maple Leafs had been forced to make a decision on whether to keep him or expose him to the draft. Now the Bruins had to make the same decision. The league was expanding, adding six new teams for the 1967 season. The players would be drawn from the six established teams. Each club could freeze, or protect, eleven forwards and defensemen and one goaltender before the expansion clubs drafted. With the previous season's goals-against numbers, one would think the Bruins wouldn't have that much of a problem. But they did. Boston owned four goalies at the time—Cheevers, Johnston, Parent, and Gerry's Oklahoma City sidekick—Doug Favell. They could protect only one; then, after losing one, they could protect another, and lose number four.

By this time, Hap Emms had departed the Boston scene, so there was no special prejudice in Parent's favor. Sinden liked Cheevers better than Favell and the Bruins decided to protect Gerry, exposing the other three goalies. Philadelphia picked Parent and then Boston protected Johnston, leaving Favell for the Flyers' second goalie selection. Expansion had forced a decision and the Boston commitment was to the wandering goalie from St. Catharines.

Cheevers reported to Boston's training camp knowing for the first time that he had a major-league goaltending job in the palm of his hand. All clubs carried two goalies and Boston's tandem would be Gerry and Johnston. Boston also had some other important new faces in camp that fall. The Bruins had swung a six-player summer trade with Chicago and centers Phil Esposito and Fred Stanfield and right-wing Ken Hodge moved to Boston.

Ever since losing a half-dozen teeth to Red Berenson's backhander in Rochester a couple of years earlier, Cheevers had been experimenting with masks. He had been unhappy with the ones he tried because he couldn't find one that held firm to his chin and that did not slip and slide, impairing his vision. Then, Ernie Higgins, an ex-plumber who lives in a Boston suburb, developed a mask that held. Higgins delved into the mask problem a few years earlier to protect his son, who had decided to guard the nets in a kid league. Higgins's masks are custommade affairs that require a special mold of his customer's face. He slips a silk stocking over his subject's hair and then covers the face with Vaseline and plaster of Paris.

The thing that impressed Cheevers about the Higgins creation was the chin strap, which eliminated the slipping and sliding problem the goalie experienced with other masks. He ordered one and took it to the Bruins' camp. For the first time, he wore a face-covering constantly and adjusted to it. He has never again stepped in front of a net without one. "It is a goalie's best friend," said Cheevers, fingering the mask. "Without the mask, I'd be a coward out there. I have always said that I had an awful lot of confidence. If I didn't have confidence, I wouldn't stop one shot in a hundred. But the day I toss away the mask, I'll be leaving the rink in a strait jacket."

Cheevers's mask is a ghastly looking thing, primarily because it is pockmarked with crayoned stitches that represent the needlework the mask has saved on Gerry's face. Some goalies paint their masks so they look like sunbursts. Others prefer the original plain white color. Cheevers's design is the most unusual idea.

Cheevers's stitch tradition started in his first full NHL season. During a practice session, Freddie Stanfield unloaded a hard shot that ricocheted off Ted Green's arm and caught the goalie in the mask. Gerry, having some fun, went into a dramatic dive, hoping to get at least a breather from practice, if nothing else. He appeared to be on death's doorstep—unless you knew Cheevers's penchant for a gag—lying across the goalie crease. The Bruins, though, knew their net-minder. John "Frosty" Forristall, the club's assistant trainer, rushed onto the ice with smelling salts and called for a stretcher. Cheevers blinked up at Forristall and muttered, "How many stitches? How many stitches?"

Frosty, feigning deep concern for the goaltender's survival, reported dutifully that it was somewhere between forty and one hundred. Cheevers sank back to the ice, lapsing again into his put-on unconsciousness. He "recovered" and after the practice Cheevers approached Forristall and asked him to paint the stitches on the mask. Before Gerry started covering his face, he had been sliced for about fifty stiches. They added those to the mask. Since putting it on, Cheevers has painted more than one hundred new stitches. "Better on the mask," he said, "than on my face."

Goalies who take life too seriously can wind up cutting out paper dolls in serene, quiet surroundings. The art of placing one's body in the way of one-hundred-mile-per-hour shots requires a certain amount of flakiness and ability to laugh at adversity. Cheevers laughs at everything and often is the center of dressing-room buffoonery. He is not what one would term a brooder. Occasionally, though, the jokes back-fire. But Gerry can laugh at that, too.

The key to whether a Cheevers's gag works or not is who the perpetrator of the stunt is. If Gerry plans it, it works for him. If not, he's liable to emerge on the short end. There was, for example, a game at Madison Square Garden against the New York Rangers a few years ago. Cheevers showed up at the Garden early and, with a couple of teammates, wandered around the cavernous building. There was a pet show in one of the exhibit halls and the Bruins peeked in on it. Cheevers was particularly repelled by the snakes, a fact that some of his teammates noted carefully.

Later, the Bruins went into their dressing room to prepare for the game against the Rangers. Bobby Orr intercepted the goalie and nodded toward Johnny McKenzie's corner of the room. "Listen, don't say anything," whispered Orr. "We put a four-foot snake in Pie's shin pads." Cheevers chuckled and nonchalantly watched McKenzie as the gritty forward dressed for the game. Nothing happened. Finally, Gerry was distracted and moved across the room. When he returned to his cubicle, there still had been no anguished screams from McKenzie. Gerry wondered what was taking Pie so long to find the snake.

"I was just climbing into my pants when Frosty, the assistant trainer, came over," said Cheevers. "He reached into my pants and pulled out this four-foot snake. I freaked out. I leaped up and then I started to run. I knocked over Eddie Johnston and Kenny Hodge. I must have set a twenty-yard-dash mark. I had my skates on and I tore across the concrete floor, absolutely wrecking the edge on them."

The old "rubber-snake" gag had worked to perfection on the goalie, and left the rest of the Bruins in a state of hysterics.

Gerry has been a horse fancier since he was a teenager. "I've been interested in horses since I was thirteen years old when I worked around the barn at Fort Erie track in Ontario, which is about twenty miles from my home in St. Catharines. I did the usual stuff—walking hots, raking out stalls, and I got to enjoy the people and being around the horses." Because of his love for the sport, Cheevers worked summers at Fort Erie after joining the big leagues. The track hired him to help promote its summer meeting and Gerry went about it the same way he does everything else—enthusiastically.

One of his promotions was a donkey race featuring NHL players as jockeys. He invited teammate Freddie Stanfield and defenseman Wayne Hillman of Philadelphia, who looks about as much like a jockey as Racquel Welch looks like a grandmother. There were other players too and, of course, the goalie entered himself in the race. "What they didn't know," chuckled Cheevers, "is that I knew the fella at the starting gate."

Donkeys have minds of their own and it is not easy to get them moving in the direction in which you'd like them to go. The others struggled with their mounts as Cheevers got his headed properly. As soon as that happened, Gerry's starter pal began the race. The goalie won easily. "Stanfield finished second," Cheevers said, "driving."

Actually, the donkey ride was one of Cheevers's rare appearances in the saddle. He loves horses and has owned several, but doesn't fancy riding them. "Oh, no," he said. "I don't ride. In fact, I'm afraid of horses. But I'll overcome that. I'll just keep working with them until I'm not afraid any more."

Cheevers enjoys the total track scene—the horses, the people, and the atmosphere of the sport. He spends as much time as he can at the track, during the hockey season as well as during the summer months. One of the goalie's early racing friends was a trainer named Bob Warner, who had several horses at the Fort Erie track.

"Warner knew I was a junior goalie at the time," said Cheevers. "And he loved hockey. He once explained to me that a stable was trained the way a hockey team was coached. That is, every horse is different and has to be treated that way. A young horse, like a rookie player, has to be worked hard and taught how to run. There are horses that have to be pampered the way some hockey players have to be babied. Then you have stake horses in racing and stake horses in hockey. In hockey, they're Bobby Orr and Phil Esposito. They'll run their own race."

After the expansion draft cost the Bruins two goalies, Cheevers was promoted to the varsity for keeps, teaming with Ed Johnston in the Boston nets. Two other Boston-organization goalies, Ian Young and Claude Dufour, suffered

Cleveland Crusaders

As a Cleveland Crusader
in the first year
of the WHA,
Gerry led the league
in goals-against average.

serious eye injuries, ending their careers. That meant that from six goalies the Bruins' complement of net-minders was down to two. "That put pressure on both Johnston and myself," said Cheevers, "but as far as I was concerned I was anxious to prove that I belonged in this league as a matter of general principle."

He did that, turning in a 2.83 goals-against average in forty-seven games that season and helping Boston into the playoffs for the first time in nine years. The Bruins were eliminated in the first round by Montreal, but gained important Stanley Cup experience. "Add up all the guys on our team who'd never played together in playoff competition before," said Boston General Manager Milt Schmidt, "and you'll get the picture."

Cheevers was in the nets for each of the losses in the four games with Montreal. Gerry gained something beside playoff experience that season. He also came out of it with a nickname—"Cheesy." That's a derivative of his last name and it fit in nicely on the nickname-mad Bruins. Johnston was "E.J."—his initials. Phil Esposito was "Espie," and another last-name product. "Johnny Bucyk was "Chief" because he looks Indian. Johnny McKenzie was "Pie" because of the round shape of his face. Derek Sanderson was "Turk" because of his style on the ice. They were all integral parts of the Bruins' Gashouse Gang, now hockey's most potent team.

The Bruins advanced to the Cup semifinals the next year, only to be eliminated again by Montreal, the eventual champions. Then, for the next three seasons, the Gashouse Gang twice won the Cup, finished first in the East Division twice, and missed a third division title by the narrowest of margins, being beaten out on the basis of goals scored. Led by Esposito's remarkable shooting—he won three scoring championships and set an all-time record of seventy-six goals in a single season—the Bruins assembled one of the most awesome attacks in modern hockey. They totaled a record-shattering 399 goals in 1970–71, averaging five goals per game. The scoring pyrotechnics overshadowed Boston's defensive game and its goaltending.

"We realize," said Cheevers, "our machine consists of scoring a lot of goals. That means we're going to be open on defense when we get big leads. When you play for a club with so much firepower, you often find your concentration wandering in one-sided games."

The result was that goaltending was considered the weakest link in the Boston armor. But Cheevers destroyed that suggestion in 1970 when the Bruins won their first Cup in twenty-nine years. He backstopped the team to ten consecutive Cup victories, an all-time record. And then, in 1972, when Boston captured the Cup again, he set another record, going unbeaten through a stretch of thirty-three regular-season games. He had twenty-four victories and nine ties over that stretch and his string was ten games longer than the best previous NHL streak by a goalie—twenty-three games by the Bruins' Frank Brimsek thirty-one years earlier. When Boston eliminated first Toronto and then St. Louis, it put the Bruins in the Cup finals against New York.

Boston took the first two games of the series and after the Rangers took game three, the Bruins won the fourth, edging within one game of the Cup. But New York stayed alive by winning game five, sending the series back to Madison Square Garden for a sixth game. If the Rangers took that one, it would set up a winner-take-all seventh game, a situation the Bruins weren't interested in creating. They wanted to finish the Rangers off once and for all. In goal, they started number thirty, Gerry Cheevers. At the other end of the ice, the Rangers' eyes lit up. They had strafed Cheevers for ten goals in the two previous games they had played against him in this series. They had not done nearly as well against Ed Johnston—six goals in three games. If New York could choose the goalie they wanted to see, Cheevers would've been the man.

That was before the game. Afterward, Cheevers did the laughing. He shut New York out, turning in an array of dazzling stops and protecting a slim 1–0 lead until the final fifteen minutes of the game when Boston added two more goals. When it was over, Cheevers danced a little jig in front of the Boston net. "The old boy is vindicated," he said to a friend in the bubbly Boston dressing room.

That was to be the last game Cheevers played in the Boston net. All that season a new group, the World Hockey Association, trumpeted its intention to start a twelve-team league in the fall of 1972. Many NHL officials took the WHA with a ho-hum and a shrug, but unfortunately many players did not approach the new league that way. When Bobby Hull accepted a $2.75-million offer to switch leagues, several NHL players followed. One was Cheevers.

Nick Mileti, a Cleveland sports baron, had been turned down in his bid for an NHL expansion franchise. Mileti had been prepared to pay the NHL's six-million-dollar entrance fee, but when rejected, he went to the WHA. They accepted him for considerably less than six million; the Cleveland Crusaders then had a considerable amount of money to offer interested players, one of whom was Cheevers.

The first numbers kicked around in print mentioned $500,-000 but that wasn't close to what Gerry wanted. "Where do they get those figures?" asked Cheevers. "A half million dollars isn't even close to what I'd want to leave Boston for. What does that amount to, about $100,000 a year?" Cheevers continued to negotiate with the Bruins. Then came a dramatic change in the various conversations. Cleveland doubled its offer. Mileti would package one million dollars over six years for Cheevers's autograph. "Where do I sign?" asked Gerry.

"I'm sorry to be leaving the Bruins," said Cheevers, "because it was a great-knitted team. But I weighed a lot of things in the past two weeks. My priorities got down to one thing—security for my family. I hope to finish my career in Cleveland." Gerry figured he could play until age thirty-seven.

Sharing the goaltending load with Bob Whidden, Cheevers led the new league with five shutouts. The Crusaders allowed fewer goals than any other team in the WHA's first season and Whidden and Cheevers earned a four-thousand-dollar bonus for winning the league's equivalent of the Vezina Trophy, something Gerry never managed with Ed Johnston in the NHL. Cheevers was also named to the WHA All-Star team. Ironically, his goals-against average was 2.83, the same figure he achieved in his first full season with the Bruins. It rose only a bit to 3.03 in Cheevers's second WHA season. Obviously, he was the same goalie he has always been.

Asked to describe his style, Cheevers laughed. "I fall, stand, and skate a lot. I'll skate out and blitz the shooter. I'll leave the cage to clear the puck to a forward. I've been known to skate to the blue line with the puck to start a play. I'm quite unnatural."

Then Cheevers reflected for a moment and added a final note on the subject. "I figure," he said, "it's not how you stop the puck—it's how many you stop." He has stopped more than his share in fourteen professional seasons. If you don't think so, take a look at his mask.

Johnny Bower
was somewhere in his
mid-forties—nobody is
sure exactly how old
he was—when he
retired as a
Toronto goalie.

14
JOHNNY BOWER:
AGE IS WHAT YOU MAKE IT

Johnny Bower, goaltender, and Punch Imlach, general manager-coach, arrived in Toronto at the same time in 1958. They stayed together for eleven seasons, leading the Maple Leafs to four Stanley Cup championships. What made them unusual as a pair was that the star goalie was only a half-dozen years—maybe less than that—younger than his boss.

"I told him a long time ago to throw away his birth certificate," said Imlach, whenever Bower's age was questioned. "Who cares how old he is when he plays the way he does?" For the record, Bower's official date of birth is listed as November 8, 1924, but he only chuckled whenever reporters asked him if that was accurate. "I've lied about my age so often," he would say, "I'm not even sure about it myself any more."

If Bower was indeed born in 1924, that would have made him thirty-four when he arrived in Toronto, and forty-five and eligible for the pension when he finally retired in early 1970. During his decade-plus with the Maple Leafs the old goalie carved a remarkable record. He was the oldest player in the game, performing at the game's most precarious position. "He's the greatest athlete in the world," Imlach once said, following one of Bower's birthday parties.

It all started for goaltending's Satchel Paige on the frozen ponds of Prince Albert, Saskatchewan, in Canada's prairie belt, where he was born sometime after the turn of the century. "I don't know too much about any other position," Bower once said. "I've been a goalkeeper since I was nine years old.

"In those days, I didn't have any skates, so when all the kids went out on the pond back home after school, I used to go along and stand in the goal. My pads were my school books. Later on, an older boy made me some pads out of an old mattress and my father carved me a goal stick out of a spruce tree. Those sure were solid sticks—solid, one piece. No splice."

There were other innovations for an aspiring goalie who couldn't afford the regular equipment, but who possessed a good imagination. For a stick glove, a heavy chunk of cardboard was sewn on the back of a wool mitten. The catching glove was just an old work glove padded at the palm with a pair of heavy socks.

Bower's first skates were a gift from a local hockey player named Don Deacon, who performed for the senior team, the Prince Albert Mintos. Johnny was a rink rat who carried Deacon's skates to earn his way into the arena for games. One night, the little goalie inherited a worn-out pair of skates from Deacon. They didn't fit, but that hardly mattered. "I worshipped those skates," said Bower, "even if I couldn't get used to them."

Johnny learned his hockey the hard way, skating in temperatures that often dived below zero. "We'd skate for miles," he said. "We'd skate and skate. Then our faces would get so cold we'd have to skate home backwards to keep from freezing." It wasn't easy, but then few things were during the Depression years of the 1930s when Bower grew up.

When war clouds gathered in Europe in 1939, Bower enlisted in the Canadian Army. "What war was that?" ex-teammate Frank Mahovlich often asked Bower. "The Boer or First World?"

Punch Imlach remembered Bower telling him how he'd enlisted in the Queen's Own Cameron Highlanders. "So, you were born in 1924, eh?" needled the coach.

"Yes, sir," replied the goalie.

"But you also say that you joined the Canadian army in 1939," Imlach continued.

"Right," replied Bower.

"Then that means you were only fifteen, just a wet-nosed kid when you were allowed to enlist. I knew the army was stupid, but not that stupid."

It was at his enlistment, claims Bower, that the confusion

about his age started. At fifteen, he could never get into the army: So he just added a couple of years onto his age to satisfy the recruiting sergeant. Then, in later years, when he tried deducting those years, he found it a lot tougher than it had been to add them.

To add to the mix-up, Bower, who was orphaned at an early age, went under the name of Kiszkan for a while, adopting the name of the family that brought him up in Prince Albert. His age and his name may have been a source of confusion, but one thing was clear: young Mr. Bower was one fine goaltender. After his military hitch was up, he played junior hockey in Prince Albert and then was invited by Jim Hendy to try out for the Cleveland Barons of the American Hockey League. It was a big jump, but Johnny made it, turning pro with the Barons in 1945 when he either was or was not twenty one years old.

For the next four years, Bower had plenty of goaltending competition in Cleveland. He shared the job first with Harvey Teno, then with Roger Bessette, and finally with Al Rollins. "When Kansas City folded up, Cleveland brought in Rollins," said Bower. "He only played three games when Toronto came looking for a goalkeeper. I thought I was ready and should have been picked, but Al was chosen and he finished the season in Pittsburgh. The next year he was with the Leafs."

Finally, in 1949–50, Bower inherited the full-time net-minding job for the Barons. He led the league in shutouts that season with five and two years later he produced the top goaltending average in the AHL, a sharp 2.43. The next season, he again was the shutout leader with six and in the playoffs he added four more in eleven games with a 1.91 goals-against average.

Bower became a Cleveland fixture. But, like any other standout minor leaguer in those days, he was available for the right price. And it was the New York Rangers who came up with that price. When goalie Charley Rayner neared the end of his career, New York searched for a replacement. The best goalie available, they soon determined, was Bower. But Hendy's asking price always seemed too high.

When New York came up with stumpy Gump Worsley in 1952 and the little guy won the Calder Trophy as the NHL's Rookie of the Year, the Rangers' need for Bower was reduced. So was Hendy's asking price. The following summer, the long-simmering deal was finally completed. New York shipped journeyman goalie Emile Francis, forward Neil Strain, and cash to Hendy for Bower, the AHL's all-star goalie. Why did New York still covet Bower with Worsley on hand? Mostly for insurance. The next season they cashed in on the policy.

At the Ranger training camp, nobody told Bower he wasn't supposed to be New York's regular goalie. So that's exactly what he turned out to be. In a head-to-head competition with Worsley, John showed utter disdain for the Gump's rookie honors and simply went out and beat the Ranger regular right out of the first-string job. When the season opened, Worsley was on his way back to the Western League and Bower was the New York goalie. Bower hardly believed that after eight long minor-league seasons, he was finally getting that one big-league shot players always hope for.

"I guess I began to wonder several times if I'd ever get a chance," he said. "I was sure I was good enough and my record was all right. But every year I was back in Cleveland. I liked Cleveland and they treated me fine there. But there's nothing like the big time. I got my chance though before I grew any gray hairs. There are lots of years left, and I'm going to work hard. I've never been so happy as I am right here in New York."

The Rangers too, it seemed, were happy with Bower. "He's wonderful," exulted General Manager-Coach Frank Boucher. "If there's one thing wrong with this team, it isn't the goaltending. With all that minor league experience behind him, Bower is no nervous, fidgety rookie. He's cool and poised. He's smart and he's an awfully hard worker. He waits to make his move. Only the smart ones fool him, and not too often. The first thing I noticed about him was his sense of anticipation. You can see him getting set when the play develops on center ice. He's always ready for what comes."

Bower played all seventy Ranger games that season and his 2.60 goals-against average was considerably better than the 3.06 which had earned Worsley rookie honors the season before. But a front-office shuffle developed in New York. Muzz Patrick replaced Boucher behind the bench and eventually moved up to the front-office GM's desk when Phil

Watson took over as coach. Somewhere along the line, Bower's stock sunk. And the next fall in training camp, Worsley was back from an MVP season in the Western League and the Gump turned the tables on Bower, winning back the goaltending job he had lost the season before. Bower was dispatched to Vancouver to replace Worsley.

Bower had played solidly in New York's nets in his one full season as a Ranger. The season also had some comical moments, too. There was, for example, the night the Rangers protected a slim one-goal lead against Boston late in the game. The Bruins yanked their goalie for an extra attacker and swarmed into Bower's zone.

As Boston's attack formed up, Bower girded for a slap shot from the point. Just as the Bruin player fired, a Ranger defender cut in front of the goalie, blocking his sight of the shot. Bower, effectively screened, took a chance, thrusting his gloved hand out blindly. Somehow, the puck found its way into John's mitt. Save!

On the ensuing faceoff, the puck came to New York defenseman Harry Howell, whose only job was to get the rubber out of the Ranger zone. Howell whacked the puck off the boards and it skidded out of danger, caroming erratically toward center ice. Suddenly, the disc headed down the center of the ice, rolling straight for the vacant Boston net. The crowd howled as Howell's 180-foot carom shot rolled into the net for the insurance goal the Rangers needed.

All of the New York players thrust their sticks sky-high to salute the goal. One did not. That was goalie Bower. Instead of thrusting his stick, he threw it. The law of gravity brought the big wood hurtling back down shortly and landed squarely on Bower's forehead, inflicting a sizable gash. "It was worth it," exclaimed Bower later, "but I don't think I'll ever try it again."

When he went to the Western League in 1954, Bower did an instant replay of Worsley's super 1953 season. Gump had been named the league's best goalie and Bower earned the same honor. Johnny's 2.71 average included seven shutouts and rated the invitation to compete with Worsley in the Ranger camp the following fall.

Again, Bower played strongly in training camp and held his own in the battle for the goaltending job with Worsley. Watson, the new Ranger coach, couldn't decide which goalie he'd keep even though GM Muzz Patrick pressed him for a verdict. Then one night the Rangers played an exhibition game in Providence and afterward, Patrick told Watson, "Worsley is your goalie."

"What gives?" asked Watson. "I'd practically decided on Bower."

"Bower stays in Providence," replied Patrick. "And don't ask why, Phil. There's politics in everything."

Patrick apparently meant that a deal had been arranged with Providence to provide the AHL club with Bower in exchange for some future players and/or favors. And what of Bower's NHL aspirations? Well, we're sorry about that, John. That's the way it goes.

Bower shuffled off to Providence, convinced that Watson had delivered the kiss of death to his hopes of becoming an NHL goalie. He stayed with the Reds for two seasons and was the AHL's Most Valuable Player in each of those seasons. He played so well that his coach, Jack Crawford, climbed right out on a limb, proclaiming, "Johnny Bower is the best goalie in all professional hockey. Look at his record. He has come up with sensational games time and again. Everyone in the American Hockey League is raving about him. Bower is a big-league goaltender right now. I have always considered him a major leaguer and because of the amazing way in which he is playing now, I would take Johnny over any goalie in the National Hockey League."

The Rangers decided to take Bower all right—away from Providence and back to Cleveland. New York swapped the goalie for Ed McQueen in 1957 and, reunited with the Barons, Bower flourished. He turned in eight shutouts and a league leading 2.19 goals-against average. At the age of thirty-three—or thereabouts—Bower was resigned to settling down and finishing his career with Cleveland. "It was like coming home and I was satisfied to stay there," said Bower. "I was sick of jumping around the country and I wanted to settle down with my family. Cleveland was going to be my home."

At just about that time, Toronto became convinced that its goalie, Ed Chadwick, needed help. Coach Billy Reay searched for another net-minder. His first stop was Calgary, Alberta, where Al Rollins, a former Leaf, was working. Reay looked in on Rollins at a WHL playoff game against

Vancouver and saw him blitzed for a half-dozen or so goals. That performance turned Billy around and he beat a direct path to Cleveland's old-man Bower. "He's two years older than Rollins," admitted Reay, "but he's got to be better than Rollins looked."

So the Maple Leafs packaged some fifteen thousand dollars to Cleveland in exchange for Bower. There was one problem, though. The goalie wasn't exactly anxious to leave town. "I honestly didn't want to go," he said. "I was happy in Cleveland and I wanted to stay there." Old friend Jim Hendy convinced Bower to try Toronto. It was good advice. Bower, however, admitted that he was bewildered at being plucked out of the minors at the age of thirty-three.

"When the Leafs brought me from Cleveland, I thought they were crazy," said the goalie. "Goaltenders my age didn't get a second chance in the NHL." If the Leafs wanted him, Bower decided, he would make them prove it. He asked for a two-year contract. Toronto wasn't thrilled with the idea, but President Stafford Smythe agreed. "When I took Bower from Cleveland," said Smythe, "I figured it would be a one-year deal." The Leafs' boss couldn't have been more wrong.

Goalies have long memories and when it became apparent that Bower was going to stick with the Leafs, the goalie took a run at his old friend in New York, Phil Watson.

"Watson didn't give me a fair chance to stay in the NHL," said Bower. "He got on me three years ago in training camp. And his big gripe is why I look behind me when a goal is scored. Where else should I look?"

Watson didn't take the blast sitting down. "He's full of baloney," responded the Ranger boss. "I thought Gump Worsley was a better goalie three years ago and I still think so now. What I did tell him [Bower] was to look in front of him when there was a scramble in front of the net. He automatically looked behind him and took his eye off the play. Actually, age was the determining factor in sending Johnny down to the minors. Worsley was four years younger and we were starting to rebuild."

Except for his conflict with Watson, Bower remained Toronto's good-humor man, loose and carefree rather than uptight about his job like some goalies. "I think everybody realizes that old John is completely grateful for getting a shot in the

NHL long after he'd given up hope," said teammate Dick Duff. "He's a thoroughly humble guy who believes he's lucky. You can't help but like him."

The Leafs also liked to play practical jokes on their elderly goalie. A lifetime of goaltending had left Bower with exactly one natural tooth. Like all hockey players, he left his dental plates in a paper cup in the locker room when he went out on the ice. During one practice at Maple Leaf Gardens, a fun-loving soul exchanged Bower's choppers for another set of falsies. When the goalie galumphed in from the work-out, the whole team was aware of the gag and watching Bower.

Bob Pulford tells what happened: "He came in, picked up the teeth, held them just right, opened his mouth, and popped them in. Well, you know how it is usually—a couple of twists and turns of the tongue, lips, and jaws and they're in place. You should have seen him this time. At first, his face was working just normally, and then this puzzled look came. He kept right on working his jaws harder and harder, looking more puzzled all the time.

"We'd all been pretending to dress, watching him. Finally, we couldn't help laughing. When we told him what we'd done, he bounced them right out on the floor."

In his first year with the Maple Leafs, Bower drew George Armstrong as his roommate. Army was part-Indian and Bower an addict of television Westerns—not the very best combination. Once Armstrong pointed to a particular redskin on the tube and said, "See that guy, he's my cousin." Bower didn't know quite how to take that piece of intelligence. So he just let it drop. Often, just as the cavalry was ready to turn the tables on the TV Indians, Armstrong pulled Bower away from the set. "He'll never let me watch the Indians get killed," said Bower. "I never get to see the end of any of them."

On the ice, Bower often resembled the wagonmaster standing off the attack of rampaging redskins. A mistake on defense often put him in a hole, but Bower rarely complained. "Nobody makes a mistake deliberately," he said. "It's high speed out there. One goof can set up a series of them. Me? I'm paid to make the stops. The boys expect them."

Once, during a Stanley Cup series against Detroit, a Leaf defender failed to stop Gordie Howe, with whom it is a very bad idea to make mistakes. Howe steamed in on Bower and had the Leaf goalie at his mercy. Hockey's all-time scoring king waited for Bower to make the first move, but it never came. Finally Gordie fired and the puck banged off Bower's suddenly upthrust stick and deflected over the net and into the crowd behind Toronto's goal.

"I just got lucky," said Bower, describing the big save. "I threw up my stick in a sort of reflex action, I guess. The puck hit the stick right above my glove. Pure luck. I got it and more like it, so we won. But I think I've lost a fishing partner."

"Who's that?" he was asked.

"Howe," replied Bower. "Right after that save, he came up to me and said, 'Wait till next summer. I'm going to throw you out of the boat.' I've got a feeling he might do it too. I'm afraid I'll skip fishing with him if he suggests it this summer. Lake Waskesiu is deep and darned cold. And you know how strong Gordie is."

Shortly after the Leafs acquired Bower, Punch Imlach arrived, wearing both the general manager's and coach's hats. The two men hit it off immediately. Many Leaf players complained about Imlach's gruelling practices, but not Bower. "I think his coaching methods have added at least six years to my NHL career," the goalie said.

"Punch believes that hard work leads to success and I agree 110 percent," Bower continued. "There's no easy road to success. You have to give it that little extra and strain yourself until it hurts. If I had returned to the NHL at thirty-three under an easy coach, I'm sure I'd be a fat, complacent forty-one-year-old sitting on the sidelines just watching instead of playing."

In 1960–61, Bower had the best defensive record in the NHL, winning the Vezina Trophy. The next three years, Imlach piloted the Leafs to the Stanley Cup with Bower carrying a huge part of the load. Then, in 1964–65, he had his name inscribed on the Vezina Trophy for a second time, sharing the honor with Terry Sawchuk, with whom he divided the Toronto goaltending chores that season.

As he got older, Bower got better and maybe that's because he also got smarter. "When I was younger," he said, "I used to run around the goal a lot, knocking myself out for no good reason. Now I stay in one spot and play the angles. I may be a little slower, but I make up for it by using my head."

His teammates marveled at Bower's resiliency. "Bower wins games for us," said George Armstrong, his playful roomie. "By that I mean he makes the key stops when we're in trouble. He might give up four, but when it's touch and go he'll stop the other team cold and pull us through a bad time until we get going again. There have been countless times when we've started badly and Bower has held the other guys out until we get warmed up. He's a clutch goalie and there's just no way of telling how much this team owes him, how much money he's put in all our pockets."

Once, during the playoffs, Bower had to be particularly sharp to hold off the young New York Rangers. Eventually, the Leafs won the game, but it was Bower's show. As the goalie waddled off the ice, Rudy Pilous, a longtime NHL coach, called to him. "God, but you made it look easy," said Pilous.

Bower, his happy-go-lucky nature somewhat eroded by forty or so Ranger shots, scowled at Pilous. "You think it's easy?" John snapped.

"Sure," wisecracked Pilous, "you're playing from memory."

Bower turned, hands on hips to face the bushy-browed kibbitzer. "Two more minutes out there," said the goalie, "and both me and my memory would have collapsed."

Each year, when the club reported to training camp, Toronto's players, like all others in NHL hockey, underwent physical examinations. In 1964, when Bower was forty by his own scorecard and a few years more than that by the reckoning of others, Dr. J. P. McKenna conducted the training camp checkup. When he got to the goalie, he was stunned.

"If you didn't know something of this controversy about his age," said the doctor, "you could guess it was 25—assessing him physically. I have never seen a man of his reported years in such wonderful condition. I don't know what he does to stay in shape. Definitely, he is doing something."

Asked about special exercises he might be using to retain his youth, Bower laughed. "When you play goal in this league," he said, "you get enough exercise."

Bower admitted that as the years rolled by, he found this

grueling game a strain on his body. "It's tougher for me to get in shape, tougher to recuperate after a hard game. But, heck, I take a cold shower and start looking forward to the next game. Hockey is a demanding game, but I enjoy it. As long as I get a kick out of playing, I'll be around, unless they lock me out of the rink."

It was no surprise that Bower's eyes were the keys to his success. "My eyes are my most valuable possession," he said. "When they go, I'm gone." He often chomped carrots because of their reputed aid to vision. The formula must have worked because Bower just rolled along.

But even Ponce de Leon found that the Fountain of Youth wasn't bottomless. There is a limit for all men and Bower reached that limit in 1969. Imlach had left the Leafs and younger goalies were coming along. It became obvious after a while that Bower could stick with the club as long as he wanted to, but as a fifth wheel. That's when Jim Gregory, Toronto's new general manager, suggested a combination scouting and goalie coaching job for John. "Only," said Bower, "if I can still work out with the boys."

When Bower announced his retirement from hockey during the 1969–70 season, Lefty Reid, curator of the Hockey Hall of Fame, asked if he could have the goalie's skates for a display in the shrine. "Sure," said Bower. "But just one pair. I'll need the other pair for practice."

Bower's official retirement came on March 19, 1970—four months after his forty-fifth birthday, according to the record book. The goalie was asked if, in light of his retirement, he might at last want to come clean about his age. "C'mon John, how old, really?"

"If you don't know by now," responded Bower, smiling, "you never will."

The Canadiens' Bill Durnan,
who could catch the puck
with either hand
and handle a stick
both ways, shakes
right-handed with
Maple Leaf Turk Broda.

15
BILL DURNAN:
THE AMBIDEXTROUS GOALIE

Imagine you are a hockey player, a forward, and your team needs a goal. Suddenly, you find yourself with the puck on your stick. Instinctively, you dig your skates into the ice, pivot, and start out of your end. Your blades carry you over your own blue line to center ice. You look up for a quick glance at the enemy net to size up the other goalie. He starts to glide out of his crease to meet your charge. You mentally note his position as you hit the enemy blue line. Now you shift your weight and swing your body to the left to avoid a defenseman. You're past him and in the clear.

You zoom toward the net, picking up momentum. Now you have your chance. You draw back you stick about to unload your shot. At the last moment you look up again at the goalie to direct your shot. You blink when you realize that the guy in the nets, who was holding his big stick in his right hand when you looked at him the first time, now has the stick in his other hand. It occurs to you to ask, "What the heck is going on here?" But by the time you've recovered your composure, the puck has been taken by the other team and your opportunity is gone.

Now it's perfectly reasonable for a hockey player to expect that a goalie who begins the game by holding the stick in his right hand and using his left to catch the puck will remain that way throughout the game. It is the least the opposing forward can expect. And just about every goalie who has ever strapped on a pair of pads has been conventional enough to keep his stick in the same hand throughout the game. One goalie didn't subscribe to that convention. He was Bill Durnan of the Montreal Canadiens.

Durnan was ambidextrous, handling the stick equally well in either hand. In fact, he had a specially constructed pair of gloves that were combination stick and catching mitts, enabling him to shift whenever the fancy struck him.

"It was a tremendous asset," said Durnan, who had a brief but dazzling career in the National Hockey League. "I owed that gift to Steve Faulkner, one of my coaches in a church league that I played in as a youngster. He insisted that I try to perfect it. If it hadn't been for Faulkner I might never have had the skill to even get into the NHL."

Faulkner came across Durnan when the goalie started playing bantam hockey in the east end of Toronto, where he grew up. "Steve showed me how to switch the stick from one hand to the other," said Durnan. "Frankly, at the age I was then, I wasn't sure it was a hockey stick I was moving from hand to hand because it felt more like a telephone pole. But Faulkner kept after me and, gradually, the stick seemed to get lighter and lighter. It finally became so easy that I was changing automatically from hand to hand and often didn't realize I was doing it."

In those days, Durnan was a combination athlete. He was a sensational young goaltender as well as one of the finest softball pitchers in Canada. In one bantam season with the Toronto Westmorelands, he played an entire schedule without ever allowing even a single goal. As a midget, he performed the same feat during a playoff series.

Ironically, Durnan almost never played ice hockey. He never had skates as a youngster and he never learned to skate. His first exposure to the ice came in a pair of borrowed skates, but his goaltending brilliance stood out, even in somebody else's blades. Because he was a native of Toronto, Durnan automatically became the property of the local NHL team, the Maple Leafs. But the Leafs weren't particularly interested in the big guy and he went north in 1933 to play for Max Silverman's Sudbury Wolves, a junior team in the Ontario Hockey Association.

A year later, he twisted his knee badly while wrestling with a friend on the beach; shortly after that he broke a leg playing softball. It began to seem that his hockey career was over. He got a job in the mines in Kirkland Lake, Ontario.

"That was during the dirty thirties and I did a lot of traveling because in those days everyone went where he could get a job. At that time," he added with a touch of irony in his voice, "there was a little unemployment in Canada."

For one full year, there was no hockey for Durnan and the Maple Leafs lost interest in him. It was one of the worst mistakes the Toronto hockey organization ever made.

"They dropped me when I was injured and I became extremely disenchanted with hockey," said Durnan. "Until that wrestling accident, I had been one of those zealous kids who just lived for an NHL career, but suddenly I wasn't especially concerned about playing hockey at all. I don't think I was particularly mercenary, but hockey didn't pay much then and I figured it was time I lined up some sort of permanent job."

At Kirkland Lake, Durnan hooked up with the Lake Shore Blue Devils, a senior hockey team. At first, his affiliation was purely as a hobby, but on the ice the goalie realized that his knee was sound again and that he could move just as well as ever. It took a while to shake off the rustiness of a year's inactivity, but soon Durnan was sharp again. And the Blue Devils were making overtures at the Allan Cup, symbol of senior amateur-hockey supremacy in Canada. The Blue Devils zipped through the Allan Cup Tournament in 1940, defeating the Calgary Stampeders for the championship. Along the way, Kirkland Lake had eliminated the Montreal Royals, the farm club of the NHL Canadiens and favorites in the Allan Cup struggle. Among the interested observers at the Royals-Blue Devils clash was Tommy Gorman, general manager of the Canadiens. He was impressed by the Kirkland Lake team and, most of all, by their big, ambidextrous goaltender.

Gorman remembered his first impression of Durnan. "He was big and hefty, but nimble as a cat and a great holler guy," the Canadiens' executive said. Montreal approached Durnan. They wanted him for the Royals. They would guarantee a job in Montreal if he agreed. Durnan thought it over and said yes.

For the next two years, Durnan worked in the office of a steel company in Montreal and tended goal for the Royals in the Quebec Senior League. Then, in 1943, Paul Bibeault, the Canadiens' goalie, went into the service, opening up the net-minding job with the NHL team. The Montreal front office simply assumed that Durnan would move right into the job. They forgot, however, to consult Durnan about that.

Bill was invited to Montreal's training camp at St. Hyacinthe, Quebec, and played well enough to convince Coach Dick Irvin that he could replace Bibeault with no trouble. But there was plenty of trouble when Gorman approached Durnan and tried to get his signature on a Montreal contract. The goalie was less than enthusiastic about turning professional at the age of twenty-nine. He told Gorman to forget it.

"I've got a good job in a war plant and I kind of like playing for the Royals," Durnan told Gorman. "Besides, I'm a little too old to be starting in the National Hockey League."

Durnan's refusal to sign stunned Gorman. But he didn't give up. He kept after the goalie throughout the training camp, helped by Durnan's steel-company boss, who just happened also to be a director of the hockey team.

Training camp closed and the Canadiens headed for Montreal, where they would open the season against the Boston Bruins. There was one small problem. The ambidextrous goalie they counted on still hadn't signed a contract—with either hand. An hour before the puck dropped, starting the 1943–44 season, Durnan had a date with Gorman.

For fifty minutes they haggled. "He was hesitant, very hesitant," said Gorman. "I don't know what turned the tide. But Durnan finally put his name on the dotted line just ten minutes before game time. Bill hadn't even put the pen down when I informed him that he was going into the nets that very night, and I pointed at the clock."

Durnan nodded and raced across the Forum to the Canadiens' dressing room. Irvin waited for him at the door. "Am I playing?" asked Durnan. "If you want to," answered the coach. "You bet I do," said the goalie.

Suddenly, all the boyish enthusiasm Durnan had once felt for playing in the NHL resurfaced. Signing that first professional contract for the sum of $4,133 had transformed him from a factory worker who played hockey as a pastime into a pro being paid to do what many men do for fun.

Hurriedly, Durnan donned the Canadiens' uniform and

rushed out to the Forum ice. The greeting was less than enthusiastic from the Quebecois. After all, here was an En-
glish-Canadian replacing Frenchman Paul Bibeault in the
heart of French Canada. But Durnan solved that problem
with some of the most spectacular goaltending the home
fans ever witnessed.

The Bruins didn't make Bill's debut easy. For one thing,
a brand-new rule worked in their favor. The NHL introduced the center red line in 1943–44, an innovation of New
York's Frank Boucher. Boucher contended that the regulation requiring teams to stickhandle out of their own zones
was simply too restrictive. "Why not allow teams to pass
their way out of trouble?" reasoned Boucher. "Use a center
red line to divide the ice. It would open the dam and re-
store end-to-end play." With the red line, teams could pass
the puck halfway up the ice without penalty. The new rule
speeded up the game considerably and created more scoring
chances for the offense and more work for goaltenders like
Durnan.

Against the Bruins, Durnan was tested early. Herbie Cain,
who was to win the NHL scoring championship that year,
took a pass from Dit Clapper at the center red line and
raced into Montreal's end. From about forty feet, he fired
at the rookie goalie. Durnan blocked the shot with his left
pad, but went down. The rebound bounced to Cain, whose
momentum had carried him to the goalie's doorstep. Again,
the Bruin forward fired. Durnan was down and out of position. It looked like a sure goal. But the net-minder threw
out his catching glove in a desperate try. Like a magnet, the
puck hit the mitt and stuck there.

That was how it went throughout the opening game. The
Bruins shot; Durnan saved. When it was over, the score was
2–2, a tie earned mostly on the merits of a goaltender who
hadn't even signed his contract when the warmups started.

Durnan's debut was a preview of what lay ahead for the
Montreal goaltender. He beat New York 2–1 in his next
start and just kept going from there. Until he came along,
most goalies were short men who darted and dived to keep
the puck out of the net. Durnan was a big man, over six
feet tall and weighing more than two hundred pounds. He
was a stand-up goalie, the first hockey had seen. He rarely
left his feet to make a save. And he believed that his size

was an asset in doing his difficult job.

"I think I fooled the opposition," he said. "I used to go into a crouch with only my head over the crossbar, so a lot of players assumed I was fairly short. If I turned my feet sideways they, combined with my bulk and height, used to block a large portion of my net. Then, of course, I also had a pretty big stick."

In Durnan's rookie season, Irvin's Canadiens lost only five of the fifty games they played. Their large goaltender surrendered only 109 goals and earned the Vezina Trophy for posting the best defensive record in the NHL. The Vezina was named for the legendary Canadien goaltender of the team's early years and no Montreal goalie had captured the award in thirteen seasons before Durnan ended the dry spell.

Still, Durnan had his detractors. It was, after all, wartime and many NHL stars served in the armed forces. Some observers argued that the competition had been watered down and that the dilution was responsible for Durnan's success as well as that of his teammate, Maurice Richard, who scored fifty goals in Durnan's second season in the Canadiens' nets. While the Rocket blazed his way into the NHL record book, the bulky goaltender captured his second consecutive Vezina Trophy with a 2.42 goals-against average.

One of those who believed Durnan was the real thing was Detroit boss Jack Adams. "Don't hand me that stuff about a weak league making Durnan a star," snapped Adams when he heard the argument. "He's a terrific goalie. He would have been a star before the war and he'll be a star after the war. Just watch."

Adams, as usual, was right about the Canadiens' netminder. Durnan proved it the next year when the war ended and the big names drifted back from the service and into the NHL. He captured the Vezina Trophy for the third consecutive season and dazzled the returning players with his lightning fast hands.

"Some of my NHL rivals were unaware that I was ambidextrous until it was pointed out to them," remarked Durnan, laughing. "I was credited with being fast and I believe that particular trait gave the illusion of speed, for the simple reason that I didn't have to jump around quite as much as some of the other goalies. I had catching hands; they were large and quick, which was an added asset."

Durnan brought an interesting philosophy to his job. He considered every player with the puck as an equally dangerous scoring threat. "Once a goalie starts typing players, he runs the risk of getting fooled over and over again," he said. "I believe there are only four basic ways to score a goal, and I felt that anyone who was in the NHL was capable of making such a play. Consequently, every man who had the puck was my enemy and I still contend that all goaltenders should fear every opponent who gets in front of him."

In 1946–47, Durnan captured the Vezina Trophy for an unprecedented fourth consecutive year, posting a 2.30 goals-against average and also earned, for the fourth straight year, first-team All-Star honors as well. The NHL schedule was increased from fifty to sixty games that season and Durnan wondered whether teams were wise to carry only one goalie. Perhaps, he said, two men sharing the job would be a better idea. He thus became the first man to suggest the two-goalie system. Some fifteen years later, most teams adopted Durnan's idea to ease the pressure on the goalie.

Durnan always was a cool, rarely flustered customer on the ice. But inside his nerves were as taut as those of any man who ever put on a pair of pads.

In 1947, after four straight first-place finishes, the Canadiens suddenly flopped. The blame was put, naturally, at the door of the goaltender. Durnan, who had been a first-string All-Star and winner of the Vezina Trophy in each of his four years in the league, suddenly was a patsy as far as the fans were concerned.

"We want Bibeault . . . we want Bibeault," the Forum fans chanted at Durnan. And after being blitzed badly by Detroit one night, Durnan decided they were right. He went to General Manager Frank Selke. "You'd better get Bibeault," the goalie said. "It looks as though I'm about through."

"Nonsense," said Selke. "You're still a good goalie. Forget the fans."

But Durnan couldn't forget. His average ballooned to 2.74 goals-against and the Canadiens sagged to fifth place. The criticism knawed at him and the next season he pledged to prove to the fickle fans just how good a goalie he still was. He played every game that season, allowing a mere 2.10

goals per game, and reclaimed the Vezina Trophy. Ten of his performances were shutouts, including four in a row during a streak of 309 minutes, 21 seconds of scoreless goaltending. It was the longest siege of shutout goaltending in modern NHL history.

The shutout streak came to an end against the Chicago Black Hawks when Gaye Stewart jammed a shot through his pads for a goal. The memory of that goal had faded with time when Durnan was asked about it.

"I can't say I remember that Stewart goal as if it was only yesterday," he said. "But as near as I can reconstruct the scene, he came barreling in off left wing. I went out to cut down the angle, we collided, and he managed to stuff the puck through my legs. He earned the goal."

Durnan insisted that the streak did not bother him. "I can't recall that I was eaten up by pressure," he said. "I think it was tougher on my wife Mandy, sitting in on the games at home and listening to the radio on our road games."

Still, the pressure of going into the nets night after night with no relief began to erode the Montreal goalie. A basically placid man, he found himself growing short-tempered. "It got so bad that I couldn't sleep on the night before a game or on the night afterwards either," Durnan said. "Nothing is worth that kind of agony."

Before the 1949–50 season, Durnan went to Dick Irvin and told the Canadiens' coach that he would retire following that season. "I came into the league late, just before my twenty-ninth birthday and, at thirty-five with only three years of high-school education, I felt I had to start a new career in order to take care of my wife and family."

With the light at the end of the tunnel, Durnan turned in another first-rate season in the Canadiens' net, winning his sixth Vezina Trophy in seven years with a 2.20 goals-against average. But during the season, he was injured in a goal-mouth collision with Chicago's Jimmy Conacher and sidelined for six games.

"Conacher cut in front of our goal and I dropped in front of him," said Durnan. "It was a pet move of mine. I'd fall and get my arms up like a fighter warding off a blow. Nine times out of ten the puck carrier tripped over me, losing control of the puck. That was one time I failed to get my arms up. I think the toe of his boot did more damage than the skate."

Durnan refused to go to the hospital and insisted on ac-
companying the Canadiens when they left town. "My head
really blew up on the train ride home," he said. "I thought
I was going to die when we passed through Toronto on the
way to Montreal. It wasn't a bad cut, just a lump that
looked like a badly shaped goose egg, but the pain was almost unbearable."

With Durnan hurt, the Canadiens called up Gerry Mac-
Neil to fill in for their goalie. MacNeil was sensational in
the six games he played, allowing just nine goals and posting
one shutout for a 1.50 goals-against average.

When Montreal went into the opening round of the playoffs against the New York Rangers, Durnan went back in
goal for the Canadiens. But he wasn't the same goalie. "I
was just bone-weary," he said. "Maybe I came back too
early. I don't know for sure."

What Durnan did know was that the Rangers blitzed him
for ten goals in three playoff games, "While we weren't
beaten badly in any of the games with the Rangers, I
thought that maybe I wasn't sharp enough. Call it lack of
confidence or weariness."

On the day of the fourth game, Durnan called Irvin. "I
told him that I thought Gerry MacNeil might give the club a
lift," said Durnan. Irvin took his goalie's advice and started
MacNeil. The series lasted just two more games before the
Canadiens were eliminated and Bill Durnan never played
another game in goal for Montreal.

After retiring, Durnan coached some junior hockey and
piloted a team that defeated a touring Russian squad during
the late 1950s. In 1964, he was elected to the hockey Hall
of Fame and called the honor "the ultimate glory for almost
any hockey player."

A few years later, Durnan was asked if he was glad that
his career had ended before the advent of the curved stick
and slap shot that menaces modern goalies. He laughed.

"For the money they pay now," the old goalie said, "I
wouldn't care if they used a gun."

They might have had more success using one against him.
In seven seasons, he turned in thirty-four shutouts and a
2.35 goals-against average. His playoff average was an even
more impressive 2.20. When he died in 1972, he was ac-
claimed as the finest goaltender of his era.

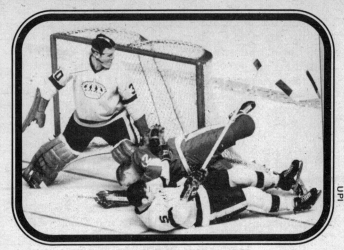

UPI

As a Los Angeles King in 1969,
Gerry Desjardins is an
interested bystander
while teammate Brent Hughes
and Detroit's Bruce MacGregor
go at it.

16
GERRY DESJARDINS:
OUT OF THE
MINES

The thermometer hugged zero and a cold wind swept across the frozen lake adjacent to one of Sudbury's (Ontario) many nickel mines. On the lake, a knot of kids did what kids all over Canada do during the winter—chose up sides for a hockey game. Most of the group had been picked by one side or the other when a chubby little guy standing on the fringe said he'd like to play, too.

It was a fine idea except for one small detail: Chubby was missing a piece of equipment. "I didn't have any skates," said Gerry Desjardins, who was about eight years old at the time. "So the kid organizing the game said I would have to be the goalkeeper."

Bundled up in rubber boots and multiple pairs of shirts, socks, mufflers, and pants, young Gerry waddled out to defend the goal. His young friends made sure he had enough work to keep him occupied. They threw about thirty shots his way that first day.

"The rule was that the players couldn't shoot high on me," said Desjardins, "so I just started rolling and falling in front of the net. Somehow, I stopped most of the pucks."

He wasn't exactly agile. "We wore so much clothing we could hardly move," he said. The forwards and defensemen kept warm by skating up and down the ice. But the goalie remained in one place, making it more difficult to stay warm—another reason young Gerry didn't have much competition for the net-minding job.

Still, there was something about tending goal that captivated Gerry. There is a fascination with their jobs that seems to entrance net-minders and hold them to a task that most other players view with distaste. Desjardins had been bitten. By the end of that first winter, Gerry had skates and pads and was in the nets for keeps.

Gerry moved through Sudbury's network of youth hockey programs, playing all the hockey he could fit into each day. "I loved the game," he said. "I could never play enough. I was young. I didn't know what it was to be tired. I had nothing else I wanted to do." One year, he backstopped Sudbury's team to the All-Ontario midget championship—the equivalent of a little-league regional title. "It was my first championship team," said Desjardins, "and also the first team I ever traveled with. I guess I'll always remember those experiences."

Desjardins's team finished third during the regular season and Gerry had a chance to play regularly when the team's other goalie developed an infected finger. With Desjardins sparking them, the Sudbury kids moved to the provincial finals. "It was very exciting," said Gerry, "sort of like being in a World Series. No matter how long you play or how well you do, I don't think you can ever forget that first big one. That tournament was the turning point of my life. It turned out to be my first big success and the first time people took real notice of me."

Among the people who noticed the young goalie were the National Hockey League's Detroit Red Wings. Desjardins was invited to play for their Sudbury affiliate the next season. Gerry jumped at the chance and even though he was only a spare it was a step up the hockey ladder.

The following year, the Wings invited Gerry to try out for their Hamilton farm club in the prestigious Ontario Hockey Association, Canada's top junior-hockey league. It was a major step for Gerry and he was thrilled by the invitation. OHA graduates often step straight from junior hockey to the NHL, so one can understand how important the Hamilton trial was for the young goalie.

Desjardins played his heart out in the Hamilton camp, competing with perhaps a dozen other goalies. And it all but cut his heart out when Jimmy Skinner, the Red Wing scout who ran the camp, told him he hadn't made the team. "I wanted to make it so much, I couldn't believe it when they told me I'd failed," said Desjardins.

"We could see Gerry might be a good one," said Skinner, "but he wasn't quite ready."

"They called me into the office and told me all the spots were filled and I'd have to go home," said Desjardins. "There was one ray of hope, though. They said they hoped I would keep in touch with them and they said they thought I'd have a good chance another year." That wasn't enough for Gerry. "I just couldn't take it. I cried. I went back home, badly disappointed and let down."

Back home, Desjardins considered the possibility that his hockey career had run its course and that his future might be in the Sudbury mines, working next to his father, who had spent his life there. "I didn't know what my future was going to be," said Gerry, "but the mines are a tough way to go. I've never been down there, and I wouldn't ever want to go down there. Off and on, I thought about it, but just to hear Dad talk about it . . . well, I'd rather play hockey."

A couple of weeks after sending him home, Skinner and Hamilton called Gerry again. A spot had opened up and they asked if he'd be interested in trying for it. Desjardins jumped, his spirits rising again. And again, the Red Wings stuck a pin in his balloon, sending him back to Sudbury. But Desjardins wasn't ready to throw in the hockey towel for the mines. He tried out for a local team named the Garson Native Sons and made the club.

The team was sponsored by the Toronto Maple Leafs and after Gerry enjoyed a standout season, Bob Davidson, chief scout of the Leafs, invited him to try out for the Toronto Marlboros of the OHA. Visions of revenge danced in Desjardins's head. He would make the team and show the Hamilton Red Wings what a mistake they had made when they let him go. It all seemed perfect—except for another of those small details that kept popping up for Gerry. The Marlboros also released him.

Part of the problem was that Desjardins just hadn't played up to par during his tryout. The young goalie was jittery and it showed. "I didn't do badly, but I wasn't at my best," he said. The bottom just about fell out of Gerry's world when Coach Turk Broda, himself a great goalie, gave him the bad news. Desjardins took it glumly and got ready to go home to Sudbury and probably to the mines. But he figured that as long as he was in Toronto, he'd stick around for the Marlboros' OHA season opener. Broda had supplied some tickets and Gerry ambled over to Maple Leaf Gardens for the game.

Sitting in the stands, he must have decided that he just wasn't a very good goalie. After all, here was Toronto's number-one goalie absorbing an awful shellacking. And when Broda lifted that youngster and substituted the number-two man, he got thumped too. These were the guys who had beaten Desjardins out. If they were good enough to make the squad and he wasn't, what did that say about his goaltending ability?

After the game, Gerry visited the dressing room. Broda saw him and the thought occurred to the old goalie that this kid couldn't have been as bad as the two he had used in the nets that night. So the coach told Desjardins to stick around, that the team would take another look at him. Gerry tore up his ticket to Sudbury and, a week later, he was a member of the Toronto Marlboros.

Things started well for Gerry in Toronto. He played regularly for Broda and benefitted from being coached by a Hall of Fame goaltender—an asset most young goalies don't enjoy. But after a while, problems cropped up again for Desjardins, most of them located in his right leg and hip. Calcium deposits caused pain and the young goalie suffered silently, afraid that if he complained he would lose his job. Eventually, the pain became so intense that Gerry had to go for x-rays. The calcium was diagnosed and treated, but after only thirty games Gerry's season was over. He was sent home for the balance of the year to heal and to reflect on his performance. He had achieved a 3.27 goals-against average, which isn't so good, but he also had two shutouts, which isn't so bad.

It wasn't the first time that an injury had cut short a hockey season for Desjardins. A couple of years before, he had been pole vaulting in his high-school gym. The bar was set at eight and a half feet, but Gerry didn't make it. He tumbled backward, landing on his elbows so hard that the force of his fall cracked his left shoulder. The break had to be repaired with a pin and finished him for hockey that year.

Rest healed the shoulder and it did the same thing for the calcium problems in his hip and leg. Desjardins returned to

the Marlboros in 1963, ready for another OHA season. But
he had a surprise waiting for him—a surprise that stood
about six feet, four inches, and also wore pads and carried a big stick. Gary Smith had beaten him out of the
Marlie goaltending job. It was another disappointment in
what had become a depressing string of disappointments.

There was one difference this time. Instead of being
handed a ticket back to Sudbury again, Desjardins was given
a bit of encouragement. The Marlboros weren't quite ready
to give up on him completely. They felt he needed regular
work and that he could get it playing Junior B hockey at
London, Ontario. At the same time, Kitchener's Junior A
team suffered the goaltending shorts and requested the loan
of Desjardins from Toronto. It was up to Gerry and after
some soul searching and a long talk with Marlboro officials,
he decided to go to London and Junior B hockey. The deciding factor was Kitchener's ragged defense and last-place
standing which, Marlie officials convinced him, would hurt
Desjardins more than playing Junior A hockey would help
him.

Junior B hockey is a wide-open type of action where high-
scoring games are routine and pucks fly at goalies with dis-
tressing regularity. Desjardins responded well to the shooting gallery, leading the team to a second-place finish and
turning in a 3.87 goals-against average. That sounds high,
but it was good enough to earn Gerry an All-Star berth and
a ticket back to Toronto and Junior A hockey for the following season.

Gerry was twenty now and going into his final season of
junior hockey. He made it count. His steady goaltending
helped Toronto to a second-place finish and the Marlies
made it through two rounds of the OHA playoffs before
being eliminated. His shutout won the deciding game of the
first round against Toronto's traditional rivals, the Montreal
Junior Canadiens.

Watching that first round of playoffs with considerable
interest were a host of scouts, including Claude Ruel of the
Canadiens. The Montreal man was impressed by several
players, but perhaps most of all by the chunky goalie guarding Toronto's nets.

After the season, Desjardins worked in a hockey school
and contemplated the fall, when he figured he'd be starting

his professional career in the Toronto organization. He was right about the first part, but wrong about the second. The Maple Leafs had roster problems and had dropped Gerry from their protected list during the summer. He was technically a free agent, although the Leafs still had plans for him, assuming they could slip him through the summer without another team noticing. There was only one thing wrong with that plan. Claude Ruel noticed.

Desjardins was unaware of his free-agent status when Ruel called with an offer to sign him for the Montreal organization. Of course, the Canadiens aren't just another hockey team to French Canadians. They are something special, something to strive for. And here they were, trying to sign Desjardins, a French Canadian who'd get chills when one mentioned names like Rocket Richard, Jacques Plante, and Bernie Geoffrion. Gerry couldn't believe it. It seemed too good to be true. But he didn't jump at Ruel's offer, because he felt a certain obligation to the Toronto organization for whom he had been performing at the junior-hockey level for three years. He reported Ruel's contact to the Maple Leafs, adding, with a bit of imagination, that the Canadiens had offered him twelve thousand dollars to sign for two years.

The Leafs offered to match that figure. Now Gerry went back to Ruel and said Toronto had offered him twelve thousand for two years. The Canadiens countered with fourteen thousand. It took Desjardins almost no time to tell Ruel he had a deal.

Gerry showed up at a training camp chock-full of good goalies. Charlie Hodge and Gump Worsley were Montreal's holdovers; behind them stood a bunch of promising goalies including Rogatien Vachon, Ernie Wakely, and Les Binkley. Desjardins wasn't surprised or disappointed when he was shipped to Montreal's Central League farm club at Houston. He was enthusiastic when he got to the Texas town, but his enthusiasm soon dipped.

Carl Wetzel had the regular goaltender's job with the Apollos and Gerry stationed himself on the end of the bench, sitting and waiting. He spent most of the season doing just that. Only when Wetzel was called up to the Canadiens in an emergency did Desjardins get a chance to play. He worked in nineteen games, posting a disappointing 3.78

goals-against average. When he hurt his knee, he left the lineup and never got back in again. "I got pretty discouraged," he said. "That first season, I played so little. I couldn't keep in shape and my record was bad. I felt all I needed was a better chance."

He got the chance the following fall when the Canadiens again assigned him to the Houston club. Wetzel was gone and this time Gerry would be the first-string goalie. He played well throughout training camp and things looked promising as the regular season got underway. And they continued to do so—for fourteen games. Then the old injury jinx caught Gerry again. He went down for a save against St. Louis and felt pain flash in his right knee. He completed the game, but the next day his knee was badly swollen.

Desjardins spent the next three weeks having his knee treated by Houston's trainer, hoping that rest would speed his recovery. But it was no use. Finally, in mid December, x-rays revealed torn cartilage and surgery was ordered. "I was disgusted," said Desjardins.

With Gerry sidelined, his backup man, Rogatien Vachon, took over. Vachon played well and when the Canadiens began having goaltending problems, they called him up to the NHL. Desjardins was all but destroyed by the kick in the teeth he had been dealt. Here he had been the regular goalie, playing ahead of Vachon. Then the injury and backup goalie Vachon moved up to the NHL, while the number-one man, Desjardins, stayed stuck in Houston.

"I felt like I'd been cheated," said Gerry. "I felt it should have been me starring in a big-league pennant race. I felt it should have been me instead of him getting a chance in the majors. I had been playing ahead of him and felt I was better than he was."

If Vachon's lucky break hurt Desjardins's feelings, an incident with Omaha Coach Fred Shero just added to Gerry's despair. Rusty from his injury-enforced layoff, Desjardins played badly when he returned to action. After one performance, Shero was moved to term Gerry "the worst goaltender in pro hockey."

Shero, of course, had company in that harsh assessment of Desjardins. Gerry struggled through the remainder of the season, finishing with a bloated 3.61 goals-against average for thirty-six games. That summer, at the NHL expansion draft that added six new teams, the Canadiens made Gerry available but found no takers. "A lot of people didn't think I was going very far," said the goalie. "It didn't exactly make me feel like the hottest prospect in hockey."

The expansion draft did do one good thing for Desjardins. It distributed some of Montreal's excess goaltending talent around among the new teams. One of the Canadiens' net-minders drafted was veteran Les Binkley, who had been tending goal for Montreal's American League farm club at Cleveland. Desjardins set his sights on that job when he went to training camp. "I didn't want to go back to the Central League," said Gerry. "I wanted the opportunity to prove myself in a tougher circuit, which the American League sure was."

The Canadiens decided that perhaps the tougher challenge of the AHL competition was what Desjardins needed. So they sent him to the Cleveland club's training camp in Sherbrooke, Quebec. It turned out to be a major turning point in the young goalie's life. One day, several of the Barons' players were driving along when they stopped at a railroad crossing. The goalie struck up a conversation with the young lady driving the car next to his. Soon Michelle Parenteau and Gerry Desjardins became an item.

Desjardins hit it off immediately in Cleveland, getting considerable help and encouragement from the Barons' coach, veteran AHL star Fred Glover. For the first time since his days at Toronto under Turk Broda, Gerry received concentrated coaching and, although Glover was not a goalie, he had scored on enough of them to learn a few tricks of their trade. He worked long and hard with Gerry and soon Desjardins improved.

He opened the season with a shutout and continued to carry the Barons after that. He was an iron man in the nets, playing sixty-six games—eleven more than he had played in the previous two seasons combined at Houston. He posted a 3.45 average—deceptively high because the Barons' defense greatly resembled the one he had in front of him a few years earlier in Junior B hockey.

Desjardins was voted the AHL's Rookie of the Year and first-team All-Star. He was runnerup in the Most Valuable Player balloting, but perhaps the most important endorsement came from an opposing coach, old friend Fred Shero, who was then piloting Buffalo and was the one who, a year earlier, had termed Gerry "the worst goalie in pro hockey." Now Fred had a change of heart. "He's a changed man and a changed goalie," said Shero. "He's really improved. He's shown me something." Then Shero went out on the limb again, calling Gerry "the best goalie in the league."

Gerry gave Fred Glover all the credit for his improvement. "He gave me the confidence," said Gerry, "and without confidence a goaltender is nothing. Coming under him was the best thing that ever happened to me in pro hockey."

Two other very good things happened to Gerry Desjardins in the summer of 1968. The first was that he married Michelle Parenteau and the second was that the Los Angeles Kings traded a couple of amateur draft choices to Montreal to get him. "That may have been the biggest break of my life," said Desjardins, reflecting on the trade to the Kings. "I didn't think I'd ever crack the lineup of the Canadiens. Playing for Montreal was my childhood dream, but the public there demands too much of hockey players. It would have been tough playing there."

Gerry assumed the trade to the Kings meant a switch from Cleveland to Springfield for the 1968–69 season. The Kings' AHL farm club seemed to be the most he could anticipate. After all, Los Angeles had finished just one point away from the West Division pennant the previous season with Wayne Rutledge and Terry Sawchuk in goal and there was no reason to expect them to break up that duo. But the Kings had other ideas. Sawchuk was pushing forty and when Desjardins played well in training camp, LA traded Sawchuk. Gerry had made it to the NHL. He shared the Kings' job with Rutledge.

"That's what hockey is all about," said Gerry. "Some guy's loss is somebody else's gain. I was very fortunate. I was just happy for the chance to play. I knew I wasn't supposed to make the team, but no one told me I couldn't."

Desjardins figured he would sit most of the time while Rutledge played the majority of the games. Again he was wrong. Coach Red Kelly wanted both his goalies sharp and so he divided the work load. Early in November, it was Gerry's turn in the nets when the New York Rangers invaded Los Angeles' fabulous Forum.

It was only his fourth NHL start, but Desjardins played

like a veteran. The high-powered Rangers buzzed him almost continuously and over and over Gerry blunted their attacks. Finally the Kings got him a goal and then another, and LA was sitting pretty with Desjardins hanging on tenaciously to his shutout. Finally, in one sudden change of direction by the puck, it seemed that Gerry's luck had finally run out.

Veteran Ron Stewart had sneaked behind the Los Angeles defense and a teammate hit him with a pass that caught the old pro in full stride. It was one-on-one, me-against-you, hockey's moment of truth.

"I braced to meet his breakaway," said Desjardins. "He came at me off his wing, and I moved out a little to cut down his angle, then backed down slowly, watching him, waiting for him to make the first move." Stewart had plenty of moves to choose from and he'd made all of them at one time or another over his long NHL career. But the rookie goalie wasn't buying any of them. "I refused to commit myself," said Desjardins. "He shot low and hard and I kicked at it and felt it smack off my skates and skid to one side." Save!

It went like that the rest of the night. "I felt good out there, like there was no way they were going to get the puck past me," said Desjardins. "It's a funny feeling, like you're ten feet tall and as strong as a man can be. Whatever they shot, I got."

The Rangers had not been shut out in sixty games, but they were shut out in this one. "It was the best game I've ever played anywhere," said Desjardins. "Everything just went right for me. You have games like that sometimes." Gerry came right back and had another one just like it a few nights later, beating Toronto 3–1. Now he was the toast of LA.

Desjardins was hot and Coach Kelly couldn't resist the urge to stay with him. When Rutledge pulled a groin muscle, Gerry's job became permanent. Rutledge dressed for games, but he could not play. Desjardins was it and knew it. Gerry played seventeen consecutive games before Rutledge had the green light to play again. His return lasted just thirty-one minutes before he was hurt again and back into the box went Desjardins, completing that game and playing in nine more in a row. He had another streak of thirty consecutive games and one of fifteen straight as well. He was cool about the work load.

"That's the way it happened, that's all," he said. "That's what I get paid to do—play hockey." Kelly was more enthusiastic. "He's been just great," the coach said. "He's done everything we've asked—and more—because he knew he had to do so much of it alone."

Desjardins saw plenty of pucks in that first season with Los Angeles, but the year wasn't just a rain of rubber. It had some smiles too. There was, for example, the time he showed up at practice with a terrible toothache. He told trainer Norm Mackie about the pain and Mackie set up an appointment for the goalie with the team dentist. Gerry struggled through the practice and then stripped off his uniform and dressed for his visit to the doctor. Then he realized something. He didn't know the dentist's name. The goalie asked defenseman Bill White for some help. It was the wrong place to go.

"What's the dentist's name?" asked Desjardins.

"Dr. Pull," replied White, quite casually.

Gerry wasn't born yesterday. "You're kidding," he said to White.

"No, really," answered the defenseman. "It's Dr. Pull."

Off the goalie went, looking for Dr. Pull.

Following Mackie's directions, Desjardins reached the medical center. He scanned the directory for Dr. Pull, but couldn't find him. He tried one of the other buildings, thinking perhaps he had mistaken the address. Still no Dr. Pull. He went back to the first building and tried a drugstore in the lobby, asking the pharmacist if he knew Dr. Pull. No Pull. By then the time of his appointment had come and gone, so the goalie, disgusted and still battling his toothache, headed back for the Forum, where he found White.

The defenseman broke up, confessing that there was no Dr. Pull. While the other King players roared, Desjardins just smiled. "That's okay," said the goalie. "I just realized today is Monday. My appointment isn't until tomorrow."

In between grins, Desjardins played sixty games in his first season and finished with a 3.26 average—the best he had ever posted. He was labeled "the fastest glove in the West," and voted the Kings' Most Valuable Player. Jack Kent Cooke, exuberant owner of both the Kings and basketball's Los Angeles Lakers, called his goalie "the man with the fastest reflexes in all pro sports. I used to think Jerry West, who plays for my Lakers, had the fastest hands. After watching Desjardins, I have changed my mind."

Desjardins has huge confidence in his catching hand. "One thing I do," he said, "is when I leave an opening, I give it on my glove side. This tempts the shooters and I have quick hands to make the catches."

His rookie season earned Desjardins widespread praise. "He has a chance to be a great goalie," said Coach Red Kelly.

"He is fast becoming one of the best goalkeepers in the league," added Larry Regan, general manager of the Kings.

The praise sounded very nice and the following fall, when he negotiated a contract with the Kings, Desjardins decided it ought to be translated into dollars. He and his wife developed a presentation for Regan, complete with a point-by-point resume of all of Gerry's trophies and clippings for his five professional seasons.

When Regan beckoned Gerry into his office for the contract talks, in marched mini-skirted Michelle instead, armed with her ammunition. Regan is used to dealing with attorneys and players' agents, but this was the first time he negotiated with a player's wife. "She impressed me more than any of the lawyers I've had to deal with," said the LA general manager, "although I didn't agree with her salary figures."

Eventually, the wife and general manager came to terms and Desjardins went to work for the Kings. And, like the previous season, he was a workhorse, taking the bulk of the punishment when opposing teams filtered through Los Angeles' less than awesome defense. The constant barrage of shots got on his nerves and he made it known that he wasn't thrilled with his situation. A few weeks later, the Kings solved the problem for the goalie, trading him to Chicago in a six-player swap. Moving to the Black Hawks with him were defenseman Bill White, his old friend from the Dr. Pull episode, and forward Bryan Campbell. In exchange, the Kings got goalie Denis DeJordy, defenseman Gilles Marotte, and forward Jim Stanfield.

Chicago Coach Billy Reay was enthusiastic about the trade, which was completed on February 20, 1970. "Desjardins had an outstanding rookie season in 1968–69," said Reay. "He will be a great backup man for Tony Esposito." Desjardins, who had a 3.89 average in forty-three games for the Kings that season, played in four games down the stretch for the Black Hawks, allowing only eight goals. The future looked bright for Desjardins as the 1970–71 season got underway.

He shared the Black Hawk net-minding with Esposito, just as Reay had planned, and did quite well, too. Then, around the first of the year, he sprained his ankle badly and was forced to sit out four weeks. When the injury healed, he really got hurt.

"It was frustrating," said Desjardins. "I came back on a Saturday against Montreal and beat them 4–1, and then the next day I went out and broke my arm." That's not entirely accurate. Actually, it was Chicago defenseman Keith Magnuson who broke Desjardins's arm. It happened on national television in a game against St. Louis.

"Craig Cameron took a shot and as I went to grab it Magnuson crashed into me and pinned my arm to the goalpost," said Gerry. "I knew it was broken right away because my arm was wrapped completely around the post. I managed to straighten it out before I skated to the bench. It was strange. It didn't really hurt. Instead, my arm was just numb."

But his season was over. He had a cast on the arm until April and even after it came off there was no way he could get into the playoffs. "The doctor said I could play with a partial cast, but if it ever cracked I'd be back where I started," said Desjardins. So Gerry sat by idly, watching Esposito play the iron man and the Black Hawks lose the playoff finals in seven games against Montreal.

It was a hard-luck season, but nevertheless it was his best in the NHL. In twenty-two games he allowed only forty-nine goals for a 2.41 goals-against average, by far his best ever. He posted a 12–6–3 won-loss-tied log and had been unbeaten the season before in the four games he played for the Hawks following the trade from LA. That meant that in two seasons in the nets, Desjardins had come away with either a tie or a victory in twenty of twenty-six games for Chicago. It was not good enough for the Hawks.

Concerned over the condition of his arm and anxious to

solidify their team with a solid number-two goalie, the Black
Hawks dealt Desjardins and two other players to California
in exchange for Gary Smith. The same Gary Smith had beaten
Gerry out of the goaltending job with the Toronto Marlboros several years earlier. The trade came during training
camp, September 9, 1971, and Desjardins wasn't all that disappointed because it meant he rejoined Fred Glover, his old
coach from his days at Cleveland, who was now piloting
Charlie Finley's Seals.

There was only one problem when Desjardins showed up
at the California training camp. He couldn't move his arm
properly. It was bent grotesquely and it was next to impossible for him to tend goal. Finley had been hoodwinked,
or at least that's what he said. The Hawks had sent him dam-
aged goods and he demanded a settlement. Chicago didn't
rush to Finley's rescue, letting him stew for a while and
think about the NHL's policy of *caveat emptor*—let the
buyer beware.

Finally, the Black Hawks benevolently offered to take back
Desjardins, giving the Seals goalie Gilles Meloche and defenseman Paul Shmyr for the injured goalie. It was listed as
a trade, but it really was an adjustment of the first deal five
weeks earlier.

"The arm hadn't healed properly," said Desjardins. "It
had to be rebroken and set again. It wasn't until February
that I even got into a game with Chicago and by that time
Gary Smith had become the backup. I played six games with
the Hawks and never felt really comfortable. I knew I was
going to be traded."

The Hawks went into the 1972 expansion draft with three
goalies—Tony Esposito, Smith, and Desjardins. Gerry, coming off the bad injury and virtually idle for an entire year,
was obviously the third man—the one who would be available to the new Atlanta Flames and New York Islanders.
Bill Torrey, bowtied general manager of the Islanders,
wanted Desjardins and made an advance deal with the
Hawks to insure the goalie would be available when the Islanders got their draft turn.

"The only question is his arm," said Torrey. "He has the
ability to become one of the best in the league. A year
ago, Gerry couldn't do one pushup without suffering pain in
his arm. Now he is doing thirty-five to forty a day with ease.

His arm is improving all the time."

Desjardins confirmed that opinion. "The arm has given me no problems," the goalie said. "I did a lot of exercises during the summer, swimming and water skiing and, of course, those pushups. It feels fine, but I'm going to continue to work hard anyway."

Gerry had no idea how hard. Their initial season in the NHL was, to put it mildly, a nightmare for the New York Islanders. They lost more games and surrendered more goals than any team had ever lost or surrendered in any previous NHL season. A night in the nets was no picnic.

"Pucks, pucks, pucks. Game after game, that's all I see. It's sheer frustration. Forty or fifty shots on goal makes you feel a little punchy," said Desjardins. "I stop them in my sleep. I have to kid myself about my situation. If I take it too seriously, I'd go nuts."

Although his goals-against average was an inflated 4.68, he played well. With a team like the Islanders, 4.68 isn't bad. "I had a 3.89 average in Los Angeles and went to Chicago and it was 2.41," said Gerry, explaining that statistics aren't a true measure of a goalie's worth. "I wasn't any better in Chicago than I was in LA. I had a better team in front of me and wasn't getting as many shots, so my goals-against average was better." The Islanders were better in their second season and Desjardins's average dipped to a more respectable 3.12.

Asked about that first-year 4.68 average, Torrey brushes it off, saying, "Without him, I don't care to think of what our fate might be."

Ask Desjardins about living in the shooting gallery that is the New York Islanders' net and he smiles. "After being on the injured list for the most part of two seasons, just playing this game is a pleasure. For me, just playing again is like being reborn. There have been times in my career when I thought I'd wind up in the mines."

There are some goalies who'd suggest that the Islanders' nets are just as bad. But not Gerry. At least his defensemen don't go around breaking his arms in New York.

He chopped his goals-against average to 3.12 in the Islanders' second season but there was a noticeable split between the goalie and management. When it came time to renegotiate his contract, Desjardins mentioned a no-trade clause, more playing time, and some larger numbers than Torrey was willing to produce.

There seemed to be an impasse and nowadays when that occurs, the player turns to the other league. So that's what Desjardins did, jumping to the WHA's Detroit Stags. It was no coincidence that the day he signed with the Stags, the club also signed Johnny Wilson as coach. Wilson was behind the bench in L.A. when Gerry enjoyed his best NHL days. "I'm delighted to have him back," the coach said. "He can play as long as he wants for me."

New York Islanders

**Gerry has been
a New York Islander
since the 1972–73 season.**